Transition Scenarios

China and the United States in the Twenty-First Century

DAVID P. RAPKIN *and*

WILLIAM R. THOMPSON

THE UNIVERSITY OF CHICAGO PRESS   CHICAGO AND LONDON

DAVID P. RAPKIN is associate professor of political science at the University of Nebraska. WILLIAM R. THOMPSON is Distinguished Professor and the Donald A. Rogers Professor of Political Science at Indiana University. He is the author or coauthor of numerous books, including *The Arc of War*, also published by the University of Chicago Press.

The University of Chicago Press, Chicago 60637
The University of Chicago Press, Ltd., London
© 2013 by The University of Chicago
All rights reserved. Published 2013.
Printed in the United States of America
22 21 20 19 18 17 16 15 14 13   1 2 3 4 5

ISBN-13: 978–0-226–04033–2 (cloth)
ISBN-13: 978–0-226–04047–9 (paper)
ISBN-13: 978–0-226–04050–9 (e-book)

Library of Congress Cataloging-in-Publication Data
Rapkin, David P., author.
    Transition scenarios : China and the United States in the twenty-first century / David P. Rapkin and William R. Thompson.
        pages cm
    Includes bibliographical references and index.
    ISBN 978-0-226-04033-2 (cloth : alkaline paper) — ISBN 978-0-226-04047-9 (paperback : alkaline paper) — ISBN 978-0-226-04050-9 (e-book) 1. United States—Relations—China. 2. China—Relations—United States. 3. War—Forecasting. I. Thompson, William R., author. II. Title.
    E183.8.C5R37 2013
    327.7305109′05—dc23

                                                                                                2013003714

Transition Scenarios

Contents

Acknowledgments

W e thank our two anonymous reviewers for their helpful comments, our editor, David Pervin, for picking them, and Elissa Park, for her excellent copyediting. As usual, it is a pleasure to work with all of the folks at University of Chicago Press. Part of chapter 4 was published initially as David P. Rapkin and William R. Thompson, "Power Transition, Challenge, and the China Problem," *International Interactions* 29 (2003): 315–42. Portions of chapters 1 and 6 first appeared in David P. Rapkin and William R. Thompson, "Will Economic Interdependence Encourage China and India's Peaceful Ascent?" in Ashley J. Tellis and Michael Wills, eds., *Strategic Asia 2006–07: Trade, Interdependence, and Security* (Seattle: National Bureau of Asian Research, 2006), 333–64. Another part of chapter 6 is based on David P. Rapkin and William R. Thompson, "Kantian Dynamics and Systemic Transitions: Can International Organizations Influence U.S.-China Conflict?," in William R. Thompson, ed., *Systemic Transitions: Past, Present, and Future* (New York: Palgrave-Macmillan, 2008). We are grateful to Taylor and Francis, the National Bureau of Asian Research, and Palgrave-Macmillan, respectively, for permission to use this material.

CHAPTER ONE

Twenty-First-Century Transition Struggles

In March 1996 China engaged in military exercises in the Taiwan Straits, including the firing of missiles to offshore sites near Taiwanese ports, with the obvious intent of intimidating voters during the lead-up to Taiwan's national elections. The United States responded by sending two carrier groups to the area in a show of force that proved effective in so far as China's military exercises stopped, the carrier groups exited the area, and the crisis was resolved—though the underlying issues concerning the status of Taiwan, China's use of force, and the role of the United States were not. A little more than three years later, in May 1999, in the course of NATO's war against Yugoslavia, US planes bombed the Chinese embassy in Belgrade, killing three Chinese diplomatic personnel. The Chinese government, as well as most Chinese, dismissed as implausible the US explanation that the bombing had been an accident stemming from the use of an outdated map and rejected the US apology premised on this account. With their government's approval, large crowds of outraged Chinese demonstrators demonstrated their antagonism by stoning the US embassy in Beijing. The prospect of armed conflict between the United States and China loomed even larger in April 2001 when the pilot of a Chinese fighter aircraft was killed near China's territorial waters in a collision with a US EP3 surveillance aircraft. The EP3 then made an emergency landing at a Chinese airbase on Hainan Island, triggering a crisis over release of the crew and return of the aircraft and its sensitive surveillance equipment.

Some fourteen years later (2009), the USNS Impeccable, a small ship with a crew of about fifty and designed to detect and track submarines, experienced several days of Chinese harassment about seventy-five miles south of China's Yulin Naval Base on Hainan, an island in the South China Sea. Presumably, the US mission was to monitor new classes of nuclear submarines based at Yulin. The first day a Chinese frigate crossed the Impeccable's bow twice while Chinese aircraft flew over the ship repeatedly. Two days later, another Chinese naval vessel demanded that the Impeccable leave the area. The next day, a small flotilla of Chinese ships began harassing the Impeccable, again demanded that it leave the area, and eventually two of the ships came quite close to the American vessel. The Impeccable responded by spraying water on the closest ship. Ultimately, the Impeccable did leave the area but the Chinese flotilla continued to harass it with dangerous maneuvers as it was leaving, including an attempt to capture its towed sonar array.

The US government protested and also sent a destroyer to escort the Impeccable. In some respects, the issue revolved around maritime rights of passage. The United States claimed its ship was operating outside Chinese territorial waters and could not be hindered. The Chinese government retorted that foreign military ships could sail through their exclusive economic zone (up to two hundred miles from Hainan), but only if their passage was for "innocent" purposes—a description that did not apply to the Impeccable. More generally, though, the problem was one of adversarial frictions over intelligence gathering reminiscent of US-Soviet naval maneuvering during the Cold War.

In light of this not-too-distant series of militarized disputes, it is possible to imagine how a US-China war could begin as a quickly escalating clash at sea or somewhere in Eurasia (i.e., between Taiwan and Serbia). Beneath the flow of events that might serve as proximate causes of such a war, however, we believe there are deeper structural changes underway that will affect more fundamentally the prospects for US-China conflict in the twenty-first century. By structural change we mean long-term change in the distribution of power at the apex of the global system, that is, a power transition in which an emerging challenger draws closer to, and may eventually surpass, the existing system leader in terms of those specific power capabilities relevant to the form and maintenance of global order. Though they need not culminate in war, power transitions tend to be particularly dangerous periods, especially if the challenger is dissatisfied with the existing order and the economic benefits, security, and status it is accorded within it.

If the rates of economic growth and military modernization that China has achieved over the last twenty years or so are extrapolated into the future, not too many more decades will pass before China is able to mount a significant challenge to the predominant position of the United States, at least in East Asia and perhaps globally. There is fairly wide agreement that some form of US-China power transition looms later in this century, but a number of questions remain. When will the power transition enter the most dangerous, war-prone phase? Will China become so disgruntled with the prevailing regional and/or global order that it will risk war in order to change the way things work? How can (and should) China's interests be accommodated within the existing order so as to minimize this risk?

We view these questions as open-ended, which is to say that we do not know the answers. But there are several possibilities. China could be integrated into the world economy peacefully. China might well become so dissatisfied with the world's status quo that it would risk open warfare to alter it more to its liking. But future outcomes are not predicated solely on how Chinese decision-makers view the world and their status within it. The current status quo structure was constructed primarily by the United States after World War II. Will the United States continue to weaken, thereby encouraging a transitional supplantment effort? Might the United States revive its faltering lead economy and make the twenty-first century an American one as it did in the previous century? We have no crystal ball to answer these questions. What we do have is history, international relations theory, and some new ways of looking at transition struggles. Turning first briefly to the history of past transition competitions, it is clear that pacific adjustments to these fundamental changes in relative status at the apex of elite states have not been the rule. That does not mean that things have to work out in the future precisely as they have in the past but we do need to start with a clear understanding of how transitions have unfolded in the past. Then we can turn to crafting an approach to examining possible future transitions in a systematic and transparent fashion.

Violent Conflict and the Emergence of Great Powers

The history of status mobility at the apex of the international system is characterized quite demonstrably by considerable violence. Upwardly mobile states invariably have had to fight their way into the elite subset of powers referred to as great or major powers. States that ascend to the status of lead economy in the world system also have had to fight to maintain that status. The consistency of the record does not mean that contemporary or future states will have to fight because their predecessors have done so in the past. It does suggest, however, that there is ample reason to anticipate conflict being associated with the emergence of new and rising powers.

There are fairly easy ways to check this generalization. One approach involves looking at the roster of states designated as great powers over the past five hundred years. Jack S. Levy provides the following list: France, England/Great Britain, Spain, Austria, and the Ottoman Empire were great powers at his 1495 starting date.[1] The Netherlands joined in 1609, Sweden in 1617, Russia in 1721, Prussia/Germany in 1740, Italy in 1861, the United States in 1898, Japan in 1905, and China in 1949.[2] While it is easy to quarrel about the validity of some entries and the absence of a few others, this list is highly representative of those powers that international relations specialists consider to be the political-military elite of the past half-millennium. We amend it only slightly for immediate purposes by treating the 1870–71 transformation of Prussia into Germany as a new great power.

Using this list as a guideline, we can then ask what happened when new great powers emerged. Table 1.1 summarizes the outcome with a fifty-year window (twenty-five years before and twenty-five years after) the year a new great power entered the elite list.[3] Nine new great power entries are listed in table 1.1. No newly emerged great power managed to evade participation in extensive warfare. There is no single reason for this rather unambiguous outcome, but each great power's story is not entirely unique either. Instead, three factors seem most prominent. The most overarching factor is that great powers have operated like Mafioso hit men. To gain status, they have had to first "make their bones," which, in organized crime parlance, is to establish one's bona fides by killing someone. Among great powers, making one's bones means defeating another state in combat. That other state need not be a great power but it certainly helps. If the opponent is a very strong power, victory is not absolutely necessary. Merely demonstrating that a state can hold its own against major power competition may suffice—as in the case of Netherlands long struggle with Spain during the seventeenth century or China's clashes with the United States and the Soviet Union in the twentieth century. Otherwise, the victory should be a very clear-cut demonstration of the new elite's military

TABLE I.I. **Entry into the great-power ranks and warfare**

Great power	Entry date	Warfare within twenty-five year intervals before and after entry into great-power ranks
Netherlands	1609	Dutch revolt from late 1560s English intervention in 1585 Spanish intervention in France 1589 Dutch war with Spain renewed in 1621 ending a truce begun in 1609
Sweden	1617	War with Russia, 1570–95 Polish invasion, 1592–98 War with Poland over Livonia, 1600–1611 War with Russia, 1613–17 War with Poland, 1617–29 "Bloodless war" with Poland, 1634–53 Swedish intervention in Thirty Years War, 1630–48
Russia	1721	Russo-Turkish war, 1695–1700 Great Northern War, 1700–21 War with Persia, 1722–23 War of the Polish Succession, 1733–38 Austro-Russian-Turkish War, 1736–39 War with Sweden, 1741–43
Prussia	1740	War of Austrian Succession, 1740–48 Seven Years War, 1756–63
Italy	1861	Italian War of Independence, 1848–49 Crimean War, 1854–56 War with Austria, 1859 Italo-Roman War, 1860 Italo-Sicilian War, 1860 Seven Weeks War with Austria, 1866
United States	1898	War with Spain, 1898 Boxer Rebellion, 1900 World War I, 1917–18
Japan	1905	Intervention in Korea, 1882–85 Sino-Japanese war, 1894–95 Boxer Rebellion, 1900 Russo-Japanese War, 1904–05 World War I, 1914–18 Intervention in China, 1927–29
China	1949	Japanese intervention, 1927–29 Japanese expansion in China, 1931–45 Korean War, 1950–53 War with India, 1962

Source: War data are taken from Jack S. Levy, *War in the Modern Great Power System, 1495–1975* (Lexington: University Press of Kentucky, 1983), 88–91.

power capabilities (as in the cases of Sweden, Russia, Prussia/Germany, the United States, and Japan). Only Italy never really satisfied this criterion and, as a consequence, its status as a great power was always considered suspect.[4]

A second factor is that most great powers emerged in fairly tough neighborhoods. To emerge in the eastern Baltic or central Europe meant that an ascending state would probably have to fight its immediate neighbors over territory and trade. In some cases, decision-makers felt compelled to fight in order to have control over adjacent or nearby pieces of territory that either had to be taken from neighbors or the neighbors had to be prevented from taking the territories themselves: Sweden fought to acquire Pomerania, Prussia to seize Silesia, Japan desired dominion over Korea. In other cases, independence had to be wrested away from overlords (e.g., the Netherlands and Italy). It is rather difficult to emerge as a great power if one's state remains a subordinate part of an imperial order.

The third factor has to do with states that emerge not only as a great power but also as the predominant great power in their home region. Russia did this in the Baltic in the early eighteenth century. So, too, did the United States in the late nineteenth century. When this type of regional power transition occurs, there has been a tendency to resort to coercion as a way to accelerate the re-organization of the region. Evicting Spain from Cuba, preventing Russian inroads into Northeastern Asia, or punishing India over alleged border transgressions are the types of behaviors toward which newly ascendant regional hegemons are inclined. A successful demonstration of force helps to underscore their asserted position in the regional pecking order.[5]

Nothing about the history of entry into the great power ranks says that states have no choice but to fight for any of the above reasons. Yet, the historical record indicates there is considerable reason to think some increased level of conflict is quite likely because the circumstances of elite emergence have encouraged it. In the modern era (i.e., the last five hundred years) no new great power has managed to evade substantial warfare around the time of its entry into elite status.

But there is also an economic dimension to emergence and ascent that must be taken into account. Some new great powers are just that: one new member among several members of an elite club. Some leap immediately to regional predominance. Still others are viewed as challengers for the lead economy position in the world system.[6] The concept of a lead economy implies that there is some likelihood that one state is recognized as the most innovative center of economic production and ex-

TABLE 1.2. **Global lead economies and challenges**

Timing, century	Lead economy	Principal challenger(s)	Outcome
Late 15th–early 16th	Venice	Portugal	Only indirect conflict between Venice and Portugal
Late 16th–mid-17th	Portugal/Spain	The Netherlands	Extensive warfare (Dutch Revolt and Thirty Years War: 1560s–1648)
Mid-17th–early 18th	The Netherlands	France and England	Extensive warfare with England/Britain aligning ultimately with the Netherlands (1652–55, 1665–67, 1672–78, 1688–97, and 1700–13)
Mid-18th–early 19th	Britain	France	Extensive warfare (1741–48, 1755–63, 1778–83, and 1793–1815)
Late 19th–early 20th	Britain	Germany and United States	Extensive warfare (World Wars I and II: 1914–45)
Mid/late 20th	United States	Soviet Union	Cold War (1945–89)
Mid-21st?	United States	China?	?

change. The United States has occupied this position since at least the mid-twentieth century. In the nineteenth century, Britain held the lead economy position. Before Britain, the United Provinces of the Netherlands enjoyed this status in the seventeenth century. Before the Dutch, the Portuguese briefly claimed this role by finding a way around Africa and into the Indian Ocean, thereby breaking the Venetian-Mamluk lock on east-west Eurasian trade.[7]

The added complexity of a second arena of action focused on economic competition, technological and industrial leadership, and long-distance commercial supremacy suggests an additional test. Are challengers for the lead economy position any more likely to escape the heightened conflict associated with emergence into the great power club? The quick historical summary provided in table 1.2 suggests that extensive warfare has been the norm, but at least there are some exceptions.

The Portuguese took more than three generations to work their way around the African continent once they had begun their initial and largely unsuccessful efforts to expand into Morocco. Once in the Indian Ocean, the better armed Portuguese were able to establish a maritime protection racket by requiring shipping to the west of India to pay for participating in trade. For a few decades, they were also able to monopolize the delivery of spices to European markets. In the fifteenth century, a Venetian-Egyptian Mamluk combination had controlled this monopoly but the Portuguese movement into the Indian Ocean circumvented the earlier pattern of control. To hold onto their newfound market control, the Portuguese had to fight Gujarati, Mameluke, and Ottoman opposition, but the Venetian contribution to this resistance avoided any direct physical confrontation with the Portuguese.[8] That the Italian state system was under siege thanks to French and Spanish interventions over succession rights may have had something to do with Venetian restraint.

The Dutch independence movement ensured there would be Dutch-Spanish fighting in the sixteenth century. The Spanish absorption of Portugal and its empire in 1581 made the partially merged Iberian entity a broader target. This was all the more true after the Dutch decision in the 1590s to circumvent the ports on the Iberian Peninsula and establish its own networks in Asia and the Americas.[9] Dutch-Portuguese combat in Brazil, Africa, and the southern tier of Asia ensued with the Dutch attempting to displace both the Portuguese trading regime in the Indian Ocean and its enclaves along the Afro-Eurasian coastline. By the time the Dutch had established their independence, the conflict had escalated to a struggle for the global system's lead economy—a struggle that the Dutch eventually won within the context of some eighty years of intermittent conflict throughout the world.

In the second half of the seventeenth century, the Dutch lead came under attack from both the English and the French. Decision-makers in both challenging states had concluded that the Dutch controlled too much of Europe's trade volume and it was incumbent upon them to take as much of it away from the Dutch as they possibly could. While the English and Dutch fought three wars during the 1650s–70s, France's ambitions went beyond merely grabbing some portion of Dutch trade: the French wanted to supplant the Netherlands as the lead economy.[10] To accomplish this meant subordinating the Dutch to French supremacy in Europe and beyond. Warfare had begun by 1672 and continued intermittently to 1713. Along the way, the Dutch stadtholder was able to realign English foreign policy by essentially seizing the English throne by force and committing England to the anti-French coalition. Ironically, however, in the 1688–1713 combat, the Dutch were bankrupted and were forced to cede their lead economic position to Britain.

While the Dutch were eclipsed by the conflicts with the French, France's bid to translate its massive size within the European region into global predominance was not extinguished in 1713. Warfare with Britain resumed in the 1740s, 1750s–60s, 1770s–80s, peaking in the 1793–1815 French Revolutionary and Napoleonic Wars. The ultimate outcome was the failure of the French challenge and the loss of French imperial territory in Canada, the Caribbean, and India. Britain's victory was marred only by the loss of its thirteen American colonies.

Britain's Industrial Revolution in the late eighteenth century altered the terrain of global economic competition by substituting an emphasis on industrial production for the previous focus on control of commercial markets. Innovating new waves of technology henceforth became the primary criterion for economic leadership. Britain led the first two waves centered on textiles, iron, and steam/railroads but faltered as the focus shifted to chemicals, steel, and electricity. Germany and the United States were better prepared to assume the lead in these leading sectors and thus to challenge the British lead economy position. But which one posed the greatest threat to Britain's position? In the long run, the American potential was considerable and might have led to British efforts to thwart American economic ascendance. Instead, British decision-makers took the position that the US rise was nearly inevitable and that the German threat was more immediate and closer to home— both in terms of European and Middle Eastern markets and Germany's North Sea location.[11]

As a consequence, the British negotiated themselves out of three ongoing rivalries (with the United States, France, and Russia), struck a deal with the Japanese, and retrenched their naval forces in European waters to better concentrate on the German threat.[12] World Wars I and II thus were fought in part to resolve the German economic challenge to Britain's position. World War I was inconclusive although it was clear that the incumbent system leader, Britain, was unlikely to recover fully from the costs of that war. World War II was decisive in that the British were exhausted, the Germans and Japanese defeated decisively, and the United States was clearly on top of the global system and controlled the introduction of new technology to the world economy.

The one wrinkle in this global economic predominance was the withdrawal of the Communist world from full participation in the world economy and the reluctance of the Communist subsystem's leader, the Soviet Union, to acknowledge or accept the US lead. Some forty-fives years of Cold War competition ensued, ending without direct major power violence with the collapse of the Soviet Union in the late 1980s.[13] The Soviets, overextended in the Third World and unable to meet the technological requirements necessary at the highest levels of economic competition, acknowledged defeat at least indirectly and altered their grand strategy.[14] In the process of attempting to reform their approach to competing in world politics, the Soviets lost control of Eastern Europe, the Caucuses, and Central Asia. Their vaunted military prowess was revealed to be far less formidable than often feared. The Russian ability to participate, let alone compete, as a great power in world politics became questionable and still has not been fully resolved.

So, while the United States appears to retain a tenuous lead in the introduction and diffusion of information technology, the real test will come with subsequent waves of technology later in the twenty-first century.[15] How many innovative challengers will emerge? If multiple challengers do emerge, will the United States designate one as the principal threat and concede or ally with the others in an attempt to thwart at least one challenger? Or, might the United States revitalize itself once again and widen its technological lead? Can China harness its huge domestic market to technological preeminence? What about Europe's efforts under European Union auspices to consolidate European capabilities in one regional-sized competitor? Where might India fit into this picture? India also has a large domestic market and some fledgling information technology capability, but even more acute poverty and underdevelopment to overcome than China.

Although these questions are all important, they are not exactly the ones we examine in this undertaking. We are prepared to assume that there is some probability of a Chinese challenge to US global leadership sometime in the twenty-first century. What form of a challenge should we anticipate? Will the two states clash in a traditional world war? Or will one state ascend while the other declines relatively peacefully now that there are so many more constraints on global warfare than there were before? What happens if the Chinese ascent is stalled for some reason? As noted above, we should not rule out altogether a US leadership revival. What difference might this make to a succession struggle? These are the types of questions that we hope to address in this volume. We must emphasize the word "address." We cannot answer any of the questions definitively. They are future possibilities and we possess no better crystal balls than anyone else. But we can take on the questions with the help of international relations theory and outline possible trajectories for the future.

Multiple Outcomes, International Relations Theory, and Scenario Construction

Our questions cannot be answered in the near term because they refer to processes that are currently underway, that are still highly open-ended, and that may require several decades or more to reach fruition. All of the potential challengers currently visible on the horizon could undergo various types of disintegration in the next several decades, thereby undermining the intensity of their challenge(s). The rapid pace of Chinese development could founder due to resource shortages and/or political dissent. The European Union area could become quite prosperous and yet lack leadership in advanced technology and production. India may generate population faster than it can transform its still largely agrarian economy.

Though it is difficult to forecast precisely who may challenge and when, there is still reason to anticipate that some level of heightened conflict is likely to be associated with a period of structural transition. The past five hundred years of great and global power competition is more than suggestive. As established earlier, the emergence of new powers is a process characterized by substantial stresses and strains that have proven difficult to manage without resorting to large-scale violence. The payoffs linked to mobility in the world system, especially at or toward the very top of the stratification hierarchy, are apt to be seen as very high. As shown in tables 1.1 and 1.2, willingness to engage in warfare at least in the past, it is safe to conclude, appears to have been especially strong. Whether the same propensities hold in the future cannot be known at this juncture. Perhaps, though, it would be most prudent not to assume that they have become totally unthinkable. Someday, they probably will become unthinkable. The question is whether we have reached that systemic fork in the road yet and/or whether we will reach it in this century.

John Mueller is well known for the thesis that war had become unthinkable by World War I but that a few decision-makers still had not heeded the message. Hence, World War II was due mainly to Adolf Hitler.[16] But an alternative thesis is that, while the system may be moving away from primitive contests over leadership selection, the transition to less primitive leadership selection processes is apt to be more rocky than smooth. Global wars, as selection contests, did not exist before 1494 and took some time to acquire the characteristics exhibited in 1914–45. It should not be surprising if the elimination of global warfare resembles its emergence—slow and gradual—as opposed to an abrupt change in the way leadership issues are resolved. This uncertainty is reflected in much of the recent scholarship on transition issues, for example:

> As far-reaching as its impact may be, however, the future character of the U.S.-China relationship is also profoundly uncertain. Most experts have opinions

about this question but, if pressed, few would claim to be sure about what lies ahead. Such modesty is entirely appropriate. Not only are the answers to the questions posed here unknown; they are also, at present, unknowable.[17]

Over the past decade, so much has been written about China's rise and its implications for international relations that it seems there should be little left to say. . . . In many respects, the scholarly debate has been well framed and what remains is the testing of ideas and the gathering of more and better evidence as it becomes available.[18]

Reading the two citations above in juxtaposition may be confusing. If the questions pertaining to the rise of China and its implications for a possible systemic leader transition are unknowable, how is it possible that everything has already been said that needs to be said about the issue? While we recognize that the future is unknowable, we still think there is something more to say about a potential China-US transition. Accordingly, this book has three objectives. One is to think about what is likely to be a central concern of the twenty-first century—a renewed China-US rivalry this time within a systemic transition frame. The two states have been rivals before, but the 1950s and 1960s conflict between them had little to do with a potential displacement of US systemic leadership. As Aaron Friedberg notes in the first quotation above, how this relationship will play out into the future is both unknown and unknowable at the present time.[19] That said, we need to develop an analytical vehicle suitable for thinking about the unknown and the unknowable. We do this in the form of developing multiple and alternative, theory-driven scenarios about the future. Scenario construction allows us to imagine various ways in which the relationship might play out. If we are appropriately systematic in their construction, they also can generate early warning indicators of which direction the relationship might be heading. In other words, they offer possible templates for the future. None of the templates are unlikely to get it exactly right, but they may provide useful, if rough, guidelines as events unfold. In this respect, there is still something left to say contrary to Avery Goldstein's second quotation above. But, as also noted by Goldstein, the emphasis must be on testing and evidence gathering as it becomes available. Our scenarios attempt to accelerate this process, just as they attempt to shape what testing is carried out and what evidence is examined.

A second and related concern is whether international relations theory is up to the task of explicating and explaining the structural changes through which we are living. We are not so much concerned with the framing of the discourse about the transitional possibilities as we are about our theoretical materials. Are they up to the task? Here we need to note that the task is not one of predicting when or whether China will pass the United States and become the world's leading power. That is not what theory is for. Rather, theory exists to explain in general how such transitions come about and what outcomes might be anticipated. We focus on this second objective by asking whether, to what extent, and how well, our theories speak to the prospects of a future transition.

Our third objective is to reiterate that the future is contingent and not easily predictable. By developing six, theoretically driven scenarios of possible futures pertaining to the systemic transition question associated with our first objective, we offer (a) an illustration of future contingencies and (b) a set of templates for watching our future unfold. The ultimate test and the full implications of the alternative scenarios, and the power of international relations theory, thus lie sometime in the future. The templates, however, are tools that can be used right away. As the years roll by, one can check off the indicators pointing to the probability of one or more of the scenarios approximating reality. In this respect, we are creating alternative forms for interpreting the fragments of evidence as they become available.

But none of this means that we must hold our critical breath while time passes. There are problems with our theoretical infrastructure that can be addressed here and now. Just as we must watch as the China-US relationship changes in the future, we must also seek to improve our theoretical constructs for interpreting these possible changes. Part of our third objective, therefore, is to work on more specific analytical constructs for interpreting transitional processes. Whatever the merits of general international relations theory, it has major limitations when it comes to assessing specific types of behavior. The potential significance of a transition from one leading power to another in the twenty-first century is sufficiently great to warrant more focused theoretical attention. We are not content to merely evaluate the state of current international relations theorizing. We also seek to improve it.

It is a common, though certainly not unanimous, expectation among observers of the world political economy that we are in the early stages of a systemic transition in which China will challenge the United States and attempt to become the next system leader.[20] To the extent one shares this expectation, a premium is immediately placed on answering the question of whether this transition, like some of its predecessors, is likely to be accompanied by large-scale violence. Will there be another transition war (or depending on your theoretical lexicon, global, systemic, general, or hegemonic war) at the apex of the global system?

This question is complicated in several important ways. First, there is a range of potential outcomes, not just a binary war/no war outcome. Some prior transitions have been extremely violent (United States–Germany/Japan), others pacific (Great Britain–US), and still others have featured intensive competition but fallen short of full-fledged challenge and violent confrontation (United States–Soviet Union Cold War). Second, as made clear below, within the war category there are numerous potential wars to choose among. Third, a large number of variables are involved, some of which pose serious conceptual, measurement, and model specification problems and which are likely to involve complex forms of causality, that is, conjunctural causation, equifinality, and multifinality. Fourth, since we are in the early stages of what could be a protracted systemic transition, predictive models relying on extrapolation of existing trends will not allow us to peek very far into the future.

If attempts to build a predictive model are likely to founder on these complications, we think there is more (or at least a different kind of) leverage to be gained by addressing the question of the war proneness of a prospective US-China transition from a scenario-building standpoint. Chapter 2 outlines how we might go about doing it.

CHAPTER TWO

Scenario Construction

S cenarios are stories about the future. Building them involves linking a sequence of possible events that leads to some future outcome. Emphasis is placed on contingent causal mechanisms rather than on the determinism and sought for but seldom-attained precision associated with point estimate predictions. Forward reasoning can be thought of as construction of chains of theoretical logic that link causally potent drivers (variables for the moment) to particular outcomes. The objective is not to be able to predict but rather to anticipate the main processes by which the future might unfold.

Developing outcomes, the alternative ways of how things might turn out, is one among several integral elements of what we mean by the term scenario. But it is important to emphasize that the two terms used here are not coterminous. How then do outcomes fit into the broader scenario-building task? We begin with outcomes rather than driving forces because of the large number of possible outcomes that might issue from a US-China transition.

Identification of driving forces that pull or push in a particular direction is at the core of the scenario-building exercise. Drivers are similar to independent variables in the parlance of conventional methodologies, and as such exert primary causal influence in the determination of outcomes. Additional drivers derived from other theoretical perspectives can be added as we hone the scenario model. We begin with two broad sets of driving forces, which are posited to pull in opposite directions. One set of drivers reflects the kinds of *competitive forces* exerted by the main protagonists in systemic transitions, namely, an incumbent system leader and a rising challenger who aspires to the top position. The main driving force in this relationship is the structural decline of the system leader, which may give rise to secondary drivers and manifestations of intensified competition for leadership succession.

We expect these primary and secondary driving forces to pull in the direction of conflict and, possibly, transition war:

- Competition for market space
- Resource competition
- Technological innovation and competition, with both commercial and military implications
- Military competition, especially in space and in other global reach capabilities
- A dense pattern of dyadic rivalries
- Systemic bipolarization

Another set of driving forces, which might be termed Kantian dynamics, is expected to pull in the opposite, more peaceful direction:

- Pacifying effects of shared democracy
- Economic interdependence
- Shared membership in international organizations

To this set of constraining driving forces, we also add the deterrence presumed to follow from the presence of nuclear weapons.

Thus, the structure of the book first considers what role scenario construction can play in our concerns with theoretical explanations of world politics. We will amplify this initial focus with a review of fictional future wars already available. The next task is to selectively review the pertinent international relations theory literature to derive a set of driving forces. Some driving forces push toward conflict, whereas others tend to restrain conflict. Our question is which driving forces are likely to prevail in situations of contending effects. We develop an answer or a set of answers by developing future scenarios that demonstrate different mixes of conflict promoting and restraining drivers. The outcomes are not precise predictors of what will happen. Rather, they permit authors and readers to contemplate the relative plausibilities associated with each scenario and to develop benchmarks that suggest features to watch for as we move forward in time. In this respect, we have created a project with no immediate conclusion. Its utility should unfold as time passes. If we have captured likely futures reasonably well, we should have a better sense of which possibility lies ahead. If we also stimulate further theoretical work on systemic transitions, the international relations field should profit.

But why become excited about the prospects of a once and future conflict between the system's two strongest states over its leadership? Surely,
after the intense conflicts of the twentieth century, we have moved past
these primitive approaches to selecting systemic leadership. Maybe so,
but, then again, maybe not. The European region has become more pacific,
but only after a vicious, upward spiral in combat over earlier leadership-
succession struggles. It is now hard to imagine a European state challenging the structural status quo in the future as Spain, France, and Germany
did in the past. But the European region is not the world and it will take
considerable time for the rest of the world to catch up. Whether the world
will also require more intensive combat over leadership succession questions remains to be seen. The past five hundred years of international relations, as we have seen and to the extent that this is a useful guide to transition problems, is not encouraging. New major powers often have had to
fight their way into the international system's elite. Declining system leaders have often had to fight challengers who seek to usurp their predominant position.

Scenario Building and Forward Reasoning

> In complex, evolving, uncertain situations . . . the future is not easily pre-
> dictable . . . The best the analyst can do is to identify the driving forces that
> may determine future outcomes and monitor those forces as they interact to
> become the future. Scenarios are a principle vehicle for doing this. Scenarios
> are plausible and provocative stories about how the future might unfold. When
> alternative futures have been clearly outlined, decision makers can mentally
> rehearse these futures and ask themselves, "What should I be doing now to pre-
> pare for these futures?"[1]

According to Bernstein et al., scenarios are "narratives with plot lines
that map a set of causes and trends in future time" and building them
entails "the identification and connection of chains of contingencies that
could shape the future."[2] Emphasizing the desirability of reasoning from
cause to effect, Bernstein et al. counsel that scenario building should begin
by specifying the causal forces that "drive" the scenario under construction rather than by first describing the most plausible expected outcomes.[3]
Accordingly, we have selected various forces thought to "drive" systemic
transitions, and we then turn to a brief explication of other elements of
the scenario-building scheme: predetermined elements, critical uncertain-

ties, early indicators, and wild cards. More in-depth treatment is given to outcomes, which we structure into four categories for reasons that will be explained: More of the Same/Pax Americana, Pax Sinica, Transition War, and Liberal Peace.

Driving Forces

We begin with what we term the primary (or structural) transitional driver: an incumbent system leader undergoing relative decline and a rising challenger who aspires to the top position. These factors are considered to be the transition's structural drivers because they express the primary structural features of transitions that shape the actions and strategies of those involved. We would anticipate that the primary drivers associated with other structural configurations, say bipolarity or multipolarity, would be different. Secondary drivers are less abstract and tend to derive from the primary driver, though some operate independently. We specify two broad sets of secondary drivers, which will be discussed in greater detail in chapters 4 and 5, which are posited to pull in opposite directions.

As we have suggested, incumbent leaders and challengers compete over market space, access to resources, technological innovation, and the development of global reach capabilities within contexts characterized by increasingly bipolarized and complex rivalry fields. These secondary drivers push toward higher probabilities of conflict. Other secondary drivers (e.g., democratization, economic interdependence, international organizations, and nuclear deterrence) are thought to work to constrain potential conflicts.

This is surely a large number of driving forces, but as Bernstein et al. contend, "the starting point is to put on the table multiple driving forces that can be the basis, in different combinations, for diverse chains of connections and outcomes. Parsimony comes later, after not before an analysis of complex causal possibilities."[4]

One useful way to think about complexity involving sets of driving forces combining to pull in opposed directions is provided by the concept of "aleatory explanation." Humphreys distinguishes between contributing causes, which raise the probability of an effect, and counteracting causes, which lower the probability of that same effect.[5] This enables causal statements of the form "transition war occurs because of competitive forces, despite constraint dynamics" or "no transition war occurs even though competitive forces are operative, because of constraint dynamics."

This logic of aleatory explanation is similar to Bruce Russett's use of methodological terms borrowed from the epidemiological lexicon in application to the study of war: *inducers or facilitators* (of disease/conflict) correspond to contributing causes while *suppressors* (of disease/conflict) correspond to counteracting causes: "The disease, a militarized interstate dispute, becomes the product of these two additive vectors [inducements and suppressors] linked by a multiplicative term."[6] Note here the further specification explicit in Russett's formulation—inducements (or contributing) causes and suppressors (or countervailing) causes are additive within each category, whereas the two broader categories are multiplicatively linked.

Aaron Friedberg, with specific reference to future US-China relations, provides a similar conceptualization in which there are some causal forces that "are pushing the relationship toward conflict ... and other, countervailing forces ... that, operating alone, would tend to promote peace."[7] The opposing vectors each have relative strengths. Which one will win out when they collide?

Predetermined Elements

According to Bernstein et al., "Scenarios are generally constructed by distinguishing what we believe is relatively certain from what we think is uncertain. The most important 'certainties' are common to all scenarios that address the same problem or trend."[8] Put differently, predetermined elements are tantamount to assumptions that important systemic properties or trends will remain constant, within specified parameters, or not otherwise undergo significant change. Consider, for example, demographic trends, which are unlikely to exhibit rapid, discontinuous change in the short to medium term. Should assumptions, say about the rate of growth of the global product, for example, fail to hold, we would expect the relationships to and among the other elements of the scenarios to be altered and possibly to lead to different outcomes. Below are some transition-relevant examples:

- China sustains X percent economic growth, enabling it to close various gaps with the United States.
- China averts an internal collapse that might result from environmental overload, growing inequities, or deepening rural-urban tensions.
- The United States does not turn inward and withdraw from an active role in Asia.

Critical Uncertainties

In contrast to the relative certainty that predetermined elements will remain so, critical uncertainties are potential causal forces for which the probability, timing, duration, impact, and consequences are unknown. Although predetermined elements are present in all scenarios, "the most important [critical] uncertainties are used to differentiate scenarios, turning out one way in one scenario and a different way in another."[9] They are especially difficult to incorporate into scenario-building exercises in a nonspeculative manner when they combine and interact with other critical uncertainties, driving forces, and/or predetermined elements. Some examples include the following:

- Outbreak of China-Taiwan conflict across the Taiwan Straits
- Outbreak of conflict on Korean peninsula
- Both challenger dissatisfaction and incumbent's threat perceptions intensify
- Alliance configurations among major powers remain stable

SCENARIO PLOT LINES.   Plot lines are narrative stories that tie together the main elements in the scenario—driving forces, predetermined elements, and critical uncertainties—to show how they might interact so as to lead to particular outcomes.

EARLY INDICATORS.   Early indicators are described as, "observable and measurable attributes ... that allow researchers to assess, as events unfold, the extent to which a scenario (or which part of a scenario) is coming to pass."[10]

- Bipolarization of great powers around challenger and incumbent structurally signal increased probability of violent conflict.
- China-US cooperation deepens and becomes more institutionalized in both bilateral and multilateral contexts: for example, climate change, energy, and other natural resources, keeping sea lanes open.

WILD CARDS.   Wild cards are low probability, high impact events that may shatter the logic with which the scenario builder has linked together the scenario elements. As such, wild cards, which are similar to what others term "game changers," are tantamount to "strategic surprise."[11] Some possibilities include the following:

- Catastrophic nuclear accident
- Collapse of Pakistan or Indonesia
- Severe water supply problems in Asia

Outcomes

There are a large number of possible outcomes that might issue from a US-China transition. Most observers and scenario builders have envisioned that a US-China war would likely be triggered by some form of clash in the Taiwan Straits. Others have anticipated that a casus belli would emerge from events on the Korean peninsula. Still others posit escalation of naval and air conflict in the South China Sea, while some involve India. Developing de novo a separate scenario for each of these transition-war outcomes, plus all the others that might result in such a war, would be a formidable task. And, we have yet to consider either the pacific scenarios that do not result in transition war, or those more ambiguous outcomes that fall in the middle ground between the war and no war possibilities. Assuming (1) equifinality, that is, we expect there will be multiple pathways to each of these outcomes, and (2) further multifinality, that pathways launched from the same starting point can lead to different outcomes, it seems to us much easier to impose some order on these complex, contingent forms of causation if we begin by specifying the range of potential outcomes toward which the drivers might in fact be driving.

Also, the sheer number of outcomes leads us to think that the way to proceed is by building composite scenarios that can accommodate categories, or groups, of outcomes.[12] We probably do not need all the half dozen or so war-across-the–Taiwan Straits scenarios that have been generated (though not based on any explicit scenario methodology). We may want to retain elements of these plots, however, within a broader transition-war category that also includes the Korean peninsula and South China Sea outcomes, as well as others that thus far have not received much attention (e.g.,, space war scenarios).

More specifically, we follow the methodological guidelines for what Heur and Pherson term "alternative futures analysis."[13] They indicate a number of steps to operationalize.[14]

1. Define the focal issue.
2. Identify the key forces, factors, or events that are likely to influence how the issue will develop over a specific time period.

3. Group the key forces, factors, or events to form two critical drivers that are expected to determine the future outcome.

4. Define the two ends of the spectrum for each driver.

5. Draw a 2 × 2 matrix to create a square divided into four quadrants. Each quadrant represents a scenario generated by a combination of the two drivers.

6. Generate a narrative story of how each hypothetical scenario might come into existence.

7. Generate a list of indicators for each scenario that would help to determine whether events are starting to play out in a way envisioned by that scenario.

8. Monitor the list of indicators on a regular basis.

Our chosen theoretical frame is intentionally simple. We contrast factors promoting transitional conflict (inducers or facilitators in the Russett terminology) with possible constraints (suppressors) on transitional conflict. This choice yields a 2 × 2 matrix that is sketched in figure 2.1. Each of the four cells in the matrix are characterized by a unique mix of the two main categorical "variables" in which we place an appropriate scenario.

Moving clockwise:

"More of the Same" or "Pax Americana II": The combination of weak conflict inducements and weak constraints [in this cell, we develop two scenarios]

"Transition War": Strong conflict inducements and weak constraints

"Pax Sinica": Strong conflict inducements and strong constraints

"Liberal Peace": Weak conflict inducements and strong constraints

These will be constructed inductively, derived from our understanding of transition history and theory and from elements extracted from scenarios put forth by others. The four-part framework should encompass most of the outcomes we are interested in, though we shy away from suggesting that it exhausts all the possibilities.[15]

The Plan of the Book

Setting up these scenarios entails several preliminary steps. First, we need to establish what we want to avoid. Chapter 3 looks at fictional scenarios of US-China warfare already in existence. For the most part, we think

Conflict Constraints	Conflict Inducements	
	Weak	Strong
Weak	More of the Same Renewed Pax Americana	Transition War
Strong	Liberal Peace	Pax Sinica

FIGURE 2.1 The scenario framework

these fictions are not theoretically grounded and, as a consequence, do not develop storylines that are useful for our own purposes or that lead themselves to systematic comparison. Next, we need to make more explicit just what our understanding of transition history is and how we view the field of constraints that may or may not be operative in the future. Chapters 4 and 5 concentrate on different ways to interpret transitions by looking at power transition theory, offensive realism, and multiple models developed by leadership long-cycle theory. Our preference, for reasons specified in the chapter, is to integrate the multiple long-cycle models into one transitional model, which is provided more elaboration in chapter 5. Chapter 6 examines the perceived power of constraints on transitional conflict traceable to democratic regimes, economic interdependence, international organizations, and nuclear deterrence.

Our approach in this undertaking is hardly conventional. But using scenarios to probe the future is by no means unconventional. Business, military, and intelligence agencies are quite familiar with scenario construction and using it for making policy or developing strategies. But we are not making policy, developing strategies, or even advising decision makers. Our focus is the possible future associated with a transition in systemic leadership in which China could supplant the United States. We do not say that this transition will occur. We do not even know if it is probable. But, we think it is certainly conceivable as are other possible futures involving no transition. Similarly, a systemic transition could take place with or without war.

While we draw on earlier approaches to scenario construction, the emphasis on bringing in international relations theory to construct our scenario drivers is unconventional. Most people who construct scenarios may draw upon theory but they are not particularly interested in theory construction. Our interests are double- or even triple-fold. We want to embed our scenarios in international relations arguments, but we also want to use the opportunity to assess the adequacy of our theories for at least this transition question. When we run into problems with contemporary international relations theory, we also want to construct theories that better match the problem at hand.

Chapters 4–6 develop the drivers for our scenarios. Five scenarios are then constructed around the theoretical parameters discussed above and are advanced in chapters 7–10. Chapter 11 returns to the question of what it is that we should do with these scenarios. One of our answers is that they can be used to develop a slate of "early warning" indicators of future probabilities. While we do not think that all five of our scenarios are equally likely, there is no doubt that analysts and readers alike will disagree about their relative probabilities. But, as time goes by, we may be able to tell whether our future is unfolding in a more conflictual or more constrained fashion. The evolving future trajectory will also tell us something about which of our theories are most useful as well.

Scenarios of Future United States–China Warfare: What Is Missing from This Picture?

A number of US-China plot lines have already been developed by authors interested in telling stories but also very much interested usually in promoting some type of policy warning. That is, writers about future wars are often trying to scare their readers into not following the same policy paths as the incumbent decision makers they are writing about. Since this type of story telling has been around for nearly two centuries, we should first consider what fiction can tell us about constructing scenarios for transitional futures.

The main purpose of such an exercise, for our immediate purposes, is not to fill space, to borrow ideas used in the past, or even to criticize the story-telling abilities of selected authors. Rather, it is most closely akin to the old standby, newspaper feature that shows two similar pictures. One is complete and the other has five or six missing objects (e.g., hands, vases, chair legs, and so forth). The object of this type of newspaper puzzle is to determine whether the reader can find all the missing objects. There are missing objects in most (but not all) extant stories about future US-Chinese warfare, too. We deviate from the newspaper approach by not first showing what we think is a complete picture. We start instead with a review of earlier scenarios to illustrate some of the things that we think are missing and, therefore, things that we want to avoid in our own scenario building. In short, we will argue and demonstrate that most earlier scenarios are (a) only about war and not other possible outcomes and (b) only rarely about structural transitions in world politics.

Transition War Scenarios

Fictional nonwar scenarios involving future world orders in which China
has bypassed the United States peacefully or in which the United States
has revitalized its own earlier lead are pretty much nonexistent. Fictional
war scenarios pitting China against the United States are not hard to find
even though the current preoccupations with Iraq/Afghanistan and terrorism have pushed them out of the public eye in the first decade of the
twenty-first century. The odds are that that may change in the second decade. Be that as it may, most of the war scenarios that are available currently are not inherently satisfying. This observation is not meant as liter-
ary criticism. The stories are not great fiction. Readers stay with the plots
to find out how the stories end as much if not more than they may be en-
tranced by character development or scintillating prose. But great fiction
is not the goal of hypothetical war stories. They are meant as cautionary tales—this is what might happen, authors warn, if current developments play their course. Moreover, authors of future war fiction always
have their "villains"—very often inadequate military preparations for a
future war. In that respect, future war fiction is not designed for the purposes we have in mind.[1]

From the perspective of international relations theory, the stories
rarely seem to quite get it right. They tell stories about how wars might
break out, but none capture adequately the nature of transition wars—
that is, intensive conflicts between declining system leaders and ascending challengers that involve showdown confrontations involving all major
powers on one side or the other, with hegemony in the world economy at
stake.

To make this case, it should help to provide brief synopses of some
of the scenarios that are currently available. Nine representative ones, a
number of which are book-length treatments, have been selected for attention.[2] Each one has a different trigger: Korea, Taiwan, South China
Sea, and India. Our point is not that the triggers are implausible but that
the triggers in these treatments tend to become principal drivers of what
takes place. Put another way, these stories tend to be all trigger and no
drivers. One way of simplifying our criticism in advance is that we see the
triggers as substitutable precipitants in an inflammatory structural context. We think any number of local conflicts have the potential to escalate
to global conflagration given the right structural setting.[3] But triggers and

drivers are not and cannot be same thing. Given sundry drivers at work, various triggers can lead to violent (or pacific) outcomes. It is the structural setting that is not captured all that well in most of the nine scenarios outlined below.

1. A Korea-centric War Scenario[4]

This scenario is predicated on the overlapping of Chinese and North Korean ambitions. The Chinese, facing a looming natural resource shortage and hoping to head off a consequent deterioration of their position have decided that it is time to establish its control over the South China Sea and its oil-gas reserves. The North Koreans seek another opportunity to coerce reunification of the peninsula. For the Chinese, a Korean war is an opportunity to exploit as a northern diversion while it acts in the south. For the North Koreans, the Chinese activities in the south can also weaken the resistance to their own drive into South Korea.

North Korea initially attacks with infiltrations of commandos via submarines and tunnels. Anthrax is also introduced to reduce the number of defending combatants. A massive invasion from the north forces the defenders to retreat south and away from Seoul. The military question then becomes whether the entire peninsula can be conquered before South Korean and US forces can be reinforced. China focuses its attack initially on Quemoy and when that island falls quickly transfers its attention to Taiwan and the Spratly Islands. In the process, China forces clash with an American carrier group in the Taiwan Straits. However, China holds back its air/sea attack on Taiwan, hoping that Western forces will become bogged down in the Korean peninsula. Japan enters the war on the third day and sends troops to Korea, along with military forces from France, Britain, and Australia.

North Korea employs tactical nuclear weapons in an effort to break through a defensive line erected in the southern part of the peninsula. When that fails to eliminate the resistance, Kim Jong-il orders the launching of nuclear-tipped ballistic missiles. He is overthrown by his own military who fear the probable consequences of a nuclear exchange. Chinese troops then begin entering North Korea in force in order to accelerate the pace of the ground attack. Successful resistance to the Chinese–North Korean attacks leads to a Chinese use of missiles equipped with nuclear warheads and the United States responds in kind. This strategic missile exchange leaves both sides either reluctant or unable to continue fighting. A cease-fire is constructed, and negotiations lead to an acceptance of the status quo. Neither side's position is altered much from prewar circumstances.

2. A Taiwan-centric War Scenario[5]

In this scenario, China is responding in part to US antimissile defense testing and the possibility of US technical successes neutralizing the Chinese ballistic missile threat. There is also some desire expressed on the part of the Chinese to avoid repeating the Cold War missile race in which both sides competed at great expense to build more destructive arsenals with longer and longer reach. These concerns lead somewhat loosely to a scheme to take advantage of US decline and overextension by seizing Taiwan. Taiwan has nothing to do with missile superiority per se, but Taiwan is considered to be a step toward regional hegemony by the Chinese that might otherwise be thwarted should the US acquire a defensive shield against the threat of a nuclear attack.

An opportunity arises when US troops are committed to counter Indonesian instability. The Chinese plan is to secretly make things worse in Indonesia so that not only are US troops tied down in this theater, in conjunction with ongoing commitments in Korea and the Middle East, but that the American population and its governing elite will redevelop a bad taste for Asian military interventions thanks to rising casualties.

Assuming the US attention is focused elsewhere, a Chinese attack on Taiwan commences using a variety of inexpensive ploys ranging from hijacked airliners and ferries to hang gliders to insert troops into the island. Biological warfare is used to make a number of defenders ill. A nuclear device is employed to destroy the possibility of electronic communication among the defending forces. The Panama Canal is rendered inoperative for months by having a freighter explode while moving through the lock system.

The United States is initially reluctant to assist Taiwan, but some accidents force small units of US military forces to land on Taiwan after they are attacked. Under attack, they defend themselves without specific authorization and are able to do disproportionate damage to the Chinese invading forces. When they are about to be ordered to surrender by the US president, CNN footage is aired demonstrating US forces inflicting damage on the Chinese in Taiwan. This CNN effect stops the United States from withdrawing from the combat and even leads to a House of Representatives declaration of war against China. But when China threatens to launch nuclear missiles at the West Coast of the United States if US forces are not removed from the war theater, the Senate tables the war resolution, mass panic erupts in California, and the Chinese have almost won the battle over Taiwan.

The day is saved by the decision of the Quemoy-Matsu garrison to invade mainland China when they are about to surrender but hear that a local revolt against the Communist Party has erupted in an area adjacent to their islands. The local revolt, led by the Falun Gong and abetted by a few thousand Taiwanese soldiers, spreads widely throughout China. The Communist Party disintegrates as its officials are killed or imprisoned by angry mobs.

3. A South China Sea War Scenario[6]

China's most pressing problem in this scenario is its rising oil imports. The solution is to seize the Spratly and Paracel Islands, control over which is disputed among China, Vietnam, Taiwan, the Philippines, Malaysia, and Brunei, in the South China Sea. The action could actually accomplish a number of goals besides more access to oil and gas. Punishing the Vietnamese would be popular as would demonstrating the weakness of the United States. Success would help establish the unchallenged regional leadership of China.

The fighting begins with Chinese air raids on Vietnamese bases because the Chinese think that the Vietnamese are likely to provide the sole military resistance to the expansion and to the easy capture of the Paracel Islands. Military forces from Vietnam, Malaysia, Taiwan, and the Philippines are all defeated in various encounters, giving China military control of the South China Sea. Vietnam continues to fight back via guerrilla raids across its northern land border. Several complications begin to emerge. A large number of actors are inclined to accept the fait accompli in order to preserve their trade with, and investments in, China. However, a US naval vessel is sunk by the Chinese when it enters the South China Sea area. The Japanese are seriously concerned about the ability of their oil supplies to move through what is now a Chinese-controlled exclusive zone requiring Chinese permission for transit. The economic threat and perceived US weaknesses encourages Japan to test its first nuclear weapon. India offers noninterference in Tibet in exchange for China reducing its Pakistani ties and allowing India to share its bases in Burmese territory.

North Korean infiltrators begin a series of assassinations in South Korea, and South Korean commandos return the favor.

A North Korean ballistic missile launch is intercepted by the South Koreans. The South Koreans respond with air strikes on North Korean military bases. China communicates its support for the South Korean countermeasures. When the North Korean land attack begins, a Chinese-encouraged coup removes Kim Jong-il from power and halts the attack. A one country–two systems structure is created to unify the peninsula with the proviso that all foreign troops must be evacuated.

Farther south, a Chinese land attack is mauled by the Vietnamese, with French technical support. An allied fleet (United States Japan, Britain, Australia, New Zealand, and France) moves into the South China Sea to wrest its control away from China. After naval clashes, China and the United States are on the verge of exchanging ballistic missiles but agree to a cease-fire to avoid following through on the launches. Although the threat of a nuclear exchange is diminished, Chinese activities continue. Troops are massed on the Vietnamese border, a revolt in Tibet is suppressed, and coastal Taiwanese islands are seized. The United States is prepared to retreat and offers to recall all its forces west of Japan once China ceases all its Asian hostile activity. China's response is to attack Taiwan, only to be beaten back by stiff Taiwanese resistance.

The scenario ends with US troops withdrawn from the now-unified Korean peninsula. On the other hand, the United States has now reversed its trend toward military downsizing, and it and its main adversary are preparing for a Pacific War in which the participants all hope to do better the next time around.

4. An India-centric War Scenario[7]

This scenario is an explicit sequel to the South China Sea scenario. The action begins when an Indian commando force, composed of Tibetan refugees, infiltrates Tibet to rescue a jailed monk without Indian sanction. China responds with an assassination attack on the Tibetan exile community in India and accuses India of perpetrating a military attack on China. Roughly at the same time, India attacks several Pakistani villages by air in retaliation for an attack on Indian governmental elites in Kashmir, which was suspected to have been organized by Pakistan.

A military coup in Pakistan, with Chinese support, removes the civilian leadership. The quid pro quo is that Pakistan will assist in suppressing

Islamic fundamentalist attacks on western China in exchange for Chinese support against India. Pakistan then proposes that control of Kashmir be put to a referendum and threatens India with attack if it does not acquiesce. India declines the referendum. Pakistan attacks in the Kargil region while China reinforces its own border with India in the area where China attacked in 1962. The Chinese hope to force India to abandon its support for Tibetan resistance, as well as Bhutan, Nepal, and Sikkim. Arundal Pradesh would become Chinese territory. In general, India would be in a much poorer position to compete with China for Asian leadership if this war were to unfold as China and Pakistan anticipated.

India attacks Pakistan. China invades Bhutan. Pakistan, losing the war in the Thar Desert, uses tactical nuclear weapons supplied by China. Russia unsuccessfully attempts to persuade China not to escalate its attack on India. China then attacks India unexpectedly from Burmese soil. Pakistan next launches two nuclear missiles into India, prompting US intervention in the form of an air attack on the Pakistani command structure. The idea is to prevent Pakistan from launching any more nuclear missiles and to allow India to concentrate on the Chinese attack. As an auxiliary complication, an Australian, New Zealand, Britain, and Malaysian commando attack on a Chinese base in Burma occurs as part of an effort to keep the Malaccan Straits free of Chinese control. China's response is to attack a British fleet in the Indian Ocean.

A further complication is brought about by Taiwan choosing to declare its independence at a time when China appears to be heavily involved in South Asia. China responds to the Taiwanese initiative with a missile attack. The United States launches two cruise missiles at China in response. Meanwhile, India launches a conventional missile on a Chinese target only to have India respond with a nuclear counterattack. Further nuclear attacks on Indian targets, the United States warns will lead to a full US nuclear attack on China. At this point, Russia intervenes and threatens the United States with nuclear attack if the United States attacks China.

A Chinese missile destroys Mumbai, and India retaliates. The United States insists that Russia must arrange an Indian-Chinese cease-fire or it will destroy all Chinese nuclear weapon capability. If Russia should threaten to strike the United States or western Europe, the US nuclear attack on China would also include Russia. No ceasefire is arranged but no US missile strike occurs either. More Chinese and Indian missiles are exchanged but the fighting does subside. The outcome of this scenario is a loss of twenty million Indian lives with the new Indian leadership exploring cooperative ties with a more assertive Japan. Pakistan is a collapsed state. China controls Taiwan and is now regarded as a superpower.

5. A Southeast Asia War that Expands Scenario[8]

Although Samuel P. Huntington's scenario is set in 2010, much of the East Asian landscape has already been altered. Korea has reunified, leading to the withdrawal of US forces formerly stationed there. Taiwan and China have arranged a negotiated relationship in which Taiwan retains its independence while acknowledging Chinese sovereignty. Petroleum extraction is proceeding in the South China Sea with China controlling the lion's share. Some Vietnamese-US extraction efforts are tolerated. The US military presence in East Asian waters, including Japan, has been reduced substantially.

Given improvements in China's ability to project military force, a decision is made to proclaim the South China Sea an exclusive area strictly for Chinese development. Vietnam resists and fighting at sea breaks out. China escalates the dispute by invading Vietnam from its northern border and hoping to show more effectiveness than in 1979. Vietnam requests US assistance. The immediate American reaction is to impose economic sanctions and send one of its few remaining carrier groups into the South China Sea. China insists that this is an illegal invasion of its territory and proceeds to attack the carrier group from the air.

Intermittent US-Chinese fighting continues at sea while China proceeds to occupy most of Vietnam. Neither China nor the United States is prepared to escalate to a nuclear exchange, creating something of a standoff. Japan, however, declares its neutrality at this time. Domestic opposition to a dangerous war for seemingly debatable goals increases within the United States, particularly in the part of the country most likely to be hit by Chinese ballistic missiles.

Seeing China tied down in Southeast Asia, India seizes the opportunity to attack Pakistan preemptively, hoping to reduce the Pakistani nuclear/military threat. Initial Indian successes prompt Iran to come to the aid of Pakistan. Chinese successes against the United States also have stimulated Islamist movements in the Middle East to overthrow the surviving pro-Western Arab governments. This leads, in turn, to an attack on Israel that is overwhelming and too strong for the United States to block.

Back in East Asia, Japan switches from neutrality to the Chinese camp. The United States is forced to withdraw its remaining military from Japanese territory while under attack from Japanese forces. Russia, alarmed by Chinese successes and their implications for Asian predominance, pursues the opposite course by reinforcing its military forces stationed in Siberia. Clashes with Chinese settlers in Siberia soon leads to Chinese military intervention in that region. Russian forces continue to combat Chinese forces as China captures Vladivostok and eastern Siberia.

The fall of pro-Western governments in the Middle East causes oil supplies to the West to pretty much cease altogether. As the West becomes increasingly dependent on Russian sources, it does not object to Russia's increasing control of Central Asia and its oil resources. The US's European allies prove reluctant to become involved in the ongoing fighting until Chinese and Iranian nuclear missiles are moved into Algeria and Bosnia to further encourage their noninvolvement. North Atlantic Treaty Organization (NATO), however, demands their immediate withdrawal but is trumped by a Serbian attack on Bosnia that captures the missiles there and reignites Slavic-led ethnic cleansing in the region. Albania and Turkey attempt to provide assistance to the Bosnians, which prompts Bulgaria and Greece to invade Turkish territory. A missile launched from Algeria hits Marseilles. NATO responds with retaliatory strikes in several parts of North Africa.

Huntington stops his scenario narrative with fighting ongoing in southeastern Europe, North Africa, South Asia, and East Asia. Three alternative forks in the road are posed. If China and the United States drop their restraints on nuclear exchanges, both sides are likely to incur considerable damage. If nuclear deterrence prevails, the two adversaries could negotiate a cease-fire that would leave China predominant in East Asia. If fighting continued at the conventional level, the inability of the US Navy to operate effectively in the Pacific without bases offshore from the Chinese mainland would increase the emphasis on an allied land attack from Siberia into northern China.

Huntington declined to speculate on which of these alternatives might be more probable. His perspective was influenced strongly by the pessimistic calculation that, no matter which path was pursued, the main participants would suffer serious losses in wealth, population, and military power. The primary beneficiaries would be any relatively powerful states in the Global South that had managed to remain aloof from the fighting. India and Indonesia were singled out as states that were likely to improve their relative positions but that meant that their relationship was likely to become more conflictual, whether a revived China reappeared on the Asian scene. Elsewhere, the United States would become increasingly Hispanic in population and culture and dependent on economic aid from Latin America while Europe would be deluged by African migrants.

6.–7. *Two More Global Efforts*[9]

Two novels may hint at what we may expect to see more of in the future. Eric Harry's book is about a Chinese invasion of the United States. The book focuses mainly on the actual invasion and the ensuing combat, but the reader can glean some idea about the events that led up the outbreak of war between China and the United States. Unfortunately, the preceding events resemble a global Risk game. Korea and Japan are conquered in early efforts by China that require some two years of fighting. Then China moves into the Middle East after defeating the European Union in naval combat in the Battle of Diego Garcia. Israel unsuccessfully deploys tactical nuclear weapons against the invading forces and is punished with the destruction of Tel Aviv. Further naval combat in the vicinity of Gibraltar initially appeared to be won by the European Union fleet, only to be overwhelmed by Chinese reinforcements in the guise of a large number of carriers that the Chinese were not known to possess. Earlier, China had destroyed Western military satellites—a favor to which the United States and Europe had responded to in kind. However, a compromise had been worked out to demilitarize space, thereby leaving the West with no "eyes in the sky" to monitor Chinese naval construction efforts.

The defeat at Gibraltar served to disintegrate European military unity. British and French forces returned to their national borders to prepare for invasion. But instead of striking north, the Chinese moved into the Caribbean and occupied three islands. Citing the Monroe Doctrine, the United States finally declares war but is unable to resist the Chinese island hopping tactics, aided by Latin American, and especially Cuban, support, and loses control of the Caribbean after Guantanamo falls. Invasion of the United States soon follows.

Carl Berryman's novel is a much more detailed tome about the outbreak of world war in 2013. The United States has been persuaded that military combat of the future will be of the Iraqi variety in which a United States defeats technologically inferior foes with precision weapons and advantages in information technology. No perception of the possibility of a peer challenge emerged, aided in part by a "new" China Lobby that worked to suppress criticism of China.

China is portrayed as a large population characterized by looming insecurity over access to food, raw materials, and energy. Droughts and flooding had further aggravated the inability of China to feed its growing population. The solution was to conquer South East, South and Central Asia, as well as southern Africa. Southeast and South Asia would provide new supplies of rice, grain and arable land for resettled Chinese farmers. Central Asia and Africa would provide the raw materials needed for future industrialization.

Fighting begins with intermittent raids over the Mexican border financed by the Chinese. North Korea attacks South Korea initially using biological weapons followed by a massive movement of troops southward. Conveniently, US troops had been expelled from South Korea earlier to placate popular hostility to their presence. Chinese subversion in Kashmir gives the appearance of Indian attacks on Pakistani positions. The United States has few resources to respond quickly and focuses on airlifting US citizens out of South Korea and responds to the Mexican raids with force on Mexican soil.

After a month of fighting in the Korean peninsula, a desperate South Korea launches a nuclear missile at Pyongyang and begins using tactical nuclear weapons, left behind by the departed US forces, on the battlefield. North Korea retaliates by using a nuclear missile to destroy the South Korean missile base but begins to lose the battle on the ground. The Indo-Pakistani fighting also escalates to the nuclear level after two small nuclear weapons are detonated in Pakistan. Believing this attack to have originated in India, the Pakistanis respond with a nuclear missile barrage on Indian cities. The Indians respond as well, leading to massive destruction throughout South Asia. Chinese troops are able to move into the theater two weeks later and encounter little in the way of resistance.

The Chinese invasion of Southeast Asia succeeds relatively quickly. Forces used in Southeast and South Asia are sent on to the east African theater. At the same time, China had occupied the Ryukyu Islands and seemed to be preparing to take control of Taiwan.[10] US mobilization to prepare for a total war is underway. Japan, Russia, the European Union, and the United States jointly demand that the Chinese expansion on land stop at Iran and withdraw from Africa. Southeast and South Asia are written off as successful Chinese conquests. The Chinese threaten massive retaliation if their forces are attacked. The United States attacks the Panama Canal Zone and manages to capture a number of Chinese missiles that could have been launched at American targets. Yet, it is a US threat to destroy all Chinese submarines simultaneously that saves the day. The Chinese attack grinds to a halt even though it never formally withdraws its troops from Africa.

The story ends with Russia and the European Union assuming responsibility for European defense. NATO is dissolved. Middle Eastern states draw closer to European and US protection. Two to three billion people have died, mainly in Asia. The structure of the system is focused on a four-way split among China, Japan, the European Union, and the United States, with more, unspecified combat presumed likely in a multipolar setting.

8. A Weakening China Lashes Out[11]

In marked contrast to the last two scenarios depicting Chinese juggernauts, this scenario describes a process possibly leading to a war that no one really wanted. The scenario is based on a China that is experiencing a sharp slowdown in its rapid economic growth rate, one of the main pillars of governmental legitimacy. A number of problems are converging to restrict Chinese growth in the second half of the twenty-first century's second decade. One factor is a natural fall off in high growth rates that is anticipated as the Chinese economy moves beyond its less developed status. High energy prices are another constraint on growth, as well as reduced US purchase of Chinese production that stems from the lingering bursting of the real estate bubble. A fourth factor is the aging of the Chinese population, aggravated by the long commitment to a single-child policy, which reduces the proportion of the population that is most likely to be productive. It also increases the need for, and the costs of, welfare and health support systems. Making matters worse, severe economic degradation, intensive pollution, and the increasing scarcity of water, particularly in the north China plain, are combining to reduce standards of living.

In 2016, debate within the US Congress over the desirability of trade sanctions to force China to revalue its currency (and decrease the size of the US trade deficit with China) leads to a Chinese threat to liquidate its holdings of US Treasury notes. The threat works to end the congressional debate. But a year later, Chinese unrest is increasing on a number of fronts, including the usual foci of Tibet and the Uighurs, but expanding throughout the country in response to declining living standards. Taiwan has also resumed its open discussion of the attractions of declaring independence. The Chinese government's response is to acknowledge the existence of the widespread economic problems, but the main source of its problems is attributed to malign foreign powers attempting to thwart Chinese growth.

In early 2017 the Chinese government decides to assume the offensive and announces a three-part declaration. Taiwan must cease its discussion of independence and increase its investment in the Chinese economy. The United States must withdraw from its Asian bases and abandon its efforts to encircle China. Finally, the United States should encourage its Persian Gulf clients to expand the production of oil. To go beyond mere rhetoric, China announces an immediate blockade of Taiwanese commerce. Any foreign shipping in Taiwan waters would be destroyed. Any foreign state that attempts to aid Taiwan would be considered a belligerent at war with China. Any US satellites violating Chinese air space would also be destroyed.

As Taiwan resists the blockade, the issue is discussed in the United Nations (UN) Security Council. No concrete outcome is forthcoming, thanks to the threat of a Chinese veto. In the United States, an increasing number of cyber attacks on both private and public information networks are deflected. Nonetheless, a counterblockade of Chinese ports is mounted by the United States and Japan, which the Chinese government portrays as ample confirmation of its earlier accusations of the malign intentions of foreign powers.

Chinese submarines are dispersed to positions that would maximize their ability to interrupt world oil flows and US carrier movements toward the East China Sea. US decision makers contemplate withdrawing their planes from bases in Okinawa and Guam to preclude missile attacks, but decide not to do so to avoid appearing to be abandoning Japan. At the same time, Central Asian governments are balking at approving the stationing of strategic bombers at US bases in their territories.

The scenario ends with the US and Japanese decision makers agreeing that they are not in a position to significantly aid Taiwan. This realization encourages them to offer to negotiate a resolution of the crisis in order to avoid the possibility of conflict escalation. However, China rejects the offer, leaving the United States and Japan to choose between war or capitulation. We are not told what choice is made.

9. An Eagle in Decay[12]

The last scenario almost seems a nontransition scenario, but it is instead a distinctive, possible sequence of events in which both the United States and China suffer major setbacks. At the end of the second decade of the current century, China's economic power is still increasing but not at its earlier breakneck pace. The slowdown is attributed to the inefficiencies of central planning. Moreover, China's military capability, while improving, has still not changed all that much from the decade before. In contrast, the United States is depicted as approaching the economic status of a third world state, reduced to selling timber and coal to China. Most of the US's high technology production had been transferred to India and China to reduce costs, but in the process China and India had been able to copy or steal the technology for their own economic production. In addition, an aging population had led to intergenerational political warfare over entitlements. Suffering the lingering effects of technology bubble bursts, large-scale unemployment, increasing deficits, a diminishing economy, and rising debt, social services had been reduced, defense spending was down considerably, and debt payments halted altogether. The result was declining foreign investment, increasing inflation, and an armed forces establishment that was beginning to resemble the American military in 1940 in terms of its lack of preparedness.

By 2020, the power structure of the world is decidedly multipolar with India and the European Union outspending the United States and China in military expenditures. The Indian and European Union navies are also stronger and more technologically advanced than their American and Chinese counterparts. The Indian economy is the largest in the world and growing quickly. The United States presence in East Asia has been handicapped by the inability to station a nuclear carrier in Japan. Taiwan, though, is no longer an issue of contention. Its close economic ties with the mainland have led to a compromise in which Taiwanese politicians have accepted Chinese sovereignty in exchange for a free trade zone status.

Nonetheless, changed leadership in China resolves to push for a more ambitious foreign policy agenda in 2019. Looking for an opportunity to demonstrate its claims in the South China Sea, a foreign oil exploration vessel is attacked near one of the Spratly Islands. A Malaysian warship protects the exploration vessel by sinking the Chinese ship. Unable to catch the fast-retreating Malaysian warship, a Chinese submarine is sent through the Malacca Straits to attack the Malaysian naval base at Malaka. By mistake, an Indian warship is sunk instead. India decides to retaliate by moving a carrier group into the Spratly Islands. The guilty Chinese submarine is sunk along the way.

Meanwhile, an American plane is attacked by a Chinese Mig, acting without authorization, near the Philippines. China apologizes to the

United States but a US B2 bomber is sent to destroy a Chinese air force base in response. Chinese attempts to halt the entry of Indian warships into the South China Sea fails. A similar failure to block the entry of a US carrier group into the same area soon follows. Justifying its actions by citing the need to save face, China brings into play satellite weapons to destroy a US carrier. The United States responds by neutralizing all Chinese satellites with weapons capabilities. Waiting for the right moment, a group of Chinese submarines launch missile and torpedo attacks on the remaining US forces. The US defense is not successful, but manages to attack the Indian carrier group thinking that they are part of the Chinese offensive. The Indian carrier group defends itself successfully, thereby contributing further to the damage suffered by the US naval forces. China decides to press its attack on the crippled US forces, but the Indian naval forces intervene and inflict substantial damage on the Chinese attacking force while protecting the withdrawing US forces.

This combat in the South China Sea and the Indian Ocean has taken approximately a month to unfold. Although nuclear missiles have been considered and threatened, no nuclear escalation is ordered by any of the belligerents. Peace talks ensue under the auspices of the UN Secretary General and the European Union. The substantive outcome is that China is allowed to retain control of a majority of the Spratly Islands while permitting oil exploration in 40 percent of the area. Chinese and US warships are forbidden to enter the Indian Ocean. India emerges as the leading power in a new world order, with the European Union as the second ranking power, and China and the United States rebuilding as best they can.

Comparing the Fictional Scenarios: Scenario Drivers

All the scenarios take for granted some degree of US relative decline, US overextension, and Chinese ascent and a desire for regional (or more) hegemony. Yet only the last one can be said to really stress these elements. Factors such as these might be considered to be structural drivers. They are present at least minimally in order to account for the unwillingness of the United States to act boldly or at all. Secondary drivers are the more specific ambitions of the actors involved, and these secondary motivations, not surprisingly, are given more emphasis in the story telling. The focus of these secondary drivers is always China-centric since it is China that sets things in motion—never the United States, which always responds, however reluctantly or feebly, to a Chinese gambit. The Chinese gambit, in turn, is motivated by something like concerns about resource shortages, the potential for domestic unrest, recreating Greater China, or taking advantage of favorable opportunities to score positional gains on the United States (and other powerful states in the general Asian regions, including Japan and India).

Nothing resembling a full-fledged World War III is described. Conflict often spreads in these scenarios, but they remain regional affairs, sometimes including all the other possible major powers but only in what might be best described as restricted circumstances—more on the order of allied involvement in the Korean War (1950–53), or, at best, serial, regional clashes. These last two observations are not meant as criticism. World wars have begun in limited ways (e.g., an Austrian-Prussian attack on France [1792], an Austrian attack on Serbia [1914], or a German move against Poland [1939]), but they spin out of control and ultimately bring in the other major powers in the system for a bipolarized showdown between two sets of at least nominally connected teams of great powers. The nine war scenarios oft go awry as well, but they tend to be managed confrontations that stop short of outright conflagration with all major powers fighting simultaneously.

The relative absence of constraints, other than decision-maker prudence, is striking. The democratic peace argument is not a factor because only some of the states are democracies—and they tend to be on the same side. The authoritarian states' behavior is usually determined by a small group of highly placed actors. The democratic actors are often seen as near paralyzed by domestic public opinion considerations, but never completely blocked from acting. International institutions play no significant role, although in one scenario the UN Secretary General is allowed to play a minor role in picking up the pieces. Economic interdependence often is given a role in making states, particularly the United States, reluctant to oppose Chinese aggressive moves. Other states, both in Asia and elsewhere, are depicted as having too much to lose in terms of trade and investments to contemplate a coercive strategy of resistance, until their backs are against the wall. Individual and corporate actors who have the most to gain from economic stability are depicted as taking strong stands to persuade their own governments from overreacting. Yet this constraint tends to be overcome by accident or the lack of alternatives once one's own armed forces come under attack. Otherwise, of course, there would be no war scenario story to tell.

Deterrence, especially nuclear deterrence, plays little role at least up to a point. Actors employ nuclear weapons out of desperation or as part of a more complicated strategy but always selectively and rarely with much hesitation. Missiles tend to be exchanged one or two at a time, at least at first. Either common sense then prevails and states cease launching more missiles or the barrages increase in number. But when they do increase, the nuclear exchanges tend to be between actors who have limited nuclear capabilities. Never does the possession of nuclear weapons by adversaries stop actors from attempting to do something at the outset—only toward the end does deterrence reemerge as something of a constraint on a full-tilt Armageddon.

What is missing from most but not all these scenarios is some sense of technological competition between China and the United States, or anyone else for that matter. There are two easy explanations for this omission. One is that most of the scenarios are very much fin de siècle constructions. Written in the late 1990s and usually projected vaguely into the first decade of the twenty-first century, China remains in this first wave of fiction, not unrealistically, underdeveloped in the production of industrial technology. The United States has a clear advantage in military technology but is stretched too thin to bring it to bear in East Asia at full force and is tired of getting bogged down in Asian ground conflicts. This portrayal is hardly unrealistic either, with or without having knowledge of subsequent wars in Afghanistan and Iraq and the fixation on combating terrorism. Chinese technological competitiveness begins to appear more noticeably, especially in terms of military technology, in a second, post-2000 wave of fiction. But only one story really emphasizes China as becoming the center of world manufacture.[13] In this story, however, the threat of war with China becomes a vehicle for restimulating the US economy with military contracts.

The other explanation is that we do not all fully appreciate the technological competitions that underlay earlier global wars. Students are exposed to the battles and geopolitical machinations of World Wars I and II in elementary and high school, but rarely is there much attention to political-economic competition. That, for instance, the United States entered World Wars I and II because a German submarine sank an American vessel and Pearl Harbor was attacked, respectively, suffices as reason enough for many people. If these wars have something to do with contests over which economy is the most productive in the world economy (and the perks that accompany this status), a clash between a less-developed Asian state with a large population and army and the state with the lead in industrial technology is less satisfactory as a template for transitional warfare. The most important caveat, however, is that the scenario emphases on relatively limited clashes can be seen to be more plausible in the earlier stages of a rivalry between a declining economic leader and one of its possible successors. As seen most clearly in scenario four, these are preliminary matches before the main bout.

As a consequence, the scenarios, at least in the first wave, tend to have a prominent role for some contemporary territorial revision—Korea, Taiwan, the South China Sea, Tibet, and the Sino-Indian border. The small islands that are claimed by Japan and China do not figure very large in these 1990s scenarios but are likely to play bigger roles in future fiction. Territory, after all, is something states have fought over fairly consistently. At the moment, one can draw a circle around China and point to all the most obvious places for a possible clash that escalates into something much bigger than a real estate dispute. The problem is that twenty years down the road, some of these flashpoints may have been resolved. Korea could be unified peacefully. Taiwan might peacefully accept a status resembling Hong Kong or, alternatively, never really pursue the independence card to its nth degree. Still, twenty years down the road should still leave some territorial question(s) in play. At least two decades ahead, moreover, is critical.[14] Anything sooner would give too much technological lead to the United States for anything that was premeditated and that could spread to involve all major powers as participants. An earlier war between the United States and China cannot be ruled out as improbable, but if one were to break out over, say a Taiwan misunderstanding, it would be less likely to spread to other actors.

If none of these fictional scenarios seem ideal for a transitional setting, what then are the *necessary ingredients* for a transitional conflicts?[15]

1. Absolutely essential is a system leader in relative decline and at least one challenger for succession to the lead economy position—our primary structural driver. This definitely has little to do with the absolute size of the competing economies in question. That is, it does not matter ultimately which states have the largest economies in the system. What does matter is which state(s) lead in innovating radical new technologies that expand the production frontier. If there is a strong system leader with few, if any, peer competitors in terms of economic innovation, transitional wars are not especially probable. If there is only an obvious successor to the incumbent system leader and the incumbent is not prepared to contest the economic transition, transitional wars are prob-

ably not all that probable. That leaves the situations that are most dangerous in which there is one challenger and one system leader in decline that is prepared to contest the succession or a declining system leader and more than one possible successor. More will be said (and, no doubt, will need to be said) about this factor in subsequent chapters.

2. It would not be absolutely critical but it would help if world economic conditions were depressed, thereby intensifying the degree of competition among the major economic players and especially between the declining system leader and a possible successor. The major players would find themselves producing similar products and vying for position in markets around the globe. Sources of energy (petroleum and gas) and other resources (water, food, and arable land) would become more scarce while demand remained high. Conflict over new resources becoming accessible in the Arctic might also accentuate the general feelings of acute, zero-sum economic competition in which the actors perceive their competitors proceeding ubiquitously and unfairly to maximize their own share of profits, markets, and resources.

3. Two or more decades into the future there are likely to be more major powers in play and a more genuine multipolar setting. However many major powers there are, there should also be some evident polarization with major powers taking sides on opposing teams, or at least edging toward such bipolarization. This prerequisite is one of the structural ingredients that is critical for all of the major powers to jump into, or be dragged into, an escalating conflict.

4. Another prerequisite is multiple rivalries that have become more tense. One needs the active rivalries between a declining system leader and at least one challenger successor (e.g., the United States and China) that are typically found in the fictional scenarios, but also contenders for regional hegemony (e.g., the United States and China, China and India, China and Japan, or all of them), and possibly an asymmetrical rivalry or two between major/minor and minor powers in Asia (China-Taiwan, China-Vietnam, the two Koreas, and India and Pakistan). These rivalries are often present in the fictional scenarios but they are taken for granted as part of the story arc. Currently, the United States and China agree to tiptoe around the question of whether they are each other's main major power rival. Military officials on both sides make references to their significant other in terms of war plans and move weapons platforms toward one another while heads of government deny any ongoing rivalry. That needs to change if one or both sides are to begin focusing closely and with great suspicion on the other side's every move. This type of setting allows small misperceptions to become blown out of proportion. For instance, in a "tiptoe" phase, one side can accidentally attack the other state's embassy in Serbia and not

have it spiral upward into something even uglier. Once past the tiptoe stage, the conflict escalation potential of such accidents are very difficult to manage peacefully.

But one also needs several different rivalries becoming more intense so that it becomes more difficult to keep incidents strictly dyadic in fact and in implication. In 1914, what Austria-Hungary and Serbia did also had implications for other ongoing rivalries (Russia-Austria-Hungary, France and Germany, Germany and Britain, Austria and Italy, and more). The asymmetrical rivalries may not be absolutely necessary but they serve as useful triggers. A powerful state attacks/threaten a smaller state (or vice versa), thinking the implications are relatively local and finds out differently.[16] In this structural setting, one then needs only some sort of trigger to get the ball moving. If one of the main challengers has irredentist tendencies, a plausible trigger is an attack on a nearby territory that has some security linkages or economic/strategic value to the challenger's opponents and which is undertaken with the bad assumption that something (e.g., overcommitment or surprise) is likely to prevent serious resistance to the attack. For instance, it tends to be argued that, other things being equal, China is unlikely to coerce Taiwan to accept Chinese sovereignty if Chinese decision makers were convinced that such a move would very probably invoke an equally coercive US countermove. Make the probability of a coercive response hazy or dubious, accurately or otherwise, and the setting changes considerably.

A challenger attack on Taiwan, Japan, or India then swings the declining system leader and its allies into defensive action. The composition of the defensive coalition and its various antagonisms encourage others to join the challenger team. What begins as a localized conflict then quickly escalates into a contest among all the major players. As the participation widens, the stakes escalate along with the firepower involved. It is not inconceivable that all players might start the conflict with the shared assumption, implicitly or explicitly, that the conflict would be waged on conventional terms. And it might actually be conducted along conventional lines, but there is also some good possibility that some participants would come to the conclusion that it or they needed to go nuclear to stay in the contest or accept defeat. By this time, more states would possess the capability to fire missiles at some distance from the launch point. As in some of the earlier scenarios, the exchange of nuclear missiles might be kept limited, or it might not.

Hence, the main drivers of such a transition war scenario include a structural setting of political-economic decline and ascent, multiple intensifying patterns of rivalry and acute competition, and the bipolarization of the major players. The constraints are few. The democratic peace is probably irrelevant in a setting pitting authoritarian states against democratic states. In fact, the mix of regime types only makes conflict more probable. Economic interdependence is present but is insufficient to suppress antagonisms that have become more acute. What we consider to be the flip side of interdependence—the similar nature of economic production, the contest over scoring gains in technological innovation, and the dependence on limited energy sources—makes conflict more likely. International institutions are present but largely incapable of playing a significant role in managing conflicts among the major powers. Nuclear deterrence is also present as a fourth source of constraint, but the problem is that we really do not know if nuclear deterrence works equally well in periods of postglobal war, concentrated systemic leadership (as in the US-Soviet Cold War) and periods of multipolar deconcentration that have facilitated the outbreak of global war in the past. Unlike democratization, economic interdependence, and international organization, nuclear deterrence remains an unknown quantity in the mid–twenty-first century. It could have a major effect or perhaps little at all, much like aerial bombing of cities was initially proscribed in World War II.

Nonetheless, we cannot focus exclusively on the possibilities of a future war between China and the United States, however we imagine the steps to war. A transition war is only one possible outcome and it may not even be the most likely one. We need to compare alternative futures in which drivers thought to be weak in some situations turn out to be strong and, as a consequence, alter the outcome.

In our estimation, currently available, fictional scenarios about the future of China and the United States are not very fruitful venues for our analytical purposes. We have suggested what we think are their weaknesses. But the authors of the fictional scenarios had their own objectives for constructing the stories they tell. It is unfair to criticize them for not pursuing our own, more theoretical objectives. If we want scenarios to serve our purposes, we need to develop our own stories. We cannot simply take them "off the shelf." The question then is how should one go about doing this? Our answer is that the scenarios need to be grounded in international relations theory. These theories do not tell us what will happen in the future but they do address the drivers of world politics. The constructed scenarios can then be harnessed to depict what might happen depending on the mix of drivers at play. War is only one possible outcome. So, too, is structural transition.

Chapters 4–6 focus on what we see as the main drivers at work in structural transition contexts. Chapters 4 and 5 emphasize the factors that might encourage conflict and violence. Chapter 6 stresses factors that might constrain or discourage violent outcomes. Presumably, more peaceful outcomes will be associated with situations in which the constraining drivers overwhelm the conflictual drivers. Less peaceful outcomes will be a product of the converse set of interactions.

Power-Transition, Offensive-Realism, and Leadership Long-Cycle Perspectives on Structural Transitions

If structural change is critical to understanding transition processes, which structural theory or model most accurately maps the power-transition process? Which model's main explanatory variables will better track this process and provide the best explanation of how it unfolds? Which model supplies the most attractive or useful drivers of transition conflict? The best-known approach to power transitions is the research program originated in 1958 by the late A. F. K. Organski, whose coauthors and students continue the same line of research and explicitly use the "power-transition" label. Though Organski may have coined the phrase "power transition," there are a number of other works that address the same or similar underlying questions—though with different nomenclature and explanatory variables—and thus can be grouped within a more generic power-transition category.[1] Our approach in this chapter is to compare the latest versions of the Organski-derived power-transition model with Mearsheimer's offensive-realism model and our preferred alternative, termed the challenger/transition model, which is derived largely from leadership long-cycle theory and other sources.[2] We first describe the power-transition and offensive-realism models and discuss some of their limitations. We then turn to the challenger/transition model that we believe offers some clear advantages when it comes to tracking transitional conflicts.

The Power-Transition Model

A short list of key concepts in the power-transition model includes hierarchy, economic growth, dissatisfaction, overtaking, and parity.[3] The international system is viewed as a pyramid-shaped power hierarchy. At the very top tier is the system's dominant power. The next tier contains the great powers, followed by medium and small powers. Descending down the tiers, the number of states falling into each tier increases, hence the pyramidal structure.

In a system in which all states are agrarian, economic growth involves extending the size of agricultural holdings and the number of people that reside within them. Industrialization, beginning in the late eighteenth century, altered the range of options available to state makers seeking greater power. The size of one's population continued to be of great importance, but, after the eighteenth century, economic productivity could be vastly enhanced by intensively exploiting and adopting technology instead of merely expanding the state's territorial size. Most importantly, industrialization made possible relatively rapid ascents in the international hierarchy. In particular, it made possible the ascent of hitherto underdeveloped states with large populations that, in turn, meant that larger states could catch up and surpass smaller states that had developed their economies earlier. Moreover, once states reach a high level of development, their further growth is likely to be relatively slow—thereby making them more vulnerable to rapidly ascending states with developing economies.

States at the top of the system's hierarchy take advantage of their elite status and establish rules, institutions, and privileges that primarily benefit themselves. Ascending states thus encounter a structure of benefits already established by an earlier cohort of elites. If that structure is perceived to work against the best interests of ascending states, they are likely to be dissatisfied with the way in which the system is organized, in particular with its distribution of tangible and intangible benefits and with the restrictions it places on their upward mobility.

At any point in time, some proportion of the total field of states, whether they are ascending or not, will share dissatisfaction with the prevailing system structure. Three questions are (1) whether the extent of dissatisfaction is great, (2) whether one or more of those states that are most dissatisfied are in the great power stratum, and (3) whether a sufficiently dissatisfied great power is overtaking the system's dominant power. The

probability of conflict between the dissatisfied great power and the dominant power will be greatest when the relative capabilities of these two
states are characterized by parity—the "zone of contention and probable
war" wherein the ratio of the dissatisfied great power's and the dominant
state's capabilities lies between 4:5 and 6:5.[4] Prior to attaining parity, the
rising, dissatisfied great power has little incentive to attack a dominant
power that is still viewed as too powerful. The challenger essentially lacks
the capability to do something about its dissatisfaction. Long after surpassing the once-dominant power, the rising, dissatisfied great power no
longer has much incentive to attack a now inferior, former rival. Thus, the
greatest risk of warfare is when the two states have attained rough equality in power (parity), after one state that is dissatisfied with the international order has caught up with a formerly more powerful state (overtaking) that was most responsible for creating the status quo. This is the
dangerous zone of power transition.

In addition to this conceptualization of power-transition dynamics, analysts working in this tradition employ several auxiliary concepts
and generalizations. The most stable and enduring alliances are formed
between actors that relate to the prevailing status quo similarly. Therefore, alliances linking satisfied and dissatisfied actors may occur, but their
duration will be temporary. Alliances can reinforce the pro–status quo or
anti–status quo forces, but they cannot substitute for the key structural
dynamic of overtaking in the one dyad that matters most.

Institutional similarity and economic interdependence modify the
likelihood of dissatisfaction. The more similar the institutions and/or the
more interdependent two economies are, the less likely dissatisfaction will
lead to a challenge to the system's status quo. Conversely, arms buildups
and arms races (if both sides in a transitional situation participate) reflect
substantial dissatisfaction on the part of the challenger and an attempt to
accelerate the pace of military catch-up and the development of a relative
power advantage.

Another central concept in the power-transition research program is
political capacity. More efficacious political systems can facilitate economic growth and mobilize resources for attacking or defending the
status quo. Thus, it is conceivable that a state could have a large population and a rapidly developing economy, but only limited political capacity
to bring these elements of power together in an effective package. Only if
the political capability to mobilize resources improves along with population and economic growth is a state's relative power likely to be enhanced.

Political capacity also presupposes some convergence of elite goals in mobilizing resources for international competition. Divisions within the elite or a weak, decentralized state can hold back a potential challenger's ability to take on the dominant nation.

Finally, a last caveat pertains to the speed of overtaking. The faster the overtaking, the lower is the probability of war. Should war break out in such circumstances, it is not likely to be a very severe or protracted confrontation because the ascending power is likely to gain its power advantage over the formerly dominant power in fairly short order. Slow transitions prolong the period of parity and increase the window of maximum friction. If neither side can muster a relative power advantage, the combat is likely to become a drawn-out war of attrition.

The power-transition model's history begins mid-eighteenth century with the advent of the Industrial Revolution. Events that occurred prior to this milestone are regarded as irrelevant to power-transition dynamics. After Britain established its early lead, it was overtaken by the United States and Germany. The United States, in turn, according to this perspective, will be overtaken eventually by China and India. Resistance to the long-term dynamics is believed to be futile (although perhaps not unlikely). Accommodation to the shifts in relative power is the recommended policy course.

In 2011 a very specific power-transition forecast was published. Tieh-shang Lee used purchasing power parity gross domestic product (GDP) data to calculate an explicit overtaking schedule.[5] The available data showed China first catching up to Japan in 1995 and surpassing it in 2010 and forecast that China's economy would surpass the size of the US economy in 2019.[6] By 2025, the size of the Chinese economy should surpass the combination of the United States and Taiwan, and, by 2049, the Chinese economy would be larger than the combined economies of the United States, Taiwan, and Japan. Lee goes on to say that his understanding of power-transition theory suggests that the most dangerous zone of potential conflict extends from 2021 to 2076. In 2021, China's "power" will correspond to 80 percent of the US-led group. In 2076, China will be 20 percent ahead of the group, assuming it remains together.[7]

Critique

The power-transition model sees a single hierarchy in which one state has already established an edge in relative power over other great powers.[8]

The precise basis for dominance is not fully specified but its foundations lie in having a combination of more people, a larger economy, and some capacity to mobilize these power resources. A structural problem emerges when an even larger great power emerges only to become dissatisfied with the prevailing distribution of benefits and privileges. The cartoon that depicts a string of open-mouthed fish of decreasing size, with each fish about to devour the next smallest fish in the sequence, captures this transition imagery quite nicely.[9]

As a consequence, the power-transition model offers a clear prediction about the timing of conflict.[10] Around the time that the once smaller fish catches up to the bigger fish and establishes parity, conflict between the challenger and once-dominant power becomes more likely.

How do analysts conceptualize the sources of power that are most crucial to structural models in general and to power transitions in particular? Population and economic size are critical to the power-transition model. According to Tammen et al., "[W]ithout a large population, a nation cannot hope ever to become either a great power or dominant nation."[11] The main reason underlying this generalization is that population is viewed as the basic resource pool that can be mobilized for other purposes, including economic development and the exercise of military force. Population can be influenced by slowing birth rates and/or decreasing death rates but, generally, it is a relatively fixed foundation of national power. A state either has a large population or does not. States with larger populations are likely to surpass the relative power of states with smaller populations. Accordingly, power-transition analysts expect small powerful states eventually will have to give way to large powerful states.

In the long run, the already prosperous United States cannot remain the dominant nation in the international system because both China and India have populations four times larger. This population gap cannot be bridged by a developed society. Therefore, because of the constraints that stable populations impose on the expansion of power in developed societies once Asian societies modernize and overtake the United States, no new transitions are anticipated.[12]

Consistent with this emphasis on population size, power transition analysts rely on GDP as their primary index of national economic productivity.[13] Overtaking and parity, therefore, are customarily measured in terms of the difference between the dominant nation's GDP and the overtaking, dissatisfied great power's GDP. Once the overtaker's GDP attains 80 percent of the dominant power's GDP, the condition of parity is considered

TABLE 4.1. **British, German, United States, and Chinese gross domestic product (GDP) and GDP per capita (GDP/C), 1820–2015.**

	Britain		Germany		United States		China	
Year	GDP	GDP/C	GDP	GDP/C	GDP	GDP/C	GDP	GDP/C
1820	34.8	1756	16.4	1112	12.6	1287	228.6	523
1850	60.5	2362	29.4	1476	42.5	1819		
1870	96.6	3263	44.1	1913	94.4	2457	187.2	523
1880	114.9	3556	53.1	2078	161.1	3193		
1890	143.5	4099	70.6	2539	215.0	3396	233.5	615
1900	176.5	4593	99.2	3134	312.9	4096	260.6	652
1913	214.5	5032	145.1	3833	518.0	5307	300.9	688
1920	203.3	4651	114.0	2986	594.1	5559		
1930	238.3	5195	165.2	4049	769.2	6220	384.3	786
1940	315.7	6546	242.8	5545	930.8	7018	400.0	778
1950	344.9	6847	214.0	4281	1457.6	9573	335.5	614
1960	448.9	8571	469.2	8463	2022.2	11193	585.5	878
1970	594.9	10694	723.7	11933	3045.8	14854	893.7	1092
1980	719.5	12777	946.3	15370	4161.0	18270	1434.2	1462
1995	961.0	16371	1275.7	19097	6149.5	23377	3196.3	2653
2015					9338.0	25533	9406.0	6398

Note: GDP is expressed in billion 1990 constant dollars. GDP/C is expressed in 1990 constant dollars.
Source: Angus Maddison, *Monitoring the World Economy, 1820–1992* (Paris: OECD Publishing, 1995), and *Chinese Economic Performance in the Long Run, 960–2030 AD* (Paris: OECD Publishing, 1998).

to have been reached.[14] Parity holds until the overtaker's GDP exceeds 120 percent of the former system leader's GDP. Power-transition analysts further assume that once an economy has attained developed status, rapid growth is no longer an option. Rapid growth is restricted to economies attempting to modernize and catch up with the dominant nation's mature economy.

Some of the interpretative dilemmas associated with relying on an indicator of economic bulk such as GDP as the principal measure of relative power are demonstrated in the array of British, German, US, and Chinese GDP and GDP per capita figures expressed in constant 1990 US dollars in table 4.1.[15] An examination of the relative size of the British and German economies, the key transition in the first half of the twentieth century according to power-transition arguments, reveals that Germany never actually exceeded the 80 percent threshold until well after the conclusion of World War II.[16] A better argument for a single economic indicator of relative power can be made for GDP per capita (at least in the British-German case). This measure comes closer to tapping productivity than most other single indicators because it controls for population size in estimating gross wealth. If fewer people can generate as much or more wealth as a much larger number of people, the smaller group must be using more sophisticated or complex technology. Thus, the GDP per capita indicator is more sensitive to the extent to which an economy is capable of generating and adopting the latest advances in technological change than is GDP. Illustrating this point, in 1913, German GDP per capita was equivalent to 77.9 percent of British GDP per capita. By 1940, German GDP per capita had exceeded the 80 percent threshold (84.7 percent of British GDP per capita).

This brief look at the German-British dyad underscores the problems that can arise when calibrating power transitions, parity, and overtaking in terms of economic size; we submit that similar problems attend the use of other bulk indicators (e.g., size of military and population) to map the power-transition process. In other words, we have a great deal of respect for the power-transition research program, but we think the commitment to economic and other metrics based on size distorts their view of power transition dynamics.

The Offensive-Realism Model Applied to Transition

Offensive realism offers a good "stablemate" with power transition in the sense that the main conclusion about China in the twenty-first century is similar, but the assumptions and prescribed reaction are much different. The power-transition perspective argues that Chinese economic growth is rapid and that political-economic transition is highly probable. The appropriate policy is accommodation to a changing structure. Proponents of offensive realism also think that a Chinese ascent is probable, but accommodation is the last response to contemplate. More likely is that the United States and China will become adversaries and that the United States will need to construct a containment network to thwart Chinese dominance in Asia.

This prediction is based on a 2020 forecast published in 2002.[17] John Mearsheimer's approach involves looking at a region and assessing the likelihood of (a) the emergence of a candidate for regional hegemony and (b) the likelihood that local actors will have sufficient power to contain the rise of a regional hegemon. The first question is which region we are talking about. For Mearsheimer, it is northeast Asia, which may seem too narrow of a regional definition and definitely excludes India from the analysis. Be that as it may, of Japan, Russia, and China, the strongest states

in this region, Japan and Russia, are dismissed as likely candidates for regional hegemon aspirants. Japan is too small and insular. Russia is too
poor and encumbered with various security problems in the south and
west.

China has the size and may develop sufficient wealth for regional hegemony by 2020 if its rapid growth is maintained. If the rapid growth is not
maintained, China will not become the wealthiest state in the region and
would no longer be a potential regional hegemon. In the absence of a
clear threat, US forces would likely be withdrawn from the area and Japan
would be expected to strengthen its military forces in response. If China
does maintain its rapid growth, it should be expected to become a leading
producer of high technology and to develop a sophisticated army. With a
formidable resource foundation, China could also be expected to warn
the United States, with more "teeth" than has been the case in the immediate past, that the US involvement in Asia is no longer acceptable. Since
local powers could not be expected to cope with such a strong China, US
forces would probably not be withdrawn. An attempted balancing coalition would be constructed, but it is unlikely that the structural conflict
could be confined to Northeast Asia. China's superpower resource base
would then transform the contest into a global affair.

Critique

Scenarios are "what if" constructions. As such, we can debate the assumptions and probability estimates that go into their construction. Would faltering Chinese economic growth really imply US withdrawal from Asia
and a Japanese military build-up? Presumably, one could develop a scenario that predicts exactly the opposite outcome. One might also envision a scenario in which the United States accepted the inevitable rise
of China (as in the power transition model recommendation) and, as in
the case of late nineteenth-century Britain, yielded to its eventual successor. But these alternative scenarios would be based on different assumptions than offensive realism employs. The scenario(s) forecasted by
Mearsheimer do stem from his theoretical position. If we want to evaluate the plausibility of the scenario, we need to examine the nature of the
theory on which the scenario(s) is based.

Accommodation (power transition) and coercive containment (offensive realism) are opposite policy recommendations. Our own interests are
not linked to policy recommendations per se. Rather, we are interested

TABLE 4.2. **Three approaches to realism**

	Human nature	Defensive	Offensive
Motivation for activity	Inherent lust for power	System structure	System structure
Ambition	Maximize relative power and seek regional hegemony	Defend what you have and maintain the balance of power	Maximize relative power and seek regional hegemony

Source: Based on John J. Mearsheimer, *The Tragedy of Great Power Politics* (New York: Norton, 2001), 22.

in how one selects the most appropriate transition drivers from disparate conclusions in international relations theory. We have indicated some of our problems with the power-transition perspective. Now it is time to turn to offensive-realism's theoretical problems.

Mearsheimer contends that offensive realism is a straightforward hybrid of two alternative approaches (depicted in table 4.2) to realism—"human nature" realism and defensive realism.[18] An anarchic structure forces major powers to maximize their power because other major powers have some offensive capability; one can never be sure that this offensive capability will not be used against them. Regardless of intentions that can change quickly in any event, it is the offensive capability of other powers that must be guarded against to ensure national security.

If no one can be trusted and everyone must be feared, it is incumbent on each state to look out for its own interests by acquiring as much relative power as one can. The stronger a state can become, the less likely it will be attacked. Therefore, it should strive to become the strongest state in its regional neighborhood. The acquisition and maintenance of regional hegemony is the only way to develop full security. One might think that global hegemony would be the penultimate secure position, but this possibility is ruled out by assumption. Since the world is composed of multiple regions that are difficult to get to, interregional power projection occurs at some high discount. This assumption, in turn, is predicated on the assumption that armies are the principal coercive instrument. Navies and air forces help, but they cannot win on their own. Only armies can do that. But if they must be transported across bodies of water for amphibious landings, it will not be difficult for a competent adversary to defeat them. Thus, regional hegemony—by which Mearsheimer means that a state is so powerful that it has no competitors in its region—is all that is feasible.

Yet it turns out that regional hegemony is not quite the ticket for op-

timal national security after all. Once a state becomes a regional hegemon it must then guard against other states becoming hegemonic in other
regions because they will then have a resource base to make interregional
trouble. Ideally, states in other regions will make sure no state emerges as
regionally dominant but, should that not work out, an incumbent regional
hegemon will need to intervene as an offshore balancer. This argument
leads directly to the United States needing to construct a containment
network to block Chinese regional hegemony. China will seek regional
hegemony as a matter of course. It is doubtful that other Asian states will
have sufficient resources to stop that from coming about. It follows then
that the United States, the North American regional hegemon, probably
will have to step in as the offshore balancer in Asia.

Although the logic is clear, it is less than consistent. On the one hand,
if there are multiple regions, attaining regional hegemony is no antidote
for security problems. It simply means security threats are likely to ema-
nate farther from home. If that is the case, why should we assume that a
regional hegemon will assume the defensive stance implied by an offshore
balancer role? Should not any regional hegemon simply move on to the
next adjacent region(s) and at least improve its security position however marginally by eliminating nearby peer competitors? Mearsheimer,
therefore, sees only one possibility when his own theoretical infrastructure would seem to imply more of the same power maximization as opposed to selective intervention to prevent potential challengers.

Part of this problem can be traced to Mearsheimer's argument that
the only modern regional hegemon has been the United States. Since we
know that the United States has not sought to maximize its power at least
coercively everywhere and has worked to suppress potential challengers
in other regions, it may be natural to think that is a template that any
regional hegemon would follow. Consider, however, a scenario in which
Germany and Japan won World War II. Would we assume that Germany
or Japan would have been content with predominance in their immediate
region? Would we expect that their interregional behavior would be restricted to offshore balancing?

The most probable answer to both questions is no. Germany had very
concrete plans for Africa and southwestern Russia. Japan took control
not only in East Asia but also in Southeast Asia and was approaching
South Asia. Perhaps Germany and Japan would have been content to
share Eurasia but that is highly debatable. Putting aside what they might
have done vis-à-vis the Americas, it is difficult to see either Germany or

Japan as offshore balancers. Their military expansion was primarily conducted on land. Neither state had specialized in offshore naval capability (although Japan presumably had a better start than Germany).

This turn to alternative history suggests one major problem with offensive-realism assumptions. The theory assumes that all great powers are alike in terms of motivation and fears. Therefore, all will behave the same way. But, if that is the case, then only global hegemony offers any respite for security fears and even that respite would be precarious, depending of course on how it was achieved. It is possible to be dominant in a region in which there are few competitive adversaries. Historically, it has been a quite different matter to achieve hegemony in regions in which there are multiple competitors. It is not impossible. China, the Mongols, the Moghuls, the Ottomans, and the Romans have suggested that it can be done but not for infinite periods of time.[19] Challengers tend to emerge eventually and take aim at regional hegemons who find it difficult to maintain their original sources of strength.

Fortunately, all major powers do not approach world politics in the same way. The United States ruthlessly acquired regional hegemony but then did turn into an offshore balancer. Earlier, Britain had given up on becoming a continental European power and turned eventually to offshore balancing in terms of European politics, just as the Netherlands had done in the century prior to Britain's ascent. The United States, Britain, and the Netherlands all had armies but, most of the time, they were not very large armies because they specialized in what Mearsheimer views as auxiliary military capabilities (navies and air forces).[20]

Richard Rosecrance identifies one of the principal flaws of offensive realism when he says, "The major difficulty with Mearsheimer's whole analysis is that he fails to recognize that there are powerful but nonaggressive states. The United States and Britain really have been less aggressive, ceteris paribus, than many other equally powerful countries."[21] But there is more going on here than some major powers being less aggressive than others.[22] The United States and Britain create major interpretation problems for offensive realism. The one accepted example of a regional hegemon ceased to expand territorially once it had established predominance in the region. It could have expanded south and north, and occasionally toyed with schemes to do so, but never really pursued expansion into Canada, Mexico, the Caribbean, or Central America in a concerted way.

Britain is even more of an anomaly and seems to exist in offensive realism as not having an association with any region. Its separation from the European continent is taken as a geographical fact that, of course, is accurate but still requires interpretation. Some Britons may like to think that they are not Europeans these days, but, historically, England/Britain was always linked closely to the nearby European continent. It was invaded successfully by Europeans on several occasions (e.g., the Romans, the Normans, and the Dutch under William III) and unsuccessfully on other occasions. We tend to remember the latter and forget the former. In the modern last half of the millennium, its foreign policy became fixed on preventing enemies from controlling the coasts of northwest Europe closest to Britain. Like the United States, England/Britain was usually most reluctant to acquire territory in Europe, aside from Mediterranean bases, after it had been evicted from the continent in the sixteenth century. It was even offered the northern Netherlands in the 1580s but declined. Yet Britain, along with the Netherlands, was often at the forefront of the coalitions, despite fairly small armies, that beat the regional hegemonic aspirants that most closely resemble offensive realist specifications.[23]

The United States, Britain, and the Netherlands, in their respective heydays, were not really anomalies, but their behavior was different from that of Spain, France, and Germany—their respective foes. Spain, France, and Germany were committed to territorial expansion campaigns in their home region, built large armies for their times, and conducted intermittent attempts at regional hegemony. They are or were the paladins of offensive realism.

The Netherlands, Britain, and the United States eschewed regional territorial expansion (at least, the United States did after acquiring "enough") for an orientation toward commercial-industrial expansion that focused more on markets than on expanding the state at home. Most of the time these states relied on small armies and big navies (and later air forces). They figure prominently as barriers to European regional hegemony efforts.

Why did they specialize in these "auxiliary" forms of capability? They did so because they were not particularly interested in military expansion on land. Their main emphasis was placed on developing the capability to project coercive power at long distance in order to protect their access to far away markets and resource sources. The Netherlands and Britain (after the sixteenth century in any event) did not seek regional hegemony in their home region, but they did, as defensive measures, seek to prevent other states from becoming hegemonic. The United States achieved regional hegemony in part because the competition was not all that stiff and then sought to participate in coalitions to preclude regional hegemony elsewhere, as in Western Europe and Southeast Asia. US offshore balancing thus resembles the deployment of maritime capabilities by the Netherlands and Britain, but there is one difference. Netherlands and Britain were "balancing offshore" in their home region while the United States was intervening in other regions.

The point here is that a few major powers have specialized in offshore balancing against regional hegemony, whereas a few others have focused on maximizing their land-power capabilities to gain regional hegemony. Neither approach characterizes all major powers in general or for all time. One power maximization assumption that holds for all major powers is difficult to sustain. The few that specialize in offshore balancing are not anomalies. They are critical to an understanding of European international relations in the past several hundred years. So, too, are the Spanish, French, and German attempts to control the European region of their respective eras. Yet, however one looks at it, these offshore balancing/regional hegemony activities were not persistent behaviors. In any given century (of the last five), there was usually only one state seeking regional hegemony and one state engaging in offshore balancing.

Moreover, there is considerable variation in regional hegemony pursuits. Some states have sought regional hegemony and failed. Some have sought it and succeeded. But, even in such cases, the urge to possess regional hegemony sometimes seems intermittent and not always explicit. That is, various rulers have been accused of seeking regional hegemony, but other interpretations are conceivable. Charles V in the sixteenth century, Louis XIV in the seventeenth century, and Wilhelm II in the twentieth century come to mind. The Hapsburgs and Louis XIV can be viewed as attempting to defend home real estate on a broad regional scale. The Germans certainly did not begin World War I with regional hegemony in mind. World War II was a different matter. In some respects, it matters less what the motivations were as long as others act as if a state is seeking regional hegemony. But we should be alert to the possibility that regional hegemony in Europe at least may not have been sought as often and as persistently as is sometimes portrayed. At the same time, there are clear examples of uncontroversial regional hegemony pursuits. Napoleon and Hitler are good examples. American foreign policy and manifest destiny in the nineteenth century is another. So were attempts to extend South African influence in the late nineteenth century.

Yet some major powers and, of course, many states have never sought regional hegemony. Some regions have very little experience with regional hegemony aspirants. After the revolutionary wars in the 1820s the topic does not seem to have emerged again in South America. There is plenty of conflict in postcolonial West and East Africa but no hegemonic expansion schemes have been put forward. One package simply does not fit all state behavior. To assume otherwise may make for more cohesive theories but it only works if we distort the nature of the past half millennium or more of world politics.

The evidence for European regional international relations does not even support the notion that all major powers fear all other major powers.[24] One of the benefits associated with offensive-realism theory is that there are frequent references to rivalry and rivals. But if all major powers feared all other major powers, they should consider all other powerful states to be adversaries. That does not appear to have been the case. Table 4.3 summarizes the history of European major power strategic rivalry.[25] That there is plenty of rivalry activity is not surprising since post-1500 Europe has always been considered to be a highly competitive region. With ten major powers between 1494 and 1945, there are forty-five opportunities for rivalry. However, in eight cases, the periods of major power status did not coincide (e.g., Italy and the Netherlands or Prussia and the Ottoman Empire). That means that there were twenty-two rivalries in thirty-seven dyadic opportunities (59 percent). Nearly 60 percent is an impressive figure but it still falls considerably short of 100 percent. If we were to compute the number of years in which states viewed each other as strategic rivals and divide by the total number of years at risk, the proportional rivalry activity would be even less because a number of rivalries characterize only some of the years that two states might have regarded each other as adversaries. What we find instead are a few long-running feuds between selected actors—for example, Britain and France, France and Austria, or France and Prussia/Germany—but something less than a Hobbesian war of all against all.

This brings us to Mearsheimer's critical "stopping power of water" argument. Offensive realism stipulates that global hegemony is impossible because armies cannot be projected over water without losing much of their power. Armies are the all-important military capability because only they can conquer on land. Navies and air forces can help but they cannot wage wars by themselves. These stipulations are again a matter of overgeneralization. Water has a stopping power for states fixated on developing overwhelming land-power capabilities. They have no way to

TABLE 4.3. **European major power rivalries**

	Australia	Great Britain	France	Italy	Ottoman Empire	Netherlands	Prussia	Russia	Spain	Sweden
Australia		-	1494–1918	1847–1918	1494–1908	-	1740–1870	1768–1918	1701–93	-
Great Britain			1494–1716/ 1731–1904	1934–43	-	1651–88	1896–1918/ 1934–45	1778–1956	1568–1667/ 1701–1808	-
France				1881–1940	*	1668–1713	1756–1955	1732–1894	1494–1700	-
Italy					*	*	-	-	*	*
OTT						-	*	1668–1918	1494–1595	-
Netherlands							*	-	1579–1648	-
Prussia								1744–1807/ 1890–1945	*	*
Russia										1700–1815
Spain										-
Sweden										

Note: A hyphen indicates no rivalry when both states were major powers. An asterisk indicates that the two states were not major powers at the same time.

Source: Data are taken from William R. Thompson and David R. Dreyer, *Handbook of International Rivalries, 1494–2010* (Washington, DC: Congressional Quarterly Press, 2011).

transport their troops across water or, better still, to protect their troops while they are crossing waterways, and/or they turn to the logistic problems too late to be effective. England was protected from Spanish invasion on multiple occasions because Spanish fleets could not establish maritime control of the English Channel.[26] The Netherlands had only limited insularity, but even their dykes and canals could not be breached easily by French armies. Nor did the Spanish take advantage of their northern European territories to build naval bases that might have done serious damage to the important Dutch Baltic trade. The French and Germans might have crossed the English Channel, but they too had problems in taking control of the Channel and allowed themselves to be distracted in any event by land campaigns.

In all these cases, the persistent strategic error was to focus on developing land capability without sufficient "auxiliary" capability to fight the type of wars that characterized regional hegemony campaigns in Europe. Spain had been a Mediterranean galley maritime power in the sixteenth century but had little experience with organizing and managing Atlantic, blue-water fleets. The 1588 Armada depended heavily on the Portuguese fleet acquired only a few years before. France's orientation toward land and sea power always waffled, but usually land power was favored over sea power development. At the beginning of late-seventeenth-century warfare, France actually possessed a quantitative lead in sea power but failed to use it and within a few years had fallen back on a dependence on private commerce raiding. A century later, Trafalgar, designed by the British to prevent an invasion of England, suggested that there were still serious problems in French appreciation for sea power. Still another century later, the Germans challenged British sea power with a risk theory that only made the British try harder. The development of the Dreadnought class of battleships quickly made obsolete the front line of the German navy. Falling back, as the French had, on *guerre de course*, commerce-raiding U-boats proved highly effective and might have been even more effective if they had received more attention and resources before the war began. Much the same thing can be said about World War II U-boat attacks. Once again, they were a good fallback strategy that was appreciated too little and too late.

Over five hundred years of European warfare (1494–1945), the maritime powers were not stopped by water. It was their specialty. In league with large land powers that supplied the bulk of the armies for ground campaigns, the European maritime powers blockaded the continent to ensure their opponents did not receive resources from outside the region. They moved troops here and there for landings that were sometimes successful and other times not. But even that is a better record than their opponents who consistently failed at landing troops across water when they needed to do so. Equally important, the maritime powers were able to contribute to the multiple-front problem in which aspiring regional hegemon aspirants always found themselves to be in. Depending on the century, the Spanish, French, and Germans could never focus on one front and one enemy at a time.[27] They had to deal variably with problems in the east, the south, the north, and the west.

Thus, it is certainly true that armies are needed to conquer on land. But conquering on land is rarely enough in modern times (i.e., the last five hundred years). One needs armies, navies, and air forces to win. States that have chosen to develop their armies at the expense of their navies and air forces may win quickly in the beginning but, over time, tend to lose their wars. Maritime powers have done better in this type of combat because they specialize in the "auxiliary" capabilities and have been able to find allies who supply large armies to supplement their own efforts. Water has not had stopping power for all states—only those powers that do not prepare adequately for the necessity of fighting in multiple theaters and on land, air, and sea.

The core tenets of offensive realism, explicitly predicated, we are told, on the history of great power international relations do not hold up all that well to close scrutiny. It assumes that all major powers have the same fears, goals, and desires. All powers seek to maximize their power every chance they get because, to do otherwise, would be foolhardy in an anarchic world.[28] All powers should covet regional hegemony because that is the best security position for which they can hope after becoming dominant over all local comers. There are no friends or allies, only enemies or potential enemies. The best defense is offense. Should any state become a regional hegemon, then its only concern is making sure no one else achieves the same status and becomes an interregional threat.

In contrast, we see different types of major powers—some playing offensive-realism games on occasion while others pursue entirely different sorts of commercial and industrial strategies.[29] Few states actually seek regional hegemony. Even in a highly competitive system such as Europe, serious pushes to develop regional hegemony occurred only once a century at best.[30] In Europe, more states fought to block regional hegemony than those that sought it. Offshore balancers have operated both from within and from outside the region to organize the resistance to perceived hegemonic aspirants. Sea power was both critical for and facilitative of offshore balancing. States with large armies neither could nor probably would want to play such a role. When push comes to shove, major powers that developed land power without attending to the sea and air "auxiliaries" have been defeated in their bids for regional dominance.

From our perspective, offensive realism gets most of what is most important wrong. Therefore, it is difficult to accept the China scenario that flows from the theory's distinctive interpretations, at least on the basis of the theory's plausibility. It could be that there is a high probability that China will pursue or will be seen as pursuing regional hegemony. It could also be true that the United States will either withdraw from Asia if China falters and Japan rearms or stay if China does not falter. If China continues to ascend and the United States remains very much in the Asian picture, it may also be probable that the two states will clash. But this scenario could be advanced independently of offensive realism. The problems with offensive-realism's central tenets, moreover, do not reinforce its utility for forecasting purposes.

The Challenger/Transition Model

The challenger/transition model is derived from leadership long-cycle theory's interpretation of the past millennium of struggles over position, territory, and markets.[31] The model rests on several strong assumptions. First, it distinguishes between global and regional activities. Global activities involve transregional transactions, while regional transactions remain relatively close to home. All actors engage in regional transactions to varying degrees, but only a few have specialized in global transactions. This distinction leads to a fundamental duality in strategic orientations. States that have been content to emphasize improvements in wealth and power by local territorial expansion possess continental orientations. States that have focused on long-distance trade as the principal path to wealth and power possess maritime-commercial orientations and, in time, became the most innovative industrializers as well.

The challenger/transition model is predicated on a much longer historical script than is the case with the power-transition or offensive-realism programs. It begins with an economic revolution in tenth-century Song China and traces a China-Genoa-Venice-Portugal-Netherlands-

Britain-US millennium-long sequence as successive lead economies in the world economy.[32] Halfway through the sequence, the size of the economies begins to expand but the movement of succession is never predicated solely on the relative size of the economies in competition. The primary question is which economy pioneers the next wave of radical technological innovation and thereby becomes the world economy's lead economy for a finite period of time. In fact, their main opponents—the successive continental powers, Spain, France, and Germany—often (but not always as we will see) possessed the largest Western European populations and economies and, prior to the nineteenth century, larger economies than the commercial-maritime powers. Yet, they were unable to mobilize successfully these larger economies and populations to win in global warfare. One of the reasons for defeat, especially in the Spanish and French eras, was that the larger economies were simply not as competitive as the smaller lead economies in terms of advanced technology, productivity, and debt leveraging. The smaller lead economies were also in a vastly superior position to mobilize non-European resources, both in general and in the showdown clashes with their continental opponents.

In contrast, the challenger/transition model focuses on pioneering technological changes rather than on generic economic growth. Leadership long-cycle theory argues that long-term economic growth is stimulated by paradigmatic shifts in economic production on the technological frontier. The first phase of the Industrial Revolution focused on textile and iron production techniques. A second phase emphasized the development of steam power and the expansion of railroads. A subsequent phase shift, led primarily by the US and, to a lesser extent, German economies, centered on steel, chemicals, and electrification. Automobiles came next, followed by jet engines and semiconductors, before giving way to computers and biotechnology in the ongoing information technology age. Thus, the difference in emphasis is largely one of qualitative versus quantitative considerations. The challenger/transition model emphasizes radical production shifts stemming from innovations and the emergence of new leading sectors. The power-transition model instead relies heavily on industrialization and economic growth, but does not explicitly consider the sources of this growth or the Schumpeterian processes that generate it.

As a consequence, a technologically less sophisticated economy could make substantial gains in economic growth and, assuming it is sufficiently large, it could appear to be overtaking the world economy's lead economy in terms of GDP. Even though its economy remained relatively underdeveloped by prevailing world standards, a dangerous transition would be in train from a power-transition standpoint. From the perspective of the challenger/transition model, however, this type of transition would be a matter of dubious significance as long as the expected overtaking depends on sheer size and not on cutting-edge technological innovations.

From this perspective, there is no reason that a system leader cannot significantly revitalize its economy by innovating new technologies that become the basis for new leading sectors. Earlier system leaders enjoyed only two spurts of economic growth, but Britain experienced four spurts between the late seventeenth and mid-nineteenth centuries.[33] The US economy appears to be entering its third growth spurt, based on its lead in information technology and its connections to biotechnology and nanotechnology. There may be many good other reasons why systemic leadership tends to be of finite duration, but there is no upper limit on the ability of economic growth leaders to rejuvenate themselves and their technological leads by new rounds of radical innovation.[34]

The maritime-commercial qua industrial states have predominated in global transactions. At any given time, one state stands out as the predominant global system leader. To attain this position, a state must first develop power resources that combine radical economic innovation with global reach capability to form the lead economy, or most active source of important economic innovations. These innovations are translated into a predominant economic position in long-distance trade, industrial production, or both. The profits generated by pioneering economic production in turn underwrite the development of global-reach capabilities that are needed to protect the leading position. The initial stress on long-distance trade, much of which is transported by ship, placed an early premium on naval, that is, global-reach, capabilities. This emphasis has also meant that system leaders have been the leading naval powers of their times.

The development of this global structure has been conditioned strongly by the geographical location of its most prominent actors. While a claim can be made that Song China was the first modern active economic zone, East Asian circumstances proved inhospitable for cultivating this original lead. The epicenter of the active zone shifted to the eastern Mediterranean and Genoa and Venice. By 1500, the epicenter had shifted further west to the Atlantic and a string of Western European–based leaders—Portugal, the Netherlands, and Britain—only to shift once again to the other side of the Atlantic in the late nineteenth century. Although these global leaders sought to stay aloof from European continental politics, their locations frequently made that impossible. Intermittent efforts to dominate the European region by a string of continental powers—Spain, France, and Germany between 1494 and 1945—meant that the global and European realms were unlikely to remain separate. Global warfare in 1494–1516, 1580–1608, 1688–1713, 1792–1815, and 1914–1945 amounted to showdown clashes between a coalition led by one or more global powers and a coalition led by one or more regional powers. In every instance, the global coalition won. By leading the suppression of the major continental threat, the global leader enhances its resource base and its ability to shape the rules of global order. Over time, as this positional lead gradually erodes, new threats emerge on the continent and from within the global camp as states attempt to move up the military-political and technological pecking orders.

In contrast to alternative perspectives, the challenger/transition model sees a differentiated world system in which some states pursue primarily regional strategies while others concentrate on global strategies. Each domain has a different hierarchy predicated on different attributes. The regional hierarchy is based on land power and a state's ability to increase its control of territory. The global hierarchy is comprised of states that attempt to avoid entanglement in regional politics while they compete for control of long-distance commerce and for competitive superiority in technologically advanced industries. A global power's standing depends largely on the extent to which its economy can pioneer the generation and implementation of radical innovations, as well as on its command of global reach capabilities with which it can project and protect its economic activities across the planet.

The challenger model thus concentrates on contenders for the role of global system leader. These contenders may come from the ranks of global powers but may also come from the leading state of the principal region (which, prior to 1945, was Western Europe). Regional hegemony in Europe provided a strong base for global contestation. Moreover, the aspirants for European hegemony have always made some claim to global power status even if their strategies remained primarily regionally oriented. As a consequence, global system leaders have skirmished with other global powers, but the most intense confrontations have been showdown wars between a global leader and its coalition versus an ascending aspirant for European hegemony and its coalition. After 1945, Western Europe lost its role as the world system's principal region, but one can argue that the regional focus was simply stretched to encompass the larger Eurasian land mass during the US-Soviet Cold War, and that Eurasia has regained much of the preeminence it held prior to the ascendancy of the western end of the larger land mass.

The transitional clash could be between two, similarly oriented, commercial-maritime powers, but historically it has been far more likely to be a clash between the leading global power and the leading regional power.[35] Since their orientations and specialized capabilities are not likely to be the same, it is difficult for both actors to compare their relative power precisely. Metaphorically, the leading global power is like a whale, while the leading regional power resembles an elephant. The former specializes in economic innovation and global reach capabilities, while the latter specializes in coercive dominance at the regional level. Elephants do not normally fight at sea, and whales have a difficult time negotiating sustained combat on land. Instead, elephants fight in or near their home territory, and whales have to project their power over long distances with some diminishment of power practically inevitable. This situation encourages the elephant and discourages the whale. Moreover, since the leading global power is in relative decline and the regional power is on the ascent, the latter is encouraged to think it is stronger than objective assessment of its position might otherwise warrant.

In five hundred years, only four states (Portugal, the Netherlands, Britain, and the United States) have occupied this apex position. Even this statement is contested. The global system, focused on the management of long-distance transactions and related policy problems, did not spring full blown into our collective consciousness, or elsewhere, in 1494, 1648, or 1945. It began to emerge in 1494 as large west European states began to fight over control of the remains of what had been the Italian subsystem—itself a product in part of earlier profits and problems associated with long-distance transactions in the five hundred years preceding 1494. But once the system began to emerge, it can be said to have slowly begun to acquire structural shape and patterns of behavior. Throughout this structural evolution, some significant actors increasingly specialized in global politics and economics, whereas others retained more traditional orientations toward regional issues. Other actors moved back and forth, unable to commit to primarily global or local agendas. Partly as a consequence of the emergent nature of the phenomenon and partly due to the multiple patterns of behavior of the most important powers, we disagree about which actors have been most prominent and when.[36]

Observers are most readily inclined to accept the reality of a shift from

Britain to the United States around 1945 as the leader of the global sys-tem. More controversial are the ideas that similar, earlier shifts took place with a more industrialized Britain succeeding a more commercial Britain in 1815, Britain succeeding the United Provinces of the Netherlands in 1714, and the Dutch supplanting the Portuguese in 1609. This sequence, nonetheless, is critical to leadership long-cycle theory's interpretation of international relations history. If we are to understand what leads or pre-cedes systemic transition, it follows that we need to look for patterns that can be generalized across the several transitions that have occurred in the past. There is no guarantee that past patterns will be repeated rigidly into the future—and that is something that we need to keep in mind—but given the uncertainties of the future, one viable strategy is to look to the past for regularities that just might give us some clues about the future.

Leadership long-cycle theory has developed six different models to help explain transition problems linked to structural change in the global system. While each model has a somewhat different slant, the empha-ses overlap explicitly and implicitly. Our task here is to try and make the overlap more explicit.

Six Models

(1) THE LEADERSHIP LONG-CYCLE PHASE MODEL.   Table 4.4 summarizes the past five hundred years or so of systemic-leadership phasing.[37] What is most important for our immediate purposes is that each phase is char-acterized by distinctive behavior. New system leaders emerge in periods of global war by leading the victorious coalition. The phase immediately following the global war is the best window of opportunity for establish-ing new rules and institutions for global politics. This window for optimal leadership is then followed by a period of delegitimation in which oppo-nents of the system leader challenge the leadership and its status quo (but

TABLE 4.4. **Systemic leadership phases**

Global system leader	World power	Delegitimation	Deconcentration/ Coalition building	Global war
Portugal	1516–40	1540–60	1560–80	1580–1609
Netherlands	1609–40	1640–60	1660—88	1688–1714
Britain I	1714–40	1740–63	1763–92	1792–1815
Britain II	1815–50	1850–73	1873–1914	1914–45
United States	1945–73	1973–2000	2000–2030	2030–50

falling short of global warfare). Immediately prior to the renewed outset of global war is an interim period of further leadership relative decline (deconcentration) and negotiations among elite actors to see who
will align with whom (coalition building) if there an intensive conflict over
power and influence in the global system (global war).

The utility of the phase model is that it provides us with a quick historical summary of past systemic transitions and some hints about the behavior to anticipate prior to transition. Transitions have taken place at the
end of the global war phase and the beginning of the world power phase
(1516, 1609, 1714, 1815, and 1945). They are preceded by periods of intensive warfare of generation length (1494–1516, 1580–1609, 1688–1714,
1792–1815, and 1914–1945). These global war bouts, in turn, are preceded
by periods of bargaining among major powers as they feel out potential
allies. Moreover, the two to three phases preceding the global war period
are characterized by the relative decline of the system leader. One would
expect that the peak system-leader position in terms of relative military
capabilities would be found toward the beginning of the world power
phase and the nadir should be located near the end of the deconcentration phase. In sum, we are instructed to look for periods of intensive war,
coalition building, rising opposition to the status quo, and the relative decline of the system leader as preludes to system transition. We also have
a predicted timing sequence: rising opposition to the legitimacy of the
system leader, coalition building, and global war, with deconcentration
trending roughly downward across the three phases preceding global war.

(2) THE REGIONAL-GLOBAL DISSYNCHRONIZATION MODEL. The second
model, regional-global dissynchronization, starts from the co-opted Dehioan premise that aspiring regional hegemons in Europe were thwarted
by counterweights that were able to win by introducing extraregional resources into the balancing contest.[38] One authoritarian counterweight
supplied land power from the east. The other entered from a western
position based on its sea power and commercial mediation focused on
Europe-Asia-America. Operating simultaneously, the two counterweights
were able to defeat a sequence of hegemonic attempts by forcing states
attempting to take over the region to fight on two fronts and usually without much access to extraregional resources.

A 1494 French bid for Italy was stopped primarily by Spain. France
and the Ottoman Empire combined to block a sixteenth-century Habs-
burg hegemonic effort. A true western counterweight emerged later in

the sixteenth century in the form of Dutch-English resistance to Philip II and Spanish ambitions. The same western counterweight was mobilized to help defeat Louis XIV in the late seventeenth and early eighteenth centuries. By the end of the eighteenth century, Britain alone served as the western counterweight to the regional threat posed by the French Revolutionary and Napoleonic Wars. Against the German challenges of World War I and II, Britain and the United States cooperated in the west, whereas the earlier Austrian role in the east had been taken over by Russia.

This brief summary of nearly five hundred years of European international relations is fairly familiar ground. What Dehio contributed was an appreciation for the pattern of regional-global structural change. At the regional level, peaks in concentrated land power alternated with troughs in regional concentration. New regional aspirants tended to emerge during the regional trough periods. It was during these same low regional concentration periods that western counterweight strength was greatest. Thus, the principal dynamic was one of alternating relative strength. The leading land power in the region tended to be strong when the western sea power was relatively weak and vice versa.

Moreover, the two states pursued dramatically different agendas. The leading land power used absolute royal powers and large armies/bureaucracies to expand its territorial control in the home region. The leading sea power sought to avoid territorial control by specializing in monopolizing markets at home and abroad. Yet, success for the leading land power implied a direct and indirect threat to the leading sea power. Regional hegemony either led to the occupation of the reigning or former sea power and/or created a very strong base for a subsequent challenge for extraregional colonies and markets.[39] Western sea powers, therefore, never lacked structural incentives to coordinate the suppression of regional hegemonic aspirations.

Western sea power specialized in maritime containment of would-be regional supremacy. Such a strategy could limit the expansion of a regional hegemon beyond the confines of the region but it would not suffice to defeat the hegemon on land. Someone needed to supply substantial land power for that purpose. A coalition combining the requisite naval and army capabilities could then squeeze the aspiring hegemon into overextending itself by fighting on eastern and western fronts at the same time and, ultimately, unsuccessfully.

Ludwig Dehio thought this process had ended in 1945 as the last would-be continental unifier was defeated. Since extraregional resource bases kept expanding and the European regional resource base was relatively fixed, Dehio also thought that this process of attempted unification-suppression of the attempt had gradually weakened the ability of European states to make bids for regional hegemony. The process therefore could not persist forever. At some point, no further bids would be feasible and at that juncture the European region would lose its autonomy to the greater strengths of the former counterweights.

Dehio may have been right to interpret the European experience as a relatively unique convergence of geopolitical and historical factors. If so, it may not provide us with much predictive leverage for future transitions. Still, the key argument is that declining global powers are likely to be threatened by ascending regional powers. Accordingly, maritime/commercial powers will seek to build coalitions to contain and defeat leading land powers before they become genuinely global threats. In the process, sea-power capabilities are renewed and some land-power capability is exhausted. There is no reason why this syndrome of dissynchronized global and regional structures might not play itself out somewhere other than Europe. There are other regions and other states that might aspire to become the leading land power in their home region. There are also regions that are adjacent to oceans that might encourage or facilitate the emergence of sea power counterweights to land-based takeover bids. East Asia, the other end of the Eurasian landmass, comes readily to mind. That this region has not yet duplicated the west Eurasian experience does not rule out the possibility that similar behavior could not reemerge at some point in the future.

The second model directs our attention to situations involving declining leading sea powers that are threatened by ascending or leading land powers focused primarily on regional territorial control. It is not a matter of the presence or absence of one or the other factor but their interaction that is most critical. Whether a second counterweight is present or potentially recruitable is more a question of who wins and loses regional wars than it is a concern for anticipating systemic transitions.

(3) THE TWIN-PEAKS MODEL. The third model focuses on technological change and its relationship to the onset and consequences of global warfare.[40] Technological change looms large in the leadership long-cycle research program. Long-term growth is predicated on intermittent spurts in radical technological innovation. Radical innovation is neither constant

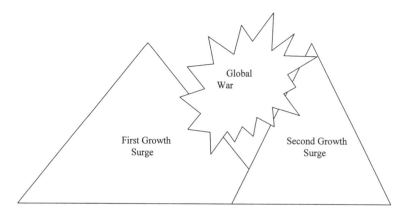

FIGURE 4.1. The twin-peaks model

nor random. Nor is it widespread geographically. Most radical innovation is pioneered by the system's lead economy. Each lead economy is associated with at least one paired set of spurts (hence the "twin peaks" depicted in figure 4.1). The first spurt peaks in the phase immediately prior to global war and contributes to the outbreak of war by destabilizing relative positions and the status quo in the world economy. The initial spurt also ends up helping to pay for the costs of coordinating the antihegemonic coalition during the consequent global war. Emerging at the end of the global war at the head of a victorious coalition, the lead economy experiences a second spurt of technological innovation in the world power phase—or the phase immediately after the global war.

The second spurt may draw upon innovations in the first spurt, either improving on them or taking advantage of the lead bestowed on the pioneering economy. The innovations of the second spurt are also likely to have been accelerated or facilitated by participation in the global war. For instance, radar, jet airplanes, and the computer were products of the World War II. Would they have been developed without a second world war? Without a doubt but their development would have proceeded much more slowly. Being on the winning side of the global war certainly helps as well.

Table 4.5 outlines the indicators of leading sectors and the anticipated and observed timing of their peaks. The expectation that lead economies enjoy two spurts of innovation seems well validated. For our immediate purposes, though, the implication is that we should look for the initial in-

TABLE 4.5. **Growth peaks in global lead industries**

Global lead industry indicators	Predicted high growth	Observed growth peak
Portugal		
Guinea gold	1460–92	1480s
Indian pepper	1516–40	1510s
Netherlands		
Baltic trade	1560–80	1560s
Asian trade	1609–40	1630s
Britain I		
Tobacco, sugar, and Indian textiles	1660–80	1670s
Tobacco, sugar, tea, and Indian textiles	1714–40	1710s
Britain II		
Cotton consumption and pig iron production	1763–92	1780s
Railroad track laid	1815–50	1830s
United States		
Steel, sulphuric acid, and electricity production	1873–1914	1870s/1900s
Automobile production, aerospace sales, and semiconductor production	1945–73	1950s

Source: George Modelski and William R. Thompson, *Leading Sectors and World Power: The Coevolution of Global Politics and World Economics* (Columbia: University of South Carolina Press, 1996), 11.

novation spike as a precursor to the outbreak of global war and subsequent systemic transition.

(4) A COMMERCIAL-RIVALRY MODEL. The commercial-rivalry model serves to elaborate some of the problems encountered in the first innovation peak.[41] A core problem is that the introduction of new commerce and industry pits pioneers and latecomers against each another. The primary competitors in the world economy are not content to engage in comparative divisions of labor. Instead, they focus on the same commodities and products roughly at the same time. The lead enjoyed by the pioneer is emulated as others attempt to catch up. Since the commercial and industrial foci are similar, the competition extends to the control of sources of raw materials and energy for which demand is increasing. Pioneers and latecomers must also compete to build and defend transportation infrastructures for access to raw materials and markets. Desired production scales lead inevitably to exports, more economic competition, and quite likely surplus capacity.

Within this spiral of increased economic competition, the nature of the strategies pursued can also aggravate tensions. Latecomers tend to practice protectionism and other perceived unfair practices against the lead of the pioneer. Depressions make these types of practices both more attractive to the people who execute them and more predatory to the perceived victims. Latecomers may also feel that the best markets are already staked out by the early leaders and require coercion to break into the pioneer's preserves. The pursuit of catch-up strategies make democratization less likely just as more centralized economic strategies (e.g., industrial policies, cooperative banks, and subsidies in particular) are apt to be viewed as more unfair competition. Of course, all these frictions reflect increased economic interdependence, but the constraining effects of shared interests can be overwhelmed by the intensification of competition.

(5) A NONLINEAR WAR-EXPANSION MODEL.   Another recently developed model contends that multiple interstate rivalries that are "ripe" for escalation generate a nonlinear influence on the probability of major war outbreaks.[42] Three conditions are advanced in this model. The first concerns serial conflicts within rivalry relationships. An increasing number of rivalries experiencing multiple clashes is one index of increasing ripeness, because successive clashes increase the probability of rivals going to war.

The degree to which antagonists are bound together or "coupled" is another indicator of increasing probability for expanded conflict. Thus, the extent to which rivals are bipolarized into two mutually exclusive camps should be suggestive for conflict escalation. Allies are not only closely linked to allies in a bipolarized situation; the sheer simplicity of the conflict pattern means that enemies are also closely coupled, even if their only shared attributes are mistrust and conflict.

Power transitions suggest a third type of conducive factor. An actor being overtaken is apprehensive about future losses. The actor doing the overtaking may be overly confident of its imminent success. As they approximate capability parity, the probability of one or the other type of actor initiating conflict with the other antagonist increases. The more central these power transitions are, moreover, the more likely the resulting conflict will lead to nonlinear conflict expansion. Examples of more central power transitions would encompass global-regional ones (as in model 2) and ones involving central regional leadership contests (as in Germany versus France or Russia in 1914 or perhaps China and India some time in the future).

The fifth model thus recommends that we look at the frequency of serial clashes within rivalries, the extent to which rivals are bipolarized, and whether multiple power transitions, especially more central ones, are ongoing. The alternative would be to look at rivalry "ripeness" more directly, but we have yet to develop a handle on how that might best be measured. Instead, the fifth model advocates looking at situations that might be expected to make rivalries more ripe for bloodshed.

(6) A CHALLENGER/TRANSITION-FOCUSED MODEL. In the initial version of the challenger/transition model, five variables—proximity, similarity, strategic orientation, innovation, and threat/frustration perceptions—were specified as especially critical to the intensity of challenges to the system leader's position.[43] This set of variables presumes that there may be a number of potential challengers and, if so, that the global system leader may play a significant role in determining just who the primary challenger is by emphasizing one challenger's threat over others. *Proximity* refers to the tendency of a system leader to be more alarmed by a nearby threat than by one that is more distant. Accordingly, challengers that are located physically nearest the home base of the system leader are likely to be regarded as greater threats than challengers located further away. If there is only one source of challenge, this factor may not have much bearing.

Similarity, a variable also found in the power-transition model, lessens the probability of a violent power transition. Similarity refers specifically to culture, language, and politico-economic institutions. Challengers that are viewed as more distant culturally and ideologically are most likely to be regarded as greater threats than are challengers that somehow seem less "alien." Dissimilarities in race, institutions, economic organizing principles, and ideology aggravate conflicts between system leaders and their challengers because the dissimilarities magnify the extent of threats perceived by all parties. They may also increase the probability of misperceptions. But this is not simply a matter of the social-psychological dynamics of perceived distance. Different types of political-economic institutions are likely to produce preferences for different organizing principles for political systems and markets. A challenger that aims to fundamentally change international regimes is likely to be perceived as more threatening than another that is expected to maintain the norms and rules that are already in practice.

The range of *strategic orientation* is limited to the duality previously mentioned; in some respects, this concepts overlaps with similarity. Challengers with continental orientations are most likely to regard territorial conquest as the best approach to defeating the system leader. This goal can be achieved in three ways. One way is to take over the European region and use this large land area with a number of maritime ports as a base of operations for global competition. A second approach is to conquer the system leader's home base. Spain did this to Portugal in the early 1580s. France attempted to do this to the Netherlands in the late 1600s but was not successful. Both Napoleonic France and Nazi Germany contemplated assaults on Britain but neither carried out their plans. A third approach, of course, is to do both—conquer the European region and the global home base. Nevertheless, the point is that states with fundamentally different strategic orientations are more threatening to global leaders than are states with fundamentally similar ones. A challenger oriented to territorial conquest is more likely to adopt coercive tactics than a challenger that is just as interested as the system leader in avoiding territorial entanglements in order to better focus on the control of markets. Put another way, the potential loss of sovereignty should be more threatening than the potential loss of market share.[44]

The last main variable has two dimensions—one is the system leader's *perception of threat* posed by one or more challengers. On the one hand, if faced with more than one potential challenger, system leaders will be forced to concentrate their defensive energies on the challenger that they perceive to be most threatening (although the existence of multiple challengers should not be assumed). The other dimension of this variable is the extent of the challenger's *frustration* (or dissatisfaction) with the leader and the world order constructed under its auspices and over which it presides. Indeed, some argue that the prospects for a peaceful power transition hinge on whether the system leader and the challenger are able to negotiate mutually acceptable agreements concerning the main elements of world order: the hierarchy of power and status; rules for managing security, including when and under what circumstances use of force is justified, as well as the laws of war; mechanisms for managing territorial changes; recognition of territorial spheres of interest; and rules that govern trade, investment, and other functional subsystems of the world economy.[45]

System leaders are often seen by challengers as obstacles to further improvements in their status. If a challenger desires a larger share of trade, most likely, it will feel the need to take it away from the leader. The question is whether the challenger is content to simply expand its share or desires to supplant the leader as the predominant trading state. This is one of the dimensions that differentiated England and France as challengers to the Netherlands in the seventeenth century. The English thought the Dutch controlled too much trade and wanted a larger share for themselves. The French wanted to supplant the Dutch lock on European trade and establish a French monopoly. So, both declining leaders and ascending challengers can contribute to the attitudinal property of threat/frustration. The greater the combined sense of threat/frustration, the greater is the likelihood of an intense struggle between leader and challenger.

Integrating the Six Models

Table 4.6 lists fifteen indicators linked to the six models.[46] All the indicators are based on some sort of empirical evidence from past iterations. Can we use this information in the twenty-first century? To borrow a phrase beloved of economists: it depends. As long as we stick to generalities, there are basically only so many alternative futures. One is that any propensity toward systemic transition will play out pretty much as it did in the past five hundred years. On the one hand, we know or have good reason to expect that Western Europe is unlikely to generate another military challenger. That might suggest that the traditional (1494–1945) fusing of regional and global politics on occasion need not work the same way as in the past. But it is not inconceivable that East Asia or Eurasia could spawn a formidable challenger in the twenty-first century.[47] Were that to occur, it is hard to imagine regional land-power concentration not increasing even as global capability concentration decayed. Thus, there is a decent possibility that regional-global dissynchronization could continue into the future, despite a substantial change in venue. It seems highly likely that we have already experienced at least one East Asian iteration of regional land-power concentration increasing as global concentration declined in the 1930s. If we look, we will find even earlier iterations of East Asian concentration dating back to the Shang and Xia dynasties and the second millennium BCE (without, of course, the global concentration).[48]

It seems implausible that the decay of the system leader's capabilities or increasing balancing activity are apt to become obsolete considerations in the twenty-first century—assuming, at least, no fundamental changes occur in the way the system operates. It is not difficult, for example, to see ongoing attempts at containing China already in motion. Some things and strategies do not seem to go out of fashion.

A second scenario is that many processes in international relations may continue as before but no aggressive challenger may emerge. The

TABLE 4.6. **Integrating the six models**

Model 1: Phases	Model 2: Dissynchronization	Model 3: Twin peaks	Model 4: Commercial rivalry	Model 5: Nonlinear rivalries	Model 6: Challenger
System leader relative decline; rising opposition to status quo; coalition building	Interaction of global and regional concentration	First of two innovation spurts	Pioneers and latecomers compete in same sectors and need same raw materials and energy sources; latecomers use more centralized strategies to catch up and break into closed markets	Multiple serial clashes, bipolarization, central power transitions	Threat proximity, similarity, orientation duality, threat perception frustration

costs of major power warfare have increased exponentially. The benefits
of engaging in peaceful economic development and trade have also expanded. In this respect, the cost-benefit calculus of global warfare may
have been altered forever.[49] The current Chinese "charm offensive" certainly seems to reflect this estimation. As one Chinese policy maker has
written:

> The ... strategy is to transcend the traditional ways for great powers to
> emerge ... China will not follow the path of Germany leading up to World
> War I or those of Germany. And Japan leading up to World War II, when these
> countries violently plundered resources and pursued hegemony. Neither will
> China follow the path of the great powers vying for global domination during
> the Cold War. Instead, China will transcend ideological differences to strive for
> peace, development, and cooperation with all countries of the world.[50]

Perhaps the Chinese path of ascent will in fact be different. It is interesting to observe, however, that the above paragraph (or the article in
which it was embedded) did not specify just how a transcendental strategy
would be forged—only that such a path would be pursued, explicitly es-
chewing traditional great power competitions à la the late nineteenth century, hegemonic resource pillaging strategies of the mid-twentieth century,
or a late-twentieth-century Cold War competition over relative influence.
At the same time as China stresses peace and cooperation, its economy
expands quickly in size, the focus of its military spending expands on land
and at sea, and it makes a point of demonstrating an ability to destroy satellites in outer space.[51] All these activities tend to contribute to regional
power concentration and may facilitate further global power deconcentration.[52] These same activities also tend to be interpreted as threatening by the incumbent system leader. Yet, faced with weaknesses in many
spheres, it makes perfect sense for a potential challenger to avoid confrontations while working on reducing the weaknesses.

   The question is whether future Chinese decision makers will feel
equally inclined toward cooperative gestures when their material base
and technological competitiveness have improved substantially. There is
also the problem that becoming the leading actor in the world system is
quite a prize—perhaps unlike any other goal in the history of world politics. It might be perceived to be so valuable that the costs and benefits of
major power warfare could be overridden in the eyes of decision makers
operating in stressful crises. This last point applies to both would-be chal-

lengers and incumbent system leaders. Whether we like it or not, there is probably at least one last hurdle to overcome before transcendental paths toward peace and cooperation might become fully plausible. That hurdle is the twenty-first-century's question of China's (re)emergence as not just a great power but also one of the most powerful states in the global system. Should it become quite clearly the most powerful and technologically innovative state in the system, some type of systemic transition, with or without global war, seems probable—all other things being equal.[53]

Yet all other things may not be equal. The United States could very well duplicate the British feat of experiencing two sets of "twin peaks," in which case one might still have an intensive conflict of some sort over global leadership but not necessarily as much of a radical transition as would be implied by a more Sinocentric outcome. From an evolutionary perspective, it would not be too surprising and certainly welcome if the next challenge simply sputters out. If so, we should be in the beginning part of a first innovation peak. It is, of course, conceivable that technological innovation will no longer be monopolized by one lead economy at a time as it has in the recent past.[54] Were the advent of new waves of technological innovation to be more widely distributed, it is equally possible that the attendant economic changes and their political-military implications might be less destabilizing. No clear evidence, however, is available that would support such an evolutionary shift in the concentration of innovation. As long as this technological concentration and uneven diffusion process remains a central feature of modern economic growth, both the probabilities of further systemic transitions and the attendant political tensions and conflicts between pioneers and later developers seem likely.

Conclusion

It is a truism to say that our expectations of what might take place in the future are conditioned heavily by the conceptual frameworks and assumptions that we bring to forecasting exercises. The expectations of power-transition and offensive-realist modelers are reasonably clear. A Chinese transition to dominant power is inevitable and fairly imminent (some time roughly within the next generation). Therefore, the main question for US foreign-policy decision makers is how best to accommodate this sea change in the international environment. Power-transition modelers counsel accommodation; offensive realists urge preparations for a showdown. Yet these forecasts are premised primarily on assumptions about the impact of population and economic size. We do not say that bulk size is irrelevant, but there are other considerations that lead to much different conclusions. If one emphasizes such factors as technological innovation, strategic orientation, and spatial domain, as are found in leadership long-cycle arguments, the inevitability of a power transition or a change in systemic leadership becomes much less evident and imminent. Structural change may be inevitable but a power transition is not. A bid for systemic leadership, as seen by the challenger/transition model, entails much more catching up than what is envisioned in the power-transition model. Nor, as suggested by the offensive realists, is regional military concentration sufficient.

Moreover, it is possible that China will continue to become larger militarily and economically without necessarily closing the qualitative gap between itself and the current system leader. The analytical question thus becomes whether we should pay more attention to the quantitative or the qualitative gap between leader and potential challengers. We argue for the latter. Such an argument by no means precludes variable amounts of Sino-American conflict in coming years, but it does imply that an intensive Chinese challenge of US systemic leadership is at least a generation away. Whether a challenge occurs will depend on how Sino-American relations unfold in the coming decades, in addition to the choices made by Chinese and US decision makers in developing economic and military capabilities for the future.

Nonetheless, these conceptual and historical abstractions about power transitions remain just that—abstractions. How might systemic-transition processes and dynamics play out more specifically in the China-US context? Chapter 5 takes on that task.

Systemic Transition Dynamics and Conflict Drivers in the China–United States Transition Context

This chapter focuses on distilling the extended, although often abstract, discussion in chapter 4 to the question of a future US-China power transition with the principal mission of establishing a foundation for the scenarios to follow. Frankly, we have a number of moving parts and no clear expectation that these parts are subject to a great deal of interpretive consensus. It is important that the reader be able to see them as a whole and how they might be applied to the US-China case in particular. Relative decline—manifest in the concentration of technological innovation and global-reach capabilities—is our primary or structural driver. One might think its meaning is fairly straightforward but that is far from the case. For many observers, quantity (as often measured in the size of the economy) is most critical. If the Chinese gross domestic product (GDP) catches up to and bypasses the size of the US GDP, the US relative share of GDP must decline relative to what others are generating. There is no question that this statement is true. The real question, though, is whether it is quantity or quality that is most important to transition issues. The qualitative dimension in this respect refers to technological innovation (often measured quickly in terms of GDP per capita). Whether one emphasizes quantity or quality makes a tremendous amount of difference when it comes time to track transition probabilities. We need to reinforce our case for our preferred emphasis on qualitative considerations in economic primacy and its link to global-reach capabilities.

But there are another twelve components in the transition-conflict set

TABLE 5.1. **Systemic transition indicators**

Relative decline of global system leader
Rising opposition to global status quo and challenger dissatisfaction/frustration
Coalition building
Interaction of global and regional concentration tendencies
First of two innovation spurts
Competitive frictions between technological pioneer(s) and latecomers
More authoritarian catch-up strategies
Multiple serial clashes
Bipolarization
Regional power transitions
Threat perception and proximity
Dissimilarity in culture and values
Orientation duality

of indicators, previously discussed in chapter 4, and listed in table 5.1. In this chapter, then, we first consider what these secondary-driver abstractions might mean explicitly and then spell out some of the various ways in which China might challenge the United States, its predominance in the East Asian region and, ultimately its global leadership.

Relative Decline — The Primary Structural Driver

Central to any structural theory of international politics is its conception of power—how it is defined and operationalized. Our preferred transitional-challenge model focuses on radical innovations in technology that push forward the technological frontier of advanced economies.

Relative decline in this context means that a leader's edge is decaying. The new technologies are becoming more routine and their market share is down, while others are learning how to produce the same products. The classical example is the automobile. Initially involving a craftsman process in the late nineteenth century, the production of a single automobile might take as long as a year. Once constructed, parts for repairs would have to be built as the need arose. The assembly line altered this process radically. People manning the line did not have to be highly skilled craftsmen. Cars could be assembled much faster and more cheaply, meaning many more drivers on the road. The products were relatively uniform which meant that generic parts could also be assembled that would fit any problems that developed later. Not only did this radical change transform the United States into the leading producer of automobiles for a num-

Capacity to Acquire Technology

```
100%        Germany, U.S.
 90            Japan
 80
 70
 60
 50
 40                              China
 30                              India
 20                              Russia
 10
  0   10   20   30   40   50   60   70   80   90   100%
              Barriers to Technology Acquisition
```

FIGURE 5.1. Capacity to implement new technology for promoting economic development and commerce

ber of decades, the diffusion of the assembly line approach also transformed the US economy into the leading manufacturing hub of the world economy.

Although this process hinges on introducing significant novelties, it is not itself a novel process. It is a characteristic of the movement away from the predominance of agrarian production and can be found repeated in the production statistics of earlier centuries. Figure 5.1 sketches the shape of the process over the past several centuries.

Robert Gilpin views innovation as a type of strategy by which a dominant state can meet the increasing costs of maintaining the existing international system when challenged by a rising state (for whom the costs of changing the status quo are decreasing): "Through organizational, technological, and other types of innovations, a state can either economize with respect to the resources at its disposal or increase the total amount of disposable resources . . . This innovative solution involves rejuvenation of a society's military, economic and political institutions."[1] We concur with Gilpin's emphasis on innovation but think that he does not take it far enough. Specifically, we view innovation as a general and defining attribute of system leaders, a kind of activity that they undertake systematically on a continuous basis, and not merely a strategy, among others, to be pulled off the shelf should challengers arise. Furthermore, we think the key feature of innovation is that it brings about *qualitative*, sometimes revolutionary, changes that enable system leaders to open initially and widen subsequently their economic and military leads; the influence on the quantity of available resources emphasized in Gilpin's formulation is a salient, but less important, consideration.

TABLE 5.2. **Sixteen technology applications by 2020**

Cheap solar energy	Solar cell conversion to electricity using new materials and nanotechnology
Rural wireless communications	Telephone and internet connectivity without relying on wired network infrastructure
Ubiquitous communication devices	Instruments that provide access to information and communication whenever and wherever one wants
Genetically modified crops	Alterations to improve food nutritional value, production, and vulnerability to pests
Rapid bioassays	Ability to verify the presence or absence of biological substances
Water purification filters/ catalysts	Ability to decontaminate water without needing skilled labor
Targeted drug delivery	For targeting tumors/pathogens without harming healthy tissue
Cheap autonomous housing	Using new materials and nanotechnology, inexpensive shelter and energy could be provided to replace traditional approaches
Green manufacturing	Reduction of waste and toxic materials from production processes
Radio-frequency identification tagging	Capability of identifying products and individuals using radio frequency techniques
Hybrid vehicles	Vehicles with propulsion systems that combine internal combustion with other power sources
Pervasive sensors	Nanotechnologically generated cameras and devices for surveillance
Tissue engineering	Development of living tissue for implantation and replacement
Improved diagnostic/surgical methods	Integration of biotechnology and nanotechnology to make assessment and intrusive procedures more accurate and effective
Wearable computers	Miniaturization of computational devices that can be embedded in clothing or auxiliary items
Quantum cryptography	Use of quantum mechanical methods for encoding information that can be used in secure transfers

Source: Richard Silberglitt et al., *The Global Technology Revolution 2020, In-Depth Analyses: Bio/Nano/Materials/ Information Trends, Drivers, Barriers, and Social Implications* (Santa Monica: Rand Corporation, 2006), 19–31.

With hindsight, it is not difficult to pinpoint past qualitative revolutions in industry. Steam engines, railroads, automobiles, electrification, jet engines, and computers come quickly to mind. The early twenty-first century is probably no different, but the nature of the qualitative revolutions has become less overt in some respects. Today biotechnology, nanotechnology, material change, and information technology interact in often subtle fashion to create new ways of doing things that are spreading throughout the economy.[2] A study by the Rand Corporation is helpful on this count.[3] Tasked to identify the most likely significant technological innovations of the next fifteen years, sixteen were singled out as listed in table 5.2. Many of them do not seem to belong in the same category as the more tangible steam engines or computers. What they reflect is the combination of new technologies that alter fundamentally the ways in which we communicate, develop new sources of energy, and cope with disease and health. Their revolutionary impact is more pervasive and stealthy but very real all the same. No single technology in table 5.2 is likely to have the same impact as the railroad or jet engine. But taken as an ensemble of new technologies, the economies that are redesigned by their implementation will be changed radically. The firms that lead the way in producing these new industries and commodities will also enjoy high profits and employment. To the extent that the firms are concentrated in a single economy, that economy is likely to become more affluent than its competitors—as long as it continues to pioneer radically new technologies.

Unfortunately, the Rand study did not allocate any attention to who leads in the production of the sixteen technologies. Since they are just coming on line, it would not be a simple matter to pin this down in any event. For instance, China appears to be an early leader in solar technology while the United States has the lead in medical biotechnology. It may be another decade or two, however, before we can tell who the 2020 or 2030 leaders in technology production are or have been. The closest the Rand study came to specifying national winners was to ask which economies were most likely to apply or implement their sixteen innovations. The list of likely barriers to implementation is impressive: costs/financing, laws/policies, social values/public opinion/politics, infrastructure, privacy concerns, environmental health, research and design investment, education/literacy, population/demographics, and governance/stability. Clearly, the world is not noted for accepting innovations readily or evenly. The Rand study, based on surveying experts, portrays the US economy as more likely to implement most or all of the sixteen technologies than the Chinese economy, but the US economy is not portrayed as a likely monopolist innovator—several economies (Germany and Japan, for instance) are given better chances, as shown in figure 5.1.

These issues are some of the more important question marks (and little discussed) of the first quarter of the twenty-first century. Are we in the midst of another upsurge in technological productivity geared to a convergence of information/bio/nanotechnologies? Will the United States economy repeat its record in twentieth-century technological leadership? Or will technological innovation move elsewhere in the world economy, either to another country entirely or to a number of advanced economies with no single state doing obviously better than its competitors? If the United States retains its technological edge, it is likely to continue being

TABLE 5.3. **China and US shares of world gross domestic product (GDP), 1940–2000**

Year	US share	China share
1940	.206	.062
1950	.273	.045
1960	.243	.052
1970	.223	.046
1980	.211	.052
1990	.213	.078
2000	.218	.115

Note: Based on Angus Maddison's historical GDP data found at http://www.ggdc.net/maddison/Maddison/htm.

the world's lead economy. If not, it will experience relative decline and fall behind the economies of other states.

Technological innovation does not always translate directly into gross domestic product (GDP), but overall wealth is one outcome that is linked to innovation and the implementation of advanced production techniques. GDP is probably one of the more imperfect indexes of innovation success since it rewards the gross size of the economy and the number of people involved in economic production and transactions. GDP per capita is less imperfect because it attempts to control for size. Tables 5.3 and 5.4 report comparative economic data for the United States and China in a fashion that is common to analyses of power transitions.

Table 5.3 reports 1940–2000 data on US, China, and world GDP using purchasing power parity estimates that also control for inflation.[4] Purchasing power parity estimates clearly favor less-developed economies for comparative purposes.[5] Recognizing that desired commodities cost less in less-developed contexts than in more-developed contexts, the attempt is to try to control for these differential costs in the creation of overall wealth indices. As a consequence, table 5.3 shows the US share of world GDP moving ahead in World War II (1940–50) but not by as much of a margin as would be delineated in GDP figures not based on purchasing power parity assumptions. The US share declines through 1980 and then rises slightly. The Chinese share remained more or less the same between 1940 and 1980 and then began an impressive rate of increase, more than doubling between 1980 and 2000.[6] It is this type of statistical movement that stimulates talk of the Chinese economy becoming larger than the US economy in the near future. What is omitted from the discussion is that the Chinese economy possessed the largest GDP in the world in much of the nineteenth century and no one worried then about China making a bid for systemic leadership because its GDP share was not based on tech-

TABLE 5.4. **China and US shares of gross domestic product (GDP), 2000–2050**

Year	US share	China share
2000	.439	.048
2010	.437	.099
2020	.389	.168
2030	.395	.237
2040	.299	.290
2050	.254	.321

Note: GDP shares based on an aggregate consisting of G6 (France, Germany, Italy, Japan, United Kingdom, and United States) and four BRIC (Brazil, Russia, India, China) economies.
Source: Based on data found in Dominic Wilson and Roopa Purushothaman, *Dreaming with BRICs: The Path to 2050* (Goldman Sachs, 2003) at http://www.goldmansachs.com/our-thinking/brics/brics-dream.html.

nological leadership but on the sheer size of the Chinese population. The sheer size problem is still with us and it means that we need to take GDP shares with a grain of salt.

The real question is whether one state can combine quantitative size with leadership of qualitative innovation. In the China case, that remains to be seen. GDP per capita indices are more useful for this purpose. The information reported in table 5.3 indicates that China has made considerable gains but still has some way to go to catch up with the United States. Between 1940 and 1950, the ratio of US GDP per capita to Chinese GDP per capita increased by some 71 percent and only began to decline noticeably after 1980. In 2000, the US GDP per capita was still ahead by a factor of eight.

What happens if we project these numbers into the future? Table 5.4 summarizes information generated by a Goldman Sachs study using US 2003 dollars and involving guesstimates of future growth rates.[7] Note that the denominator is no longer the world as a whole but has been replaced by a focus on the aggregate numbers of the G6 and the four BRICs.[8] In this analysis the 2000 GDP position of the United States is somewhat less than half the aggregate. By 2050, its share has been reduced to one-fourth of the aggregate, assuming relatively slow growth rates (or no new spurt of technological leadership). In 2000, China's share is about 5 percent and is slated to rise to about a third by 2050, passing the United States between 2040 and 2050. The GDP per capita ratio declines by half between 2000 and 2010 and then again by another half in 2020 and still again in 2030. By 2050, China will have gained the GDP per capita attained by the United States in 2000 while the US GDP per capita will have improved by 140 percent.

These numbers can be looked at in different ways. However one in-

terprets the numbers, the Chinese gains will be dramatic. Yet, qualitatively, the two economies may still be in different leagues. The problem, of
course, is that these projections to 2050 are based on assumptions about
what will happen to economic growth between now and then. They assume that the United States will continue to grow slowly and that China's
growth will slow down gradually.[9] Neither assumption may prove accurate. But, even so, the degree of economic catch up manifest in the aggregate numbers is somewhat less than is often talked about when the discussion is restricted to relative shares of GDP.

It is probably safe to assume that the United States will sustain some
relatively high rate of innovation, technologically and organizationally,
and in both the economic and military areas. Whether the Chinese do as
well or even better is something that we need to keep an eye on. But also
critical to any potential power transition will be China's ability to develop
a capacity for innovation sufficient to avoid falling further behind the US
in the revolution in military affairs.[10] There seems to be wide belief that
if China tries to emulate each and every generation of American military technology it might take a century or more to catch up with the US
military. But it may be possible for China, by exploiting the advantages
of backwardness, to "leapfrog" over some generations and thus accelerate the catch-up process. But even if one expects China to develop the
requisite capacities to innovate, it is very difficult to estimate when this
will happen, how long until the resulting innovations significantly impact
the military competition with the United States, and which technological
stages can be leapfrogged.[11]

Several recent studies have begun to address these questions by
focusing on China's thriving civilian industries as a potential source of
advanced technologies for the military sector. China's indigenous military R&D facilities have had limited success in developing new technologies and have been plagued by lengthy development times, so it is unlikely that China will rely solely on home-grown weapons systems. The
primary external sources of technology include imports of weapons systems and manufacturing technologies from other powers; previous significant upgrades have resulted from imports, mainly from the Soviet Union/
Russia (e.g., Sovremenny destroyers, SU27 combat aircraft, and Kilo-class
submarines). But China has twice experienced cutoffs of imported military technology (by the Soviet Union in 1959/60 and by Western countries after the Tiananmen Square crackdown in 1989), thus strengthen-
ing the incentives for self-reliant defense production. Another external

source is international commercial markets, where China can purchase some critical "dual-use" components and equipment and then build weapons systems around these components. But, given the wariness of governments in weapons-exporting states, neither of these external sources is likely to provide China with state-of-the-art weapons technology. The remaining external (to domestic defense industries) source is China's rapidly expanding civilian industries, which have been increasingly opened to foreign investment and the technology transfers that accompany it. In consequence, China's commercial sector has been climbing the technological gradient and now provides an advanced technological base.

Wendy Frieman emphasizes the importance (as well as difficulty) of factoring some assessment of China's scientific and technological base, and thus its capacity to innovate, into any estimate of China's overall power resources.[12] Accordingly, Frieman examines China's progress in those "technologies that will form the building blocks for information warfare and for the kind of high technology weapons envisioned by those who write about the revolution in military affairs": computer hardware and software, semiconductor manufacturing, telecommunications networking, and satellites. Frieman also considers the development of China's indigenous base of scientific and technical talent and reforms in the organization of China's scientific infrastructure, as well as the relationship between China's private industries and its defense sector. On these bases, Frieman concludes that, "in another ten years, if not sooner, China will have at its disposal the raw material, the building block technologies, to support the systems on which the battlefield of the future will depend."[13]

Roger Cliff's study of the military potential of China's commercial technology reaches similar conclusions.[14] Cliff looks at eight technology areas that are on the US Department of Defense's 1996 list of *Military Critical Technologies* and that correspond to major civilian industries: microelectronics, computers, telecommunications equipment, nuclear power, biotechnology, chemicals, aviation, and space. He reports that China has "significant production capabilities" in all these industries except biotechnology, but also that all suffer "significant limitations."[15] Cliff concludes, "that China can expect to make significant technological progress in coming years but cannot possibly catch up to, much less 'leapfrog,' the United States or Japan in the foreseeable future" [by 2020].[16] Cliff cautions, however, that despite this gap China's technological progress could still enable development of "niche" capabilities that could pose "a serious military challenge to the United States."[17]

For now, according to Paul Godwin, "A national military strategy focused on potentially high intensity limited, local war along China's extensive land and sea borders ... has called for technologies Beijing's defense R&D has thus far not developed and the industrial base cannot yet produce."[18] But if, as Eliot Cohen argues, contemporary civilian technologies of the sort examined by Frieman and Cliff, especially information technologies, are especially suitable for rapid application to military purposes, then the potential for leapfrogging may be considerable: "To the extent that the revolution [in military affairs] proceeds from forces in the civilian world, the potential will exist for new military powers to emerge extremely rapidly ... in a few years, China will quickly translate civilian technological power into its military equivalent."[19] Thus, we contend that China's capacity to innovate will provide valuable clues about how and when a power transition will develop. Expeditious improvements in China's capacity to innovate will bear out Cohen's assertion. If, on the other hand, China's innovativeness continues to lag a considerable distance behind that of the United States, then China overtaking the United States might wait until much later in the twenty-first century.

The sheer size of China and of the People's Liberation Army (PLA) would certainly pose strategic and tactical problems in so far as the United States and any potential set of regional allies would be vastly outnumbered. But sheer size is not necessarily an advantage, except perhaps in large-scale land wars, precisely the kind of war in which the United States would be least likely to engage. Furthermore, after 1985 China shifted away from the Maoist strategy of "people's war," in which adversaries were to be drawn into a protracted war that allowed China to capitalize on its considerable strategic depth and very large armies, to a strategy of "local (or limited) war." Local wars, which are anticipated to be fought on China's peripheries and to be decided quickly, are limited in geographic extent, as well as in terms of their political purposes.[20] As Mark Burles and Abram Shulsky point out, "China's vast size and population, crucial assets in the traditional 'people's war' concept, are, at best, irrelevant under local war conditions."[21] This conclusion is even stronger in light of the doctrinal shift to "local war under high tech conditions." Godwin notes that: "[W]here mass can no longer be assumed to substitute for quality, operational concepts designed to compensate for technological deficiencies are increasingly difficult to realize."[22]

It is in this context that General Zhao Nanqi, director of the China Military Science Association, argues that China's military modernization entails a change in, "armed forces construction from a quantity and size model to a quality and effectiveness model."[23] Consider, for instance, naval capabilities, as depicted by David Shambaugh:

> In aggregate terms the PLAN is the third largest in the world. It is roughly equivalent in size (but not armament) to the Russian Pacific fleet ... However in qualitative terms, when measured against other navies in Asia, one finds that the Japanese naval Self-Defense Force, the Indian Navy, the combined naval forces of the ASEAN, and elements of Taiwan's Navy are all superior to the PLAN. And of course the PLAN is incomparable to the U.S. Navy.[24]

Absent a modern air force it is likely impossible for the PLA to prevail in a local war under high-tech conditions—"the PLAAF has always been the technologically weakest leg of the PLA force structure."[25] The PLAAF fighter-interceptor inventory was once large, but many of the planes were obsolete relics, 1950s–1960s vintage Soviet aircraft that were no match for the much newer American and French combat aircraft deployed by the United States, Japan, and Taiwan. This situation has been addressed to some extent by replacing the obsolete models with newer generation planes, but China still is experiencing problems in developing jet engines.[26] The lack of AWACs (airborne warning and control systems), surveillance and target acquisition systems, airborne refueling capabilities, and sophisticated C[3]I (command, control, communications, and intelligence) combine to limit the PLAAF's and PLANAF's ability both to project force and to coordinate the kinds of joint (air, land, sea) operations envisioned by the strategic doctrine of local war. John Lewis and Xue Litai's survey of China's less than successful efforts to develop a modern air force led them to conclude that "[t]here is no near- to medium-term likelihood that China's air force could match those of its possible foes."[27] Nonetheless, China has the capability to surprise external observers as leaked photos of a new stealth-fighter prototype in 2011 indicated.[28] Whether the prototype uses western technology or not, the US monopoly on stealth fighters apparently will end more quickly than was anticipated.

In sum, the quantity of naval and air capabilities arrayed against China's potential foes currently provides a highly misleading overestimate of the country's military power. China's weaknesses in this regard stem from a variety of qualitative deficiencies that may some day be overcome but which have not yet been addressed fully. As General Chen

Bingde reiterated in a 2011 speech to the US National Defense University, the "Chinese military's strength pales in comparison with the United States."[29] Least of all would we expect such broad gauge measures as GDP, population, or PLA manpower to provide much guidance as to how and when a US-China power transition might unfold. Even if we were to allow that such measures of national "bulk" might have some predictive power, they surely do not offer much understanding. These conclusions are reinforced when we turn to the closely related issue of strategic orientation.

The significance of bulk indicators—population, economic, and armed forces size—have probably always been exaggerated in international relations. This is inherently puzzling because the states with the largest populations, economies, and armies are often beaten by smaller states with technological edges. It is as if we have never quite understood the David-Goliath parable. A small David manipulated projectile technology to topple the larger Goliath. In early modern European history, Spain and France, the largest states of their region in that time, were often beaten by smaller states such as the Netherlands or England. In more modern times, the huge Soviet Union was almost beaten by a smaller Germany that insisted on taking on Britain, France, and the United States at the same time in World War II. Moreover, the states with the largest economies in the nineteenth century were China and Russia. Neither state fared all that well in combat with their smaller adversaries. The bottom line here is that the states with the largest battalions, population, or economy do not necessarily succeed in world politics.

The states that succeed most spectacularly in modern times are the ones with lead economies that monopolize the introduction of radically new technological innovations. Their economies quickly outproduce others because lead economies are not only operating on the production frontier but also establishing the world economy's production frontier. For brief periods of time, they are without economic peers. Eventually, rivals catch up but, until they do, lead economies and system leaders enjoy substantial edges in economic and political-military advantage. As other states catch up and surpass the lead economy's head start, relative decline sets in. This relative decline is likely to be manifested ultimately in both economic and military technology.

Yet if relative decline in technological innovation is our primary driver, there are other considerations that further aggravate transition tensions and conflict. For present purposes, we can group these considerations in terms of three encompassing categories: strategic orientation, spatial domain, and perceived threat/dissatisfaction. The first two relate to the importance of global-reach capabilities, while the third is the cognitive catalyst that translates structural decline into transitional conflict and the secondary drivers of conflict.

Strategic Orientation and Spatial Domain

Strategic Orientation

Strategic orientation is a critical underlying element in the challenger/ transition model. The maritime orientation of system leaders has resulted in their development of global-reach capabilities; a strong position in global commerce, industry and finance; and the creation of global networks and institutions. In combination, these global proclivities have meant that system leaders have established a strong military and economic presence in various geographic regions, a presence that often brought about conflicts of interest with upwardly mobile regional powers. Challengers can be either regional powers that have used land power to climb to the top of a regional hierarchy (historically Europe) or other powers with a maritime orientation and global aspirations. Confrontations between globally oriented system leaders and continentally oriented regional leaders have been much more war prone, with the former invariably emerging victorious. Challenges from other global powers have tended to be resolved well short of global war.[30]

China has traditionally been a continental power with force configurations, weaponry, and strategies oriented to land warfare along its twenty thousand kilometers of borders with (presently) fourteen different countries, and to coastal defense along China's eighteen thousand kilometers of coastline. Consider the extent to which China's force structure as recently as 1998 still reflected the people's war/land-based strategy: China's army accounted for 73 percent of its 2,840,000-strong active forces, the navy for 10 percent, and the air force 17 percent; the corresponding proportions for the US army, navy, and air force in the same year were 33, 40, and 27 percent, respectively, of the 1,443,000 active forces total.[31] This continental strategic orientation continued until the mid-1980s, when China began to shift away from the "people's war" strategy. Michael Swaine and Ashley Tellis attribute this shift to "dramatic changes in China's strategic geography" brought about by the economic reforms initiated in the late 1970s: "[I]ts most valuable economic and social resources now lie along its weakly defended eastern and southeastern territorial periphery as opposed to the secure interior heartland as was the case during the Cold War."[32]

This change was reinforced by the collapse of the Soviet Union and the consequent easing of what was then China's principal threat along its northern border. The main threat was now the United States (along with Japan and Taiwan), which brings substantial air/naval force projection capabilities to the region. Together, these changes, "put a premium on the development of new kinds of conventional forces—primarily air and naval—and new concepts of operation that are quite alien to the traditional continental orientation of the Chinese military." [Owing to this continental orientation,] "[T]he PLAN's [PLA Navy] role in 1985 [had been] the coastal defense component of a continental strategy."[33] Thus, in David Finkelstein's terms, "[f]or the PLA today (and more than likely tomorrow) the essence of defending China will be defined by the PLA's ability to defend seaward from the coast in the surface, subsurface and aerospace battle-space dimensions. Despite efforts to correct this situation, this is precisely the type of warfare that the PLA is currently least well postured to conduct."[34]

Under the new doctrine of "local war under high tech conditions," maritime strategy, weapons, and operations have been deemed at least as important as the traditional emphasis on continental defense. But the PLAN's resulting attempts to extend its operational range from "brown water" (coastal defense) to "green water" (offshore defense) have been less than expeditious. The eventual development of a "blue water" navy capable of projecting and sustaining force over much greater distances from Chinese territory is even more problematic, constrained by diplomatic choices (no alliances and no forces stationed abroad), as well as technical factors [weak amphibious capabilities, poor logistics, and technological problems in making its SLBM (sea-launched ballistic missile) submarine(s) operational]. China's military, in a Chinese general's oft-cited turn of phrase, is like a boxer with "short arms and slow legs."

Consider China's efforts to improve its ability to project maritime force (an elephant's effort to develop whalelike capabilities, to continue the earlier metaphor). Chinese military strategists have declared the intention of eventually being able to project a zone of "active defense" out as far as what they term "the first island chain," which lies five hundred to one thousand nautical miles away from China's coast and extends from

Korea to the Ryuku and Spratly Islands.[35] There are three levels within this first zone:

1. Brown water: Zero to fifty miles, defended by radar missiles, coastal patrol boats and gunships, mines, and land-based aircraft.
2. Green water: From fifty to three hundred miles out, defended by missile destroyers, corvettes, ship-based helicopters, and land-based aircraft.
3. Blue water: Out to the first island chain, to be defended by submarines equipped with advanced missiles and naval attack aircraft.

Beyond that, the PLAN aspires to project force out to the "second island chain," which stretches from the Aleutians to Guam and to the Philippines.

Where does China stand with respect to realization of these force projection objectives? Godwin concludes that the PLA has improved its "ability to project and sustain forces in nearby maritime regions claimed as sovereign Chinese territory."[36] Yet, despite the improvements, China's capabilities remain quite limited, according to David Shambaugh: "In a potential conflict against the United States or Japan ... the PLA Navy could disrupt—but not defeat—operations as far as 200 nautical miles offshore."[37] Indeed, it is probably more accurate to speak of China's *force extension*, rather than projection, capabilities. In John Frankenstein and Bates Gill's terms:

> It is useful to distinguish between force extension and force projection. The latter term ... means the ability to insert and sustain military force in theatres distant from the homeland. Force projection thus requires the development of forces capable of operating on their own and the logistics capability to sustain them. Force extension, on the other hand, would require only the ability to employ force at a distance for a short time and without the intention or requirement to sustain it. An extension strategy might be suitable for certain scenarios in the South China Sea, but would be inadequate for an invasion and necessary occupation of Taiwan.[38]

Another useful perspective on power extension/projection can be expressed in terms of "three generic levels of capability," those necessary for China to (1) *deny* its adversaries free use of a given battlespace; (2) *control* a given battlespace to a degree that allows operations without inordinate risks to its own forces; and (3) *exploit* its control of a given battlespace to bring coercive power to bear against the strategic centers of gravity valued by its adversaries.[39] Combining the two standards, then, China's ability to extend air and naval force provides it with no more, at least for now, than a partial capability to deny the United States or other adversaries free use of the battlespaces along China's maritime periphery.[40] If 2049 is the target for acquiring modernized military capabilities, as Michael Swaine notes, this asymmetry will persist for some time to come.[41]

These limited capabilities have been the result of technological inferiority vis-à-vis the United States, Japan, and Taiwan that need not be perpetuated indefinitely.[42] But the idea of finding ways to defeat foes with superior capabilities has a long and venerable history, dating back to the military theorist Sun Tzu.[43] As Godwin points out, "[a] consequence of Mao Zedong's successful adjustment to Japanese (and later Kuomintang) military superiority is that the PLA's doctrinal tradition contains the principle that technological inferiority does not necessarily foreshadow defeat."[44]

The principle of "the inferior defeating the superior" has led to an emphasis on what the Chinese call asymmetric war, along with corollary emphases on deception, surprise, and preemption.[45] Pillsbury reports six approaches to asymmetrical naval warfare found in the Chinese strategic literature:

1. Attack space-based communications and surveillance systems
2. Use of shore-based missiles and aircraft rather than developing large (symmetrical) naval forces
3. Develop "magic weapons," for example, tactical laser weapons, stealth technology adapted to ships, and cruise missiles
4. Attack the naval logistics of the superior navy
5. Attack the command and information systems of the superior navy
6. Use submarines and new types of torpedoes.[46]

Note that most of these "asymmetric" methods, which are supposed to compensate until China overcomes its technological inferiority, require capabilities that lie in China's technological future. For China to become a maritime power with (regional) force projection capabilities will require that it enhance its capacity for innovation.[47]

Transformational problems, however, do not rule out early successes. Between 2003 and 2008, three manned space flights were launched. In 2007, China demonstrated that it could shoot down one of its own satellites. Early in the following year, the United States warned China against disrupting US space systems and that it should cease using missiles to destroy satellites. Less debris in space from destroyed satellites would also be another plus. A month later, the United States showed that it too could destroy one of its own satellites. China's response was essentially that it had little choice but to continue testing its space capabilities to counter the US missile defense program and thus has ignored the US warning.[48]

Another area in which China appears to have been successful involves cyberreconnaissance and warfare. The capability to invade adversary computer systems and extract classified information and to disrupt the use of computer systems by adversaries is another example of an asymmetric weapon. If one's adversaries are more technologically advanced (and dependent), the point is to take advantage of that dependence with limited means. Individual Chinese hackers have been encouraged by the state with monetary rewards just as the PLA has created specialized units to engage in this type of activity on a full-time basis. Western computer systems, both governmental and private, consequently are bombarded with many thousands of attempted intrusions per year. Much of this activity may be experimental and for practice. Certainly, some of it is nongovernmental in inspiration. However, the point is that the capability could be used to literally shut down an economy or a military coordination system in a serious political-military crisis should the occasion arise. The idea is to level the playing field by handicapping an adversary's ability to act in a major way without requiring a substantial information technology platform.[49]

Thus the questions are whether and to what extent China sheds its longtime commitment to an elephant-like strategic orientation that emphasizes security issues in the proximate environment. To reach beyond coastal waters and into outer and cyberspace, cutting-edge technological capabilities will be necessary. Since China has made concrete commitments to enhance its aerospace capabilities, its blue water, maritime capabilities, its space capabilities, and its cyberwarfare capabilities, it is not a hypothetical question about future orientations and intentions. Rather, it is an ongoing matter of China transforming its approach to security questions. How quickly and completely the transformation takes place is likely to be a critical link to the probabilities of transitional conflict.

Spatial Domain: Global or Global Regional

The central spatial regularity of challenges that have culminated in global war have all involved an emerging regional power confronting a global leader is a critical insight into transitional conflict.[50] This spatial dimension is theoretically meaningful, enjoys a large measure of empirical corroboration, and is particularly germane to the US-China case. We do not wish to suggest deterministically that a US-China war in connection with a Chinese challenge is inevitable because it fits with the historical record, but rather that, from an analytical standpoint, a transition research program that takes this aspect of the record into account is advantaged vis-à-vis those that do not.

Distance clearly influences the challenge/transition process.[51] Kenneth Boulding introduced the concept of a "loss of strength gradient" (LSG), which posits the erosion of the effectiveness of force as a function of distance.[52] Put simply, US military power erodes because the East Asian theater is on the other side of the planet from US home territory—even though the United States has invested heavily in developing weapons technologies and logistic systems that arrest the rate of decay. The network of alliances, bases, and nonalliance military relations that the US has constructed also serve to offset the LSG. Nevertheless, for various reasons, some erosion is inevitable. First, as Szayna et al. contend, "a proto-peer [challenger] with some revisionist tendencies is likely to attempt to alter regional hierarchy first. Because of its global responsibilities the hegemon will be able to concentrate only a portion of its power at the regional level, whereas the regional [challenger] is likely to be able to concentrate almost all of its power there."[53] US military advantages would be reduced further if it were already engaged militarily in another geographic theater, for example, the Persian Gulf or Central Asia. Additionally, Chinese strategists believe that in order to bring sufficient force to fight a war along China's maritime periphery the United States would have to establish very long logistics lines, which then "represent relatively vulnerable and extremely lucrative targets."[54] The relatively shallow "brown" waters around Taiwan and in the South China Sea are also seen as disadvantageous to the United States because such a maritime environment is not optimal for US antisubmarine capabilities, which were designed for deep "blue" ocean warfare.

The major implication of the LSG for a possible US-China power transition is that China need not match the United States in terms of overall military capabilities to mount a challenge. As Thomas Christensen argues, "with certain new equipment and with certain strategies, China can pose major problems for American security interests, and especially for Taiwan, without the slightest pretense of catching up with the United States by an overall measure of national military power or technology."[55] Matching American global military power may lie in the distant future, but being able to inflict punishment on the United States, should it intervene in regional matters of vital interest to China, is a much more realistic goal that is attainable in the near- to mid-term. Presently, as we have shown in the previous section, China's LSG falls precipitously at or just beyond its maritime periphery. Should China develop force extension/projection capabilities adequate to deny the United States the ability to operate with impunity (i.e., without risk to its forces) along this periphery, the point at which its LSG intersected with that of the United States would be pushed out further from the Chinese mainland.

The salience of some of the concepts discussed above—asymmetric warfare, the doctrine of "the inferior defeating the superior," and the development of "niche" capabilities—becomes apparent in this context. Thus, according to Christensen, "what will determine whether China takes actions that will lead to Sino-American conflict will likely be politics, perceptions, and coercive diplomacy involving *specific military capabilities in specific geographic and political contexts*, not the overall balance of military power across the Pacific or across the Taiwan Strait" [emphasis added].[56] Godwin explains how this perspective affects the PLA's R&D and procurement: "[I]t is useful to think about military modernization as now focused primarily on creating specific attributes designed to respond to immediate requirements while the vast bulk of the armed forces continue to pursue the complementary broader vision of a truly modern force by the years 2020–2050."[57]

For our purposes, the question here is whether the spatial domain of the challenge is regional, global, or both. If the domain is primarily regional and the issue is the pecking order in Asia, transitional conflict could come much sooner than if the issue is one of global hierarchy. The capabilities that are most significant for global challenges are different and more difficult to create than the ones most suitable for regional challenges. As we have noted in the previous section, global challenges require both specialized hardware and a change in strategic orientation. In modern European history (post-1494), aspiring regional hegemons tended to advance their challenges prior to fully developing global strategic orientations. The premature nature of these challenges strongly influenced how and when incumbent system leaders and their allies responded. It also strongly conditioned the nature of the outcomes in which defenders of the status quo have prevailed even when the incumbent system leader did not.[58]

Threat Perception/Dissatisfaction

Though we are inclined toward structural models (and their materialist bases) cast at high levels of social aggregation, we recognize that attention to attitudinal and perceptual factors is important, indeed necessary. Otherwise, it is impossible to account for how structural factors, especially structural change, translate into behavior. Accordingly, one definite strength of the power-transition model is its emphasis on the level of (dis)satisfaction with the status quo order on the part of the ascending state.[59] Although we agree strongly with this emphasis as pertains to the ascending challenger, trying to make this variable symmetrical by also assessing the (dis)satisfaction of the declining dominant power seems a questionable conceptual extension. As Tammen et al. acknowledge, "[b]y definition, the dominant power is satisfied . . . [and therefore] is the defender of the status quo. After all, it creates and maintains the global or regional hierarchy from which it accrues substantial benefits."[60] Yet the authors then proceed to develop and graphically illustrate several scenarios based on the combination of the challenger's *and* the leader's (dis)satisfaction.

A more fruitful approach, in our view, is to combine assessment of the challenger's (dis)satisfaction with the existing order and estimates of the system leader's perception of the threat posed by the challenger. On the one hand, the challenger's dissatisfaction can be mapped across the elements of order we discussed earlier: the hierarchy of power and status; rules for managing security, use of force, and the laws of war; mechanisms for managing territorial changes; mutual recognition of spheres of interest; and rules governing trade and investment. The greater the extent that a challenger feels that the existing order and its constituent rules do not afford it status, respect, and material rewards commensurate with its rising power, the more dissatisfied it is likely to be. On the other hand, the leader's threat assessment has two main elements: (1) its own future vulnerability to the challenger, based on projections of its own and the challenger's growth rates and innovative performance; and (2) the challenger's revisionist potential, that is, the likelihood that its dissatisfaction will lead the challenger to pursue a revisionist agenda aimed at overturning the existing order.[61] The more threatening the leader perceives the challenger to be, the more likely the former will resort to competitive strategies to cope with the challenger's ascent.

How to combine these two attitudinal dimensions? We propose that the most conflict-prone type of power transition would be characterized by a combination of a dissatisfied challenger and a system leader that perceived the challenger to pose high levels of threat. The least conflictual situation would result from a satisfied challenger and a system leader with low threat perceptions. The other combinations—dissatisfied challenger and low threat perceptions, and satisfied challenger and high threat perceptions—would likely fall somewhere between the first two in terms of intensity of conflict.

It may be too early to assess the full extent of China's dissatisfaction with the existing, US-dominated order, both globally and in the Asia-Pacific region. The "century of humiliation" and the succession of indignities suffered at the hands of Western and Japanese imperialism lead pessimists on this question to the view, as characterized by Richard Betts and Thomas Christensen, that "a seething set of Chinese grudges and territorial ambitions are on hold only for a lack of confidence in capability."[62] Optimists, conversely, believe that China can be constructively engaged—both bilaterally by the United States and others and multilaterally in various international regimes—to produce a generally satisfied China with a positive stake in a world order modified to account for its interests and power. The World Trade Organization (WTO) can be regarded as a kind of laboratory within which these expectations will be put to the test.

While China's level of (dis)satisfaction remains to be determined, there is considerably more evidence that China is increasingly viewed as a threat by American leaders, at least (but not only) those on the political right. The opening salvo of the so-called China threat school of thought was the ominously entitled book, *The Coming Conflict with China*, which has been followed by a bourgeoning literature pro and con.[63] There have also been a series of reports by government agencies and government-sponsored commissions that regard China in threatening terms.[64] The analytical task will be to devise systematic methods for assessing (dis)satisfaction and threat perceptions as the China challenge unfolds over the coming decades.

One of the more obtrusive hallmarks of dissatisfaction and threat perception, of course, is coalition building and bipolarization. Chinese decision makers complain about being encircled by the United States, Japan, and India, but this containment system is at best still only emerging. The Indo-US relationship, after decades of estrangement, is feeling its way toward greater cooperation. Indo-Japanese interaction and cooperation is more concrete but less than a full-fledged alliance. European powers have yet to be enlisted formally for this activity.[65] Russia and China, on the other hand, have reconciled and moved toward alignment, if not yet alliance. They share an opposition to the maintenance of the US position in East Asia and Eurasia, but they also have lingering problems of their own in terms of different growth trajectories (reversing the asymmetries of the 1950s) and long-standing Russian fears of Chinese movement into Siberia. In sum, then, coalition building has been ongoing tentatively in the first decade of the twenty-first century. Existing alliance structures have some way to go to be described as bipolarized. Aaron Friedberg predicts the possibility of a bipolarized structure along a continental-maritime divide if China continues to rise and does not change its regime and if the United States remains engaged in Asia.[66] The continental camp would be aligned around China and would consist of states contiguous to China (North Korea, Kazakhstan, Kyrgyzstan, Tajikistan, Pakistan, Myanmar, Laos, and possibly Vietnam). The maritime camp would be Japan, South Korea, the Philippines, Indonesia, Australia, Singapore, Thailand, India, and possibly Mongolia. Friedberg describes these coaslitions as continuing to be nascent, with both potentially polar powers working to break up the opposing coalition. But should a new cold war emerge between the United States and China, one could expect increasing pressures for states in the area to pick sides.[67] Both bipolarization and a period of intensive searches for alliances in preparation for a possible systemic (or regional) showdown are secondary drivers in our transitional model.

Another possibility that remains even more emergent at this point in time is that there could be more than one transitional process underway. While we are focused intensely on the possibility of a global transition, the possibility of several regional transitions should not be overlooked. The challenger model encompasses not only a global-regional transitional struggle but also intraregional transitional struggles along the lines of the Franco-German conflict in the nineteenth and early twentieth centuries.[68] It has been noted that India's growth trajectory could surpass that of China's.[69] Whether or not this occurs at some point in the future, incentives on the part of China to suppress the threatening rise of India and/or incentives on the part of India to overcome China's lead in Asia could be expected to lead to future intraregional transitional conflict. The two states have long been rivals and have already fought one war over territorial boundaries. The point here is that global-regional clashes need not occur in a vacuum. They can be made more complex and more dangerous by parallel activity at lower levels of analysis.

Challenge(s)

We have expressed some analytical ambivalence about the likely scope or domain of a systemic challenge. Based on the European historical experience, it could come in the form of a regional hegemonic bid, a genuine global contest, or some combination of the two. What specific political or military actions on the part of China would constitute a challenge to the United States and the existing regional or global order? What revisions might China seek to the regional status quo? How might these revisions jeopardize American interests? First, consider situations in which China might elect to use force, leaving the United States and others with the choice of whether and how to respond:[70]

- To vindicate claims to territory or territorial waters, principally Taiwan, but also the South China Sea, including the Spratly Islands, Diaoyu/Senkaku Islands, and, less likely, border disputes with India or Vietnam. Regional states, as well as the United States, could be expected either to accept a fait accompli (following, say, a surprise attack on Taiwan) or to acquiesce to China's territorial claims in the face of its military power.
- To suppress separatist movements, including Taiwan, Muslim Uighurs in Xinjiang Province, and Tibet.
- To prevent the emergence of new threats such as Japan or India.
- To protect overseas communities of ethnic Chinese or business interests.
- To compete for access to Central Asian, Middle Eastern, and African resources.
- Other challenges could result from China seeking to establish regional hegemony, with implications for regional states, especially those on China's periphery, as well as the United States.
- Securing deference from regional states could quickly become confrontational if the deference demanded were to include severing or significantly limiting regional states' ties with extraregional powers, especially the US; China's insistence that regional states no longer host a US military presence, for example, in Korea or Japan, or that they do not establish military ties with the US, say Vietnam, could lead to a US-China military confrontation.
- Curtailing the US military's freedom of action throughout East Asia by means of sea lane denial, disruption of US information dominance, or attacks (or threats to attack) US military bases in Japan or South Korea, well as ports, airfields or other militarily relevant facilities in the region.
- Limiting US economic access to the region's raw materials, markets, and investment opportunities.

- Shifting the region's security structure away from the configuration of formal and informal bilateral alliances between the United States and various regional states.
- Proliferating nuclear weapons and missile technology to small Asian allies and resisting attempts to apply pressure on their nuclear programs.
- Supporting authoritarian regimes in Central Asia via the Shanghai Cooperation Organization.
- Directing a program of cyberespionage, surveillance, and destruction of electronic infrastructures.

Another category of challenges could arise were China to attempt to alter the multilateral "rules of the game," which were originally set in place under American auspices and which reflect American, or at least Western, values, interests and preferences. Such a challenge could be mounted at either the regional or global level.

- Rules associated with the regional (Asia-Pacific Economic Cooperation [APEC]) or global (WTO) trade regime.
- Rules to curb proliferation of weapons of mass destruction and delivery systems.
- Rules and norms pertaining to regional security (in the Association of Southeast Asian Nations [ASEAN] Regional Forum).

None of this implies that China and the United States will go to war over these issues. Some analysts are sure that they do not imply war. Colonel Liu Mingfu, who is convinced that China will surpass the United States in the twenty-first century, has said

"The competition between China and the United States will not take the form of a world war or a cold war. It will not be like a 'shooting duel' or a 'boxing match' but more like a 'track and field' competition. It will be like a protracted 'marathon' ... The strategic competition between China and the United States will be the most civilized in the history of mankind."[71]

The colonel may turn out to be right. Then again, he may prove to be wrong. Will a transition occur? Will it be the "most civilized" in history? In the interim, we cannot be certain what the future holds. One reason the next transition confrontation might be the most civilized one in history has to do with various processes that have emerged to constrain international violence. Three of the four main sources of constraint operated prior to 1945 but all are considered to be stronger sources of constraint than they were before 1945. The question is whether they can be expected to constrain transitional dynamics. In the next chapter, we turn to a consideration of the four main sources of constraint—democratic regimes, economic interdependence, international organizations, and nuclear deterrence.

CHAPTER SIX

Constraints on Transition Conflict

Systemic transitions refer to a specific kind of potentially conflictual situation. The importance of transition conflicts stems from the location of the main contestants at the apex of the global power hierarchy and their strong implications for global order. Ascending states seek their place in the sun and may be willing to resort to force to attain it. Descending states hope to maintain their privileged status despite positional decline and likewise may be willing to employ violent means to hold on to it. Historically, such systemic transitions have seldom been negotiated peacefully. But things change. The conflict environments of the past possessed few drivers that worked to constrain conflict impulses. In chapter 2, we introduced one simple way to categorize factors thought to be associated with transitional conflict by dichotomizing them into two clusters, those that encourage conflict escalation and those that discourage it.[1] Both sets deserve consideration as potentially equal drivers of behavior in the future. Chapters 4 and 5 have already focused on transitional conflict drivers. Among the cooperation or conflict- suppressing drivers, the most prominent include the Kantian trinity of conflict-suppressing factors—joint democracy, economic interdependence, and international governmental organizations (IGOs)—and nuclear deterrence.

The relevance of these four drivers to a rising China—declining US situation varies. Joint democracy seems the least likely to have much relevance. Few scholars forecast the demise of the Chinese authoritarian political system anytime in the near future.[2] The ruling single party is thought to have strong staying power. Thus, whatever the pacifying processes thought to be associated with democratic dyads, they seem unlikely to be useful in application to the China-US pairing.

Nuclear deterrence is much more applicable, but there is not a whole lot that can be said about this possible conflict suppressor. On the one hand, we possess very strong beliefs that deterrence works, yet we have very little direct evidence that it has worked in the past. As a consequence, the likely deterrence effect in transitional conflicts require brief review but, for reasons that will become more evident, must remain somewhat elusive.

That leaves economic interdependence and IGOs. Economic interdependence has received a fair amount of attention as a pacifying influence, but we think it tends to overlook the possibilities of greater conflict associated with increasing interdependence, especially in transitional settings. We see economic interdependence as likely to have mixed effects. Why that should be the case will need some elaboration. In contrast, we see the effects of IGOs as resembling our interpretation of the effects of the democratic peace. IGOs can encourage cooperation in the right setting. It is not at all clear, however, that IGOs can be expected to play much of a role in pacifying transitional conflicts.

This chapter thus focuses mainly on the likely mixed effects of economic interdependence, the hypothesized pacifying effects of IGOs, and nuclear deterrence.[3] The principal concern is with the effectiveness of these processes in accounting for whether systemic transitions are accompanied by violence, both generically and in the context of a possible twenty-first-century transition involving the ascendancy of China. The chapter first outlines the posited interrelationships among the Kantian variables, then turns to different aspects of the relationship between economic interdependence, IGOs and peace, before turning to the nuclear-deterrence conundrum.

The Main Kantian Arguments: A Sketch

The current exemplar of Kantian-inspired research is without a doubt Bruce Russett and John Oneal, who provide a most convenient focus for our examination.[4] The basic Kantian model appears quite simple. The authors draw a triangle with each point representing one leg of the Kantian tripod: democratic regimes, economic interdependence, and IGOs (figure 6.1). A fourth variable, peace, is embedded within the triangle. Reciprocal arrows connect each set of adjacent points. Thus, democracies strengthen the effects of IGOs and vice versa. Democracies and economic interdependence share a two-way influence relationship, as do economic interde-

FIGURE 6.1. The Kantian triangle

pendence and IGOs. The main thrust of Kantian theory, however, is that each of the three Kantian variables bring about higher levels of peace. These relationships are reciprocal, so that peace contributes to the flourishing of democracy, the deepening of interdependence, and the formation of IGOs. Finally, reinforcing the notion that all "good things go together," the whole ensemble of Kantian variables combines to create virtuous spirals of higher levels of cooperation and conflict suppression.

It is the case that democracies tend not to fight other democracies. They also conduct, in general, less coercive and conflictual foreign policies than do autocracies. Since they do not have much to fear from other democracies, democracies are more apt to trade with one another, thereby generating more economic interdependence, which, in turn, raises the costs of using force against a trading partner. Severed relations will mean a decrease in imports and exports, investment, jobs, and corporate profits. People with stakes in these types of activities can be expected to lobby against harming relations with significant trading partners.

Democracies also are more likely than autocracies to initiate, join, and support IGOs, some of which will encourage democratization in still-autocratic states or in those trying to expand participation in their political systems. Expanding economic interdependence also increases the need for institutions that help to monitor, coordinate, and regulate commercial activities. All such institutions need not take the form of IGOs, but, to the extent that they do, the organizations should be expected to facilitate higher levels of economic interdependence. Some of the more visible IGOs have ameliorated international conflict through peace-keeping or peace-making operations. They can also provide an alternative arena for negotiations between disputants. If democracies are at peace with other democracies, the odds of these states remaining democratic are improved by environments in which conflict is minimized.

Downward spirals are also possible. The more states become involved in international conflict, the more likely they are to expand their commitments of scarce resources to military capabilities and to limit public involvement in foreign policy. Conflict increases economic uncertainty and risk, and therefore discourages trade and investment. IGOs are also unlikely to thrive in highly conflictual settings. Conflict among organizational members, on the contrary, is likely to paralyze the organizations into inactivity.

The main effects of these variables interacting in virtuous spirals should be less conflict and more cooperation. As the multivariate dynamic gains in strength, the beneficial effects should become increasingly strong and mutually reinforcing. A tightening web is strung that will work toward suppressing and containing conflict as it arises. These dynamics cumulate and ultimately should lead to the emergence of a Kantian world order that is expected to feature much less militarized conflict than its predecessor.

While we can easily imagine how these virtuous spirals might work as theorized, the effects of a Kantian web on transitional conflict in the twenty-first century are less than straightforward. If China remains authoritarian, one leg of the tripod is lost. If the other two legs have mixed or very weak effects in transitional situations, there is much less reason to anticipate Kantian processes working to ameliorate transitional conflicts. Thus, the Kantian virtuous spiral could be gaining ground elsewhere and still not matter all that much to the outcome of a rising China–declining United States confrontation.

Is the Democratic Peace Likely to Apply to Transitions?

It is usually presumed that democracy is one of the stronger legs of the Kantian tripod. The democratic-peace idea argues that two democracies are unlikely to go to war with one another. Why that might be the case remains disputed but it is not disputed that, other things being equal, democracies are less likely to fight each other than are nondemocracies. Of course, things are rarely equal and some definite chinks in the armor of the democratic peace have begun to appear that suggest that even this widely accepted premise of regime type conflict proneness might be on less than firm grounds.

The fact that analysts have been unable to agree on why the democratic peace works has always been a source of unease. Correlations are one thing, but explanations are another. The explanations for the democratic peace are relatively straightforward. Although a critic, Sebastian Rosato summarizes the main explanatory logics well:

1. Political elites in democracies are socialized to rely on nonviolence and negotiation. They trust that democratic elites in other states will do so as well.
2. Democratic institutions and process make leaders accountable to groups that may oppose war and punish them for war behavior. This constrains democratic decision makers by making support for war more difficult to mobilize and by making war initiation without widespread support less likely. Other processes associated with accountability make war mobilizations slow, surprise attacks difficult, and misperceptions about the degree of resolve less likely.[5]

The problem is that it is difficult to test these explanations directly and analysts invariably fall back on the presence or absence of joint regime type. Finding that democratic dyads are less likely to fight does not tell us much about the explanatory value of the putative accounts. It is possible that democratic decision makers are socialized into reflexive approaches to compromise and, therefore, are more likely to be prepared to engage in, and to expect, compromises from decision makers in political systems who have been socialized in the same manner. It is also possible that decision makers in democratic political systems are apt to be constrained by divided powers and institutions that make going to war more difficult. Democratic systems also tend to be more transparent so that it is difficult, if not impossible, for a democratic state to gain an advantage against an enemy by secretly preparing to attack. Yet we also know that compromises can be difficult to achieve even in democracies, chief executives can ignore other institutions in going to war, and transparency alone is unlikely to stop democratic regimes from going to war when they have decided to do so.

Even the correlation of regime type and the absence of war is now being attacked successfully. Perhaps the first weakness in the empirical findings was the discovery that the generalization that democracies do not fight other democracies seems to apply best to the post-1945 era.[6] If shared regime type was the main driver, one might expect the relationship between joint democracy and conflict to be consistent across time. But then perhaps it is an emergent relationship that required time to develop its full strength. A second major caveat is that the democratic peace generalization applies only to economically developed dyads.[7] Less developed democracies may still fight. In a similar vein, there is an argument with mixed empirical support that new democracies are more likely to fight than are old democracies. To the extent that this finding is judged to hold up, that would suggest both economically less developed and politically less developed democracies operate differently than older, richer democracies.

Four other interpretations have appeared that suggest the democratic peace may be a function of other considerations and that the empirical support for the causal role of regime type is being misinterpreted. The oldest alternative interpretation questions the direction of the causal arrow between democracy and conflict. Does democratization have pacific effects? Or, is it that less threatening environments are more likely to sustain democratization? Of course, the causal arrow could work both ways. If so, the question then becomes which directional arrow is stronger in effect? If the environment to democratization arrow is the stronger of the two, we may be bestowing too much credit on the arrow pointing in the opposite direction.[8]

Another argument focuses on economic development and capitalism to suggest that the decline in conflict between democratic states should be more properly attributed to their economic wealth and not their shared regime types. Affluent states are less likely to fight other affluent states because they have too much wealth and commerce to lose.[9]

Not unrelated to this emphasis on wealth is the argument that industrialized states are increasingly unlikely to fight one another because the cost/gains ratio no longer encourages war to break out. From this perspective, the costs of war have been growing since hunter-gathering days and have finally exceeded the gains from war even though those too have improved. It took World Wars I and II to demonstrate just how costly wars between industrialized states had become.[10] One difference here, however, is that there is no argument that industrialized states will not fight other industrialized states—only that they are increasingly unlikely to do so given that the costs are greater than the perceived gains. There is a loophole in that it is conceivable for industrialized decision-makers in a particular case to either misperceive the likely costs or to perceive that the gains are so great that the costs are bearable. A general tendency over time does not preclude, in other words, a third world war between industrialized states. It only means that it has become much less likely than it was in earlier times.

The fourth source of alternative interpretations might be called the territorial peace. When one controls for disputed boundaries, the empirical support for joint democracy disappears. [11] If states are not prepared to contest where borders lie, they are unlikely to fight over adjacent territory. Disputed territory happens to be one of the most prominent reasons for states going to war.[12] From this perspective, the empirical support for regime type being significant is simply spurious.

Finally, there is the finding that whatever the case with dyads involving similar regime types, dyads pitting autocracies against democracies have been particularly prone to conflict.[13] This finding may prove to be more important than asserted tendencies for similar regimes not to fight one another. The autocracy-democracy conflict relationship is not linear. Some three hundred years ago, there were no democracies. Then one or two emerged to defend themselves against autocracies interested in suppressing their subversive influence on domestic political stability in autocratic regimes. As the number of democracies increased, the ideological antagonism could have been expected to intensify. As democracies triumph, the autocracy-democracy conflict relationship should decay as the number of autocracies diminishes. Yet if only one or two autocracies remain in the system, nothing precludes their ability to defend themselves ferociously against the democracies in the majority if the last autocracies have substantial capabilities. It just means that the frequency of ideological conflict could decline as the pool of actors changes its regime-type characteristics.

Most of these disagreements about the causal strength of the democratic peace do not negate the idea that a world composed exclusively of democracies might be a less-conflictual place. But we are not there yet. The alternative interpretations of uneven pacification tendencies suggest that we should be careful not to exaggerate the strength of the democratic peace leg of the Kantian triad. By no means has the international relations field discarded the utility of the democratic peace. There are simply good reasons to think that it is a less potent force than most people thought a decade or so earlier.[14] At the same time, it seems to possess a high probability of being beside the point if the rising China–declining United States transition pits the strongest autocracy against the strongest democracy. More telling, then, would be the argument that autocracies and democracies have had a pronounced affinity for fighting each other.

Does Economic Interdependence Suppress International Conflict?

The evidence we have briefly surveyed of violence in the emergence of historical great powers in chapter 1 seems to provide a strong basis for skepticism about the conflict-suppressing effects of economic interdependence—at the least we can say that little violence seems to have been suppressed in the past. Quite different expectations, however, flow from the central premise of economic-interdependence arguments: increased levels of interdependence, while bringing definite benefits, also raise the costs of severing or otherwise disrupting the economic relationship. Conflict between trading partners, therefore, should be less likely than between pairs of states that do not trade. More dynamically, partners that are increasing their trading activity should become more concerned with avoiding increasingly costly disruptions—again, in comparison to states that are not increasing their trading activity.

This expectation that economic interdependence serves to dampen conflict ultimately stems from the calculus of national leaders seeking to maximize their state's benefits and minimize its costs. Interdependent relationships are assumed to increase benefits, while also raising the costs of their closure. As Thomas Moore and Dixia Yang point out, an assortment of state and nonstate actors, all of which encourage deepening economic interdependence, influences China's (and other countries') cost-benefit calculations through a variety of channels: person-to-person contacts, multilateral economic institutions, transfer of economic ideas and norms, intergovernmental pressure, multinational corporations, transnational manufacturing networks, and global markets.[15]

Yet, even if we allow that such conflict-suppressing interdependence effects occur, there is little basis to expect that these will be the sole consequence of increased trade and other forms of economic interaction.[16] Historical processes in general, and interdependence processes in particular, are apt to have mixed effects. Indeed, there is ample historical evidence suggesting that the restraining effects can be offset or overwhelmed by other contrary effects. For example, increases in trade are also likely to bring increased trade frictions of different sorts. The economic interdependence argument does not tell us how strong the effect should be or whether it is likely to be stronger or weaker than other putative effects that pull in the opposite direction.

How then can we know when and under what circumstances interdependence effects are likely to constrain or, alternatively, give way to conflictual tendencies? One persuasive answer is provided by Dale Copeland, who argues that it is not the level of interdependence per se, but rather decision makers' expectations about future interdependence benefits that influence whether peace or conflict prevails. If interdependence benefits are projected into the future, then conflict is less likely. But if such benefits are cut off or sharply diminished, then the conflict-suppressing effects of interdependence are weakened.[17] What is left unspecified, however, are the circumstances that influence decision-makers' expectations.

It should not be surprising—especially absent systematic data concerning decision maker's expectations of the future economic benefits of interdependence—that the empirical evidence on economic interdependence operating as a constraint on political-military conflict is quite mixed. For every analysis finding a negative relationship (the greater the economic interdependence between two states, the less the likelihood of conflict escalation between them), there is another study finding a positive relationship, or the absence of any significant relationship.[18] Thus, we do not yet know whether interdependence in any given context will constrain or aggravate conflict escalation. One reason for these mixed findings is that the relative strength of interdependence constraints appears to be fairly weak. A number of other realpolitik-type variables—for instance, ongoing territorial disputes, rivalry, relative capability, and distance— have a much stronger impact on conflict escalation. Only regime type— whether one or both of the states in a dyadic pair is democratic—has less impact than economic interdependence.[19] Thus, the first cautionary note is that economic interdependence is hardly a "silver bullet" guaranteed to pacify interstate conflicts, especially compared to the more robust relationships involving grievance issues and military power. It is probably true that it may constrain conflict-escalation processes,[20] but it is not clear that the effects will necessarily be all that strong or consistent. Other factors that appear to be more important to conflict escalation can mitigate, trump, or accentuate any possible effects of interdependence. These findings do not mean that the effects of economic interdependence are substantively nil. They only mean that there appear to be a variety of other variables that count more when it comes time to engage in, or desist from, conflict escalation.

What features of great power competition, and especially power transitions, might help to account for these ambivalent results? We suggest that the history of the past five centuries indicates that states seeking to expand their industrial and commercial activities in the world economy, especially latecomers trying to catch up with an established system leader, have recurrently encountered at least four major types of obstacles that can diminish the constraining effects of economic interdependence: (1) the perception that the prevailing status quo is relatively closed to newly ascending powers; (2) the process of catching up to early leaders encourages the adoption of strategies that are likely to be perceived as unfair; (3) the process of catching up usually involves ascending actors converging on production and trade of the same goods as the targets of their catch-up efforts; and (4) similar economic activities demand similar and possibly scarce energy sources.

Each of these problem areas implies that increased economic interaction and interdependence might also be accompanied by increased conflict among the most important economic actors. Any of the four might alone be sufficient to override the interdependence constraints expected to prevent costly disruptions of commerce. The four combined, as well as smaller combinations, could certainly overwhelm the hypothesized pacific effects of increased interdependence.

How prominent have these four sources of trouble been in the great power conflicts of the modern era? More specifically, are they especially apt to be manifest in situations involving latecomers seeking a position at or near the apex of the world economy? We have two historical "laboratories" within which to uncover recognizable patterns that bear on the challenges posed by emerging powers: (1) the historical experience of the European region, and (2) the waves of competition over *global* elite status that followed and were often joined to the intra-European struggles. Historically, then, we have a number of trials. The question is what patterns characterized these trials? And, to what extent are the patterns found in the sixteenth through the twentieth centuries likely to have relevance for the twenty-first-century emergence of China as a leading major power and possible challenger.

OBSTACLES TO GREAT POWER EMERGENCE

Markets are already staked out. Latecomers confront a world economy in which markets and imperial territories are already staked out. States that develop control of trade routes, markets, and leading industrial sectors get "there" first. They create strategically located bases, enclaves, raw material sources, and consumer market shares.[21] Later developers, who need access to the same trade routes and markets, will desire bases and enclaves in more or less the same locations. As a consequence, latecomers perceive that they must fight their way in because the states that have preceded them are unlikely to surrender their positions and market shares peacefully.[22]

Many of the commercial commodities valued in early modern Europe were cultivated in few places. Silver came primarily from Spanish mines in South America after the 1550s. Spices came primarily from a few of the islands in the Indonesian archipelago. Sugar was grown initially in Brazil after earlier sites closer to the Mediterranean proved less productive and then migrated increasingly to selected Caribbean islands.[23] Tobacco was grown on the eastern seaboard of North America. Tea came from China and so on. The point is that traders in pursuit of these products were apt to bump into one another. Whoever controlled access to the most valued commodities could set prices to some extent and determine who gained access to the commodities. The temptation to take the sources of production away from the initial possessors must have been tempting.

As a consequence, the French and British fought in part over who would gain access to Spain's Latin American colonies. The Dutch and Portuguese fought over the control of Brazilian sugar production. The Dutch, English, and Portuguese fought over who would have access to the Spice Islands. The perception that the system was relatively closed to newcomers was not always unrealistic, but perceptions of closure could also be exaggerated. Entering the Indian Ocean, the Portuguese assumed that local markets would be closed to them because Muslim traders were thought to have total control over the distribution of traded commodities. This assumption was exaggerated but it nonetheless encouraged the Portuguese to enter Indian trading ports prepared to do battle and thus to engage in a kind of self-fulfilling prophecy.[24]

Similarly, France and England did not simply wish to compete with Dutch commerce in the seventeenth century. Rather, their assumption was that European trade was a fixed volume. Whatever they could acquire would have to come at expense of what the Dutch already controlled. British and French colonies/enclaves in North America, the Caribbean, and India might have coexisted, but each tended ultimately to work on mutually exclusive principles. Neither North America nor India was large enough for both British and French agents to compete and coexist. One or the other had to be ousted. In the Caribbean, islands initially changed hands with some frequency, but gradually an increased reluctance to surrender island territory gained in eighteenth-century warfare occurred.

Bending the rules with strategic trade policies.   As Alexander Gerschenkron emphasized, latecomers have tended to develop more centralized strategies—government intervention and protection, subsidies, and industrial policies—to improve their chances of breaking into the elite ranks.[25]

More status quo–oriented states are likely to perceive the new competitors as acting unfairly (e.g., dumping, predatory trade policies, and manipulation of exchange rates) and overreact to their efforts to catch up with punitive policies.[26]

Industrialization did not diminish the mercantilist tendency to view great power conflict in zero sum terms. It is more likely to have hardened it instead. The British lead in industrialization led Napoleon to attempt to close European markets to British exports in order to provide French industry some time to become more competitive. Later in the nineteenth century, both Germany and the United States also became highly protectionist in recognition of the need to insulate their economies from the competitive advantages of British producers. The Soviets went even farther in attempts to insulate their industries from world capitalism and the competition it would have brought. In an industrialized world, it is the challengers who are most likely to protect their domestic industries from external competition because it is clear that they cannot compete initially with the front runner(s) without some leveling of the playing field via protectionist policies. If newcomers enter the field on the frontrunner's rules, the odds are biased against winning or even holding one's own.

Catching up, therefore, encourages ascending actors to bend the rules.[27] Products are dumped at unprofitably low prices. Lies are told about competitors and the quality and safety of their products. Even if the states catching up do not engage in these predatory practices all that much, they are apt to be accused of doing so. How else to explain their unexpected success against the established industrial powers? Challengers' border measures that strategically discriminate against the lead economy's products or other less-transparent attempts to increase market shares by denying the lead economy's comparative advantages have often engendered responses in kind, sometimes leading to conflict spirals of retaliation and counterretaliation.[28]

Convergence on the same sectors and industries.   Economic development tends to result in competitors converging on the same technologies, sectors, and industries—rather than the complementarity thought to follow from specialization based on comparative advantage and a deepening division of labor. At the technological high end, and depending on the time period, all advanced economies tend to produce steel, automobiles, or computers. They also tend to require external markets to accommodate their scale of production. Similar products and finite markets predict to

surplus capacity and, ultimately, to intensified competition that is often
construed in zero sum terms. These effects are exacerbated in the case of
industries that are, or at least are thought to be, critical to national security.[29] Concepts such as comparative advantage, specialization, and division of labor are well and good for most situations. They apply less well,
however, to the elite ranks attempting to operate on the technological
frontier.

The problem is made even worse by the tendency for new technologies to appear in clusters. Textiles and iron were followed by steam engines and railroads. Chemicals, steel, and electricity came next, followed
by automobiles. More recently, aerospace and electronics, followed by information technology, have all played their respective roles as strategic
industries that represented high value added, best practices, skilled employment, and relatively high profits and wages, as well as being critically
important to military capabilities.

Modern clusters of technologies are seemingly difficult to skip. That
is, those playing catch-up industrialization do not leapfrog from textiles
to electronics without also mastering steel and automobiles in between.
To be competitive with the world's lead economy, it is therefore necessary to gain competitiveness in the same industries in which the leader
excels or has excelled. If the leader stumbles and commits prematurely
to an eventually uncompetitive path (as Britain did in terms of steel) or if
the leader becomes overly complacent and allows competitors to improve
on prevailing practices (as the United States did in terms of automobiles),
it is possible that challengers will be able to surpass leaders. But even if
they do not, the nature of modern economic development forces them
to compete in the same industrial sectors more or less at the same time.
Intraindustry trade can ameliorate but not eliminate this problem.[30] This
complication not only operates between leaders and challengers but also
applies among challengers as well: if there are multiple challengers, they
are all likely to be trying to produce similar types of widgets at roughly
the same time.

As trading complementarities are lost in the process, so too are some
of the potential constraints of economic interdependence. Economies of
scale encourage producing more than is likely to be consumed by home
markets in any event, resulting in tendencies toward chronic surplus capacity. Competitors may become even more cutthroat in their efforts to
outsell each other in third-country markets, leading back in some cases
to the type of predatory practices associated with catch-up development
strategies.

An additional element encouraging similarities in industrial structure is concern about national defense. Perceived security imperatives suggest that industrial development must be encouraged at all costs: certain industries are essential to being able to operate at the military-technology frontier. Nuclear physics are critical in an era of missiles with nuclear warheads and submarines with nuclear reactors for propulsion. Information technology is vital in an era emphasizing closer coordination and control of multiple military weapons, forces, and theaters. Both nuclear physics and information technology are important to launching satellites and space missions. Biochemistry cannot be ignored as long as chemical and biological weapons are developed, even if their use remains improbable. Even more purely commercial industries, like automobile production, are strategically linked to tank and truck production. Again, the point is that the nature of interstate competition tends to lead elite economic actors to specialize in the same production areas at roughly the same time. Less interdependence and more competition can be anticipated as a result.

Competition for access to energy.   The question of competition for energy supplies is a special case of the "markets are already staked out" category we discussed earlier, but the strategic importance of energy (to industrial production, distribution, and military-power projection) warrants separate consideration. If elite economies tend to have similar industrial structures and production orientations, it is also probable that they will all need reliable and relatively inexpensive access to energy resources.[31] To the extent that supplies of these energy sources are scarce or, worse yet, diminishing, or that growing demand for them is outpacing supply, conflict over access to the same energy resources needed to operate advanced economies becomes more likely.

In the age of maritime commerce, such competition might seem to have been fairly inconsequential. After all, building sailing ships that exploited readily available wind systems would not seem to be an insurmountable task. But, even in this context, there were supply problems. Sailing ships had to be built from tall timber.[32] Much of Europe was deforested, thereby placing a premium on Baltic and North American forests as prizes to be controlled if possible. Wind may be widely distributed, but the most efficient sailing routes were more narrowly delimited. Control of these primary trade routes gave one's own national shipping a global edge.

Industrialization has, of course, made this problem even more acute. In an age of steam propulsion, coal supplies were critical. Access to petroleum becomes indispensable if the primary source of propulsion (on land, in the air, or under the sea) is the internal combustion engine. It was therefore not surprising that the United States went to great lengths prior to World War II, in competition with Britain, to develop control of as many major oil fields as it could.[33] Concerns about access to coal and petroleum helped determine Japan's acquisitive strategies toward Manchuria and Southeast Asia.[34] And, problems in acquiring sufficient access to petroleum contributed to Germany's defeat in World War II.[35]

Coal, natural gas, and petroleum are characterized by uneven geographical distributions. Some actors have large amounts of natural coal and/or oil and gas, while others are highly dependent on external supplies. Most contemporary great powers are especially dependent on petroleum supplies controlled by nongreat powers. Courting these oil producers and competing to arrange secure access to energy sources becomes a preoccupation of ascending and incumbent powers alike.

Will these characteristic problems recur in the twenty-first century? Might we expect economic interdependence to suppress or counteract the urge to fall back on coercive resolution of the issues at stake? How might the ascent of China be affected? We do not mean to imply that the contemporary examples we present amount to evidence that historical patterns are being repeated. They do suggest, however, that certain features of great power emergence and transition appear to be at least latent in the early twentieth century.

By the turn of the twenty-first century, seizing resource-rich territories, trade routes, or strategic locations staked out by great power rivals or indigenous peoples is no longer regarded as legitimate state practice. While prevailing norms now (more or less) effectively prohibit overt forms of state conquest and direct control, the nationalistic urge to exert as much control as possible over raw materials, bases, or territory deemed essential to national welfare and/or security persists. This urge, however, takes less overt and direct forms that are more congenial to those states that possess the desired resources or locations.

The explosive economic growth experienced by China in recent decades has strained its ability to secure enough raw materials for its bourgeoning industries. Indeed, China's rapidly increasing demand for various raw materials has made it difficult to find adequate supplies. World markets for various basic commodities—from copper, zinc, aluminum, iron, and scrap steel to oil and natural gas—have been booming in consequence of China's contributions to world demand.[36] By and large, China has increased its reliance on markets to meet their needs, but China seems to harbor a residual distrust of market mechanisms and an unwillingness to rely exclusively on them when other options, such as long-term contracts with raw material suppliers, are available. In China's case, this "obsession for possession" has become global in scope, involving long-term commitments—often at above-market prices—with suppliers not just in Southeast Asia but also in Africa, the Middle East, Latin America, Russia, and Australia. As Hale puts it, ". . . like previous Great Powers, Beijing will develop a foreign policy and military strategy to protect its access to raw materials."[37]

The US response has been critical. For instance, in its March 2006 National Security Strategy (approved by President George W. Bush), the US government complains that China's leaders are "expanding trade, but acting as if they can somehow 'lock up' energy supplies around the world or seek to direct markets rather than opening them up, as if they can follow a mercantilism borrowed from a discredited era."[38] Most objectionable from the perspective of the Bush administration are China's arrangements with and support for states that the US views as foreign policy problems (e.g., Iran, Sudan, Venezuela, and Myanmar) owing mainly to their human rights or proliferation policies, as well as to their overt anti-Americanism. To date, China's efforts to secure access to raw materials have not precipitated direct confrontation with the United States. But as 1.3 billion Chinese citizens/consumers, combined with a like number of their Indian counterparts, as well as others in Southeast Asia and elsewhere, become more affluent and consume increasing amounts of housing, appliances, automobiles, and other resource-intensive products in the coming decades, great power competition to "lock up" supplies of scarce raw materials is likely to intensify. The resulting frictions may or may not lead to overt confrontation, but they can reasonably be expected to pull in the opposite direction than whatever conflict-dampening effects follow from increased economic interdependence.

The perceived imperative of securing sources of raw materials and their transport, joined with traditional geostrategic concerns, have led both China and India to begin, like past and present great powers, to establish networks of naval facilities in the Indian Ocean. China is heavily involved in establishing a port facility at Gwadar in Pakistan as part of its "string of pearls" maritime basing strategy, which also encompasses facilities in Bangladesh, Myanmar, Thailand, Cambodia, and the South China Sea. According to a Booz Allen Hamilton report, "China is building strategic relationships along the sea lanes from the Middle East to the South China Sea in ways that suggest defensive and offensive positioning to protect China's energy interests, but also to serve broad security objectives."[39] India, for its part, has opened a new naval base of its own at Karwar, aims to build a port at Dawei in Myanmar, is planning to set up a monitoring station in Madagascar, and has been increasing its coordination with the US Navy.

Complaints about unfair commercial practices, trade and investment protectionism, and state support for targeted industries—all characteristic of the Gerschenkronian catch-up industrialization model—were most fully articulated in the American critique of Japan in the 1980s and early 1990s. This critique and accompanying trade frictions subsided, however, by the mid-1990s, by which time Japan's protracted stagnation attenuated its image as a formidable economic threat. Similar issues surfaced in connection with the policies of the World Bank and International Monetary Fund toward Asia's "developmental states," particularly during the East Asian financial crisis of 1997–98.

More recently, in the context of China's large and growing bilateral current account surplus with the United States, similar complaints with Chinese economic policies have emerged in the United States, particularly in the Congress, though these complaints have not yet been translated into punitive policies. It should be pointed out that the basis for American dissatisfaction with Chinese policies is narrower than in the earlier Japanese case, because China, with some significant exceptions, has been more open to imports and much more open to direct foreign investment than Japan. Hence, US complaints have focused on lax protection of intellectual property rights, state subsidization of Chinese industries, and, most prominently, allegations that China is a "currency manipulator," that is, that it routinely intervenes in currency markets in order to maintain a significantly undervalued Chinese yuan. The undervalued "peg" in relation to the US dollar, in turn, is alleged to contribute to the bilateral imbalance as (artificially) cheaper Chinese goods flood US markets and (artificially) more expensive American goods have a harder time penetrating Chinese markets.[40]

This recurrent critique of Chinese exchange-rate policies is rooted in deeper ideological considerations centering on ". . . whether markets or government policies will be the fundamental drivers of global trade." More specifically, as put by Lawrence Lindsey, former chief economic adviser to President George W. Bush, "under an exchange rate fixed by Chinese authorities and not the market, it is the Chinese government that implicitly decides who in America benefits from our trade relationship: consumers or producers, borrowers or lenders. American sensibilities hold that this is a matter best left to the market."[41] Whether these trade frictions rise to the point where they outweigh the constraints posed by the complexities of US-Chinese interdependence is of course a question that draws much speculation and analysis.

The process by which states, both firstcomers and latecomers, converge on the same limited set of industries has in recent decades accelerated. Product cycles have shortened dramatically, partly due to the ability of highly mobile multinational firms to exploit information technologies to control far-flung production networks. Perhaps more important has been the effectiveness of developing countries, especially China and India, in enhancing the engineering and scientific skills of their workforces, in attracting world-class technology firms, including their research and development activities, and in developing indigenous technology firms. The confluence of these developments has meant that China has been able to move quickly up the "value chain" and begin to challenge more developed countries not just in "low end" manufacturing and services, but also increasingly in industries that the latter had regarded as their preserve, at least in the near to medium term.

China's comparative advantages have been in manufacturing, including computer hardware, causing costly adjustments in the United States, Japan, and elsewhere. As for interdependence between China and India, their respective hardware-software specializations have so far limited competitive frictions, but this complementarity is likely to diminish as China seeks competitiveness in software and India aims to strengthen its manufacturing capabilities. T. N. Srinivasan, for example, anticipates that, "China could surpass India as a software power in a decade."[42] Others in the industry estimate that "given three to five years they will close the gap."[43] India is not expected to catch up with China in manufacturing within such a short timeframe, but its skilled, low-wage labor force and large markets are expected to draw increasing foreign and domestic investment in manufacturing activities, especially if wages in China continue to rise.[44]

Space technology, owing to its dual (commercial and military) salience, is likely to engage the United States and China in competition at the high end of the technological ladder and thus to reflect in the twenty-first century the logic of convergence described above. Posen describes how space capabilities—specifically, reconnaissance, navigation, and communications satellites—contribute to American "command of the commons" (also encompassing sea and air power), noting that Secretary of Defense Donald Rumsfeld once "emphasize[d] the military exploitation of space and has set the military the mission of 'space control.'"[45] China, which "hasn't missed an opportunity to use its success in space to showcase China's rising power,"[46] views the prospect of American dominance of space as a serious threat.

India is also intent on developing its space capabilities, "the crown jewel of its technological achievements in the post-Independence period,"[47] viewing its space prowess as integral to its bid for great power status. Accordingly, following the successful May 2005 launch of its eleventh remote-sensing satellite, Prime Minister Manmohan Singh declared to the Indian parliament that the launch "reaffirms the emergence of India as a major space power."[48]

The United States and other space-faring countries have so far refrained from actually deploying space weapons, though the United States has various space-based weapons under development. But various satellite technologies have dual—commercial and military—applications that are strategically important without crossing the weapons-in-space threshold. The ability to launch navigation satellites, for instance, is linked directly to the launch, guidance, and accuracy of ballistic missiles; therein lie American concerns with China's participation in Europe's Galileo global-positioning project. Ballistic missile defense, which would jeopardize the integrity of China's nuclear deterrent, relies on reconnaissance satellites. And, US ability to project conventional force around the globe depends on all three types of satellites. Deployment of space-based weaponry would up the strategic ante even higher.[49] In sum, space technology exemplifies the type of dual-use industrial sector that great powers have converged on and competed over and in which strategic considerations usually trump the pacifying effects of economic interdependence.

If the availability of energy resources becomes (or is expected to become) problematic—due either to scarce supplies or to increased demand because emerging economies are expanding their energy consumption—competition among major powers for control over or access to energy supplies is likely to escalate in intensity and political significance. Both scarcer supply and mounting demand characterize contemporary energy markets, especially oil. Many industry analysts estimate that a global "Hubbert's peak"—the point at which half the world's oil reserves have been extracted and after which remaining supplies become more expensive and less price competitive with alternative energy sources—is already upon us.[50] Although there are optimists who question the dire supply-side implications made by advocates of Hubbert's peak, there can be no quarrel with the demand side facts: US demand, about 25–30 percent of world consumption, continues unabated. China and India's oil demand, while low on a per capita basis, has increased significantly.[51] The former is now the world's second largest consumer, India is the fourth largest, and other Asian countries, notably Japan, Korea, and to a lesser extent Southeast Asian countries, are also large-scale oil importers.[52] All, including also Western industrialized countries, depend on the same sources of oil supply, most of which are located in the volatile Middle East where the world's largest reserves (about two-thirds of the world total) are found.

These circumstances seem certain to lead to sharp geopolitical competition for secure access to oil and other energy sources. China's strategic vulnerabilities with respect to oil are exacerbated by the fact that the US Navy controls the sea lines of communication through which Asia's energy imports flow and thus would be able to choke off China's supplies in the event of military conflict in the Taiwan Straits or elsewhere.[53] We have already mentioned that China's efforts to ameliorate this vulnerability have resulted in long-term arrangements with various regimes, notably Iran, Sudan, Myanmar, and Venezuela, which are at cross purposes with the United States on various strategic and human rights issues, and have engendered American complaints of mercantilist attempts to "lock up" supplies of energy. As gas prices increase and American consumers' discontent grows, it is quite plausible that US-China competition for oil will intensify. China and India face what James Clad terms a "common predicament" in so far as both have very limited domestic sources of supply, both are highly dependent on the same sources of energy imports, and both are in transition from direct state control of energy decisions to a more market-oriented approach.[54] Thus there are also opportunities for the two to generate "common responses," which are not quite the same thing as cooperative responses. There have been some explicit cooperative responses, such as the January 2006 agreement "to cooperate down the entire hydrocarbon value chain,"[55] but it remains to be seen whether this cooperation will endure. Moreover, not everyone views this cooperation in altogether positive terms, as stated by Mani Shankar Aiyar, India's petroleum and natural gas minister: "India, sharing a ravenous thirst for oil, has joined China in an increasingly naked grab at oil and natural gas fields that has the world's two most populous nations bidding up energy prices and racing against each other and global energy companies."[56]

We agree with Mikkal Herberg's judgment that across Asia, " to this point the evidence suggests that cooperation is falling behind competition in the search for energy security in the region."[57] It is of course preferable that China and India, as well as all other Asian states and the United States, continue to try to temper energy competition with whatever cooperation is feasible, though we harbor some doubts that cooperative arrangements will remain intact should a direct conflict of interests arise over oil or other geostrategic issues.

Contemporary Departures from Historical-Structural Expectations?

There are two features of the contemporary global political economy that might limit the generalizability of historical-structural patterns. One is what we term the "dissymmetry" of US-China interdependence: the wealthier United States provides a relatively open market for China's growing manufactured exports, while a much poorer China translates its sizeable bilateral trade surplus with the United States (see table 6.1) into international reserves, which, in turn, are used to supply unprecedented flows of capital to finance continued US consumption of its products. In interdependence terms, the relationship between the two may be symmetrical, or balanced, in the sense that both may be comparably vulnerable to costly disruptions, but it is dissymmetric in so far as both parties have very different kinds of stakes at play. This situation is quite different from more ordinary, garden-variety forms of interdependence in which two countries increase their trade and/or investment with each other.[58]

Closure of US markets would seriously crimp China's export-led development strategy, while cessation of China's purchases of US treasury bonds would trigger a chain of consequences: the reduction in inexpensive imports would combine with dollar depreciation to increase inflationary pressures, and increases in interest rates would likely be accompanied by a slowdown in the US economy, as well as greater difficulty in financing budget and current account deficits. Plus, the costs to US firms doing business in China would be substantial. A depreciated dollar would devalue China's stock of US Treasury dollar–denominated holdings (expected to reach one trillion dollars by the end of the year) and diminish its ability to

TABLE 6.1. **China and United States trade**

Year	China-US trade	Total Chinese trade	China-US share	Total US trade	China-US share
2001	121.5	509.7	23.8	2377.2	5.1
2002	147.2	620.8	23.7	2379.2	6.2
2003	180.8	851.0	21.2	2538.0	7.1
2004	231.1	1154.6	20.0	2931.6	7.9
2005	284.7	1421.9	20.0	3283.5	8.7
2006	341.5	1760.4	19.4	3572.9	9.3
2007	384.3	2173.7	17.7	4005.9	9.6
2008	407.5	2563.3	15.9	4383.7	9.3
2009	365.9	2207.5	16.6	3531.3	10.3
2010	456.8	2972.8	15.4	4175.2	10.9

Note: Trade volumes are expressed in US million dollars.
Source: US-China Business Council at https://www.uschina.org/statistics/tradetable.html; proportional shares calculated by the authors.

manage the value of the yuan by means of intervention in currency markets. And, in view of the size and pivotal positions of the US and Chinese economies, the repercussions of an economic meltdown on such a scale would surely reverberate across the Asian region and, in all likelihood, across the global economy as well. For many observers, the centrality of such arrangements (in what is arguably the world's most important bilateral economic relationship) cannot be sustained indefinitely. What remains to be determined, from this perspective, is whether a "soft landing" can be engineered or if a much harsher adjustment, or "hard landing," is unavoidable.

It is little wonder, then, that former Treasury Secretary, Lawrence Summers describes the US-Chinese economic relationship as a "balance of financial terror," while others add an "E" (for economic) to the cold war acronym, "mutually assured economic destruction."[59] These hyperbolic formulations reflect the assessment that the costs of disrupting the economic relationship would be quite substantial. We argue that because dissymmetric interdependence rests on a kind of complementarity, it allows these higher economic stakes to cumulate. Were the United States to acknowledge balance of payments constraints, take steps to increase its savings rate, and to rein in its twin deficits; and were China to encourage domestic consumption rather than savings and to reduce the size of its international reserves, neither China's stake in access to American markets nor the US stake in continued inward capital flows would have reached such proportions.

It is improbable that decision makers on either side would enact the economic policies that would bring about the kind of meltdown described above, at least not on economic grounds alone. But what if other, say strategic, stakes are factored into both states' cost-benefit calculations? Would US-China economic interdependence be sufficient to dissuade American or Chinese decision makers from resorting to force in the event of a confrontation in the Taiwan Straits? We have no basis for anticipating the answer to this question, but we do think that dissymmetric interdependence has increased the vulnerability of both countries and thereby raised the disincentives for either country's disruption of their economic relationship.

Generalizing about the emergence of new great powers would be much simpler if the historical patterns we have examined, insofar as they are structural in nature, yielded identical implications for both China and India. Such simplicity is elusive, however, as we have to take into account variation not only in the number of simultaneous challengers but also in the responses of existing powers to the newcomers challenging them and the international order they have constructed. As mentioned earlier, incumbent system leaders facing multiple challengers have in the past focused their resistance, often taking the form of efforts to contain, on the one thought to be most threatening to the status quo. For example, Britain designated late-nineteenth-century Germany as the challenger most in need of containment, while at the same time enlisting the United States, also a rival, to help thwart the German challenge. In other words, some emergent challengers face containment and perhaps even confrontation, while others find their interests accommodated as they are in effect invited into the great power ranks.

Has a similar pattern begun to emerge in which the United States, or at least certain elements inside and outside of the US government, is in the process of defining China as the challenger posing the greatest potential threat and thus warranting containment, while at the same time enlisting (or co-opting) India to that (and other) cause(s)? Along these lines, there have been considerable references to the United States and India as "natural allies." This formulation is usually predicated on three factors: both are large, multiethnic democracies; India, though lagging China in liberalizing reforms, has a well-established, independent judiciary that enforces property rights and contracts, and thus will prove in the longer run to be a valuable economic partner; and both the United States and India share an interest in preventing the emergence of China as a regional hegemon. In this context, India is often construed as a significant

"counterweight" to rising Chinese power. Moreover, the Bush administration declared that the United States intends to "help India become a
major power in the twenty-first century." And, as Defense Secretary Donald Rumsfeld made clear, the United States already differentiates its responses to the two: "We anticipate that the relationship with India will
continue to be strengthened. With respect to China, it's not completely
clear which way they are going."[60]

It is not certain, however, that India, in view of its not-so-distant history as a leader of the Non Aligned Movement and with vocal domestic
opposition, will be willing to pay the autonomy costs entailed in being
co-opted (as some see it) by the United States. India may choose a more
independent path.[61]

From another standpoint, Ashley Tellis speaks of two power transitions
taking place in Asia. One is the much-discussed US-China power transition; the other is between China and India, both of which are, according
to Tellis, "emerging powers that, growing at historically rapid rates, having
fought wars previously, and abutting one another along the Asian landmass, remain natural competitors."[62] We think this "dual transition" approach is the most useful way to conceptualize the political economy of
Asia in the twenty-first century, though it will certainly make for more
complex regional dynamics as the century unfolds. For now, to the extent that the quite different US reactions to the emergence of these two
Asian states is perceived to facilitate India's emergence at the expense of
China's and to more deeply integrate India into the US strategic network,
we expect the two countries' trajectories, roles, and degrees of satisfaction
with the status quo will likely diverge.

This chapter has presented historical findings that depict the process
of great-power emergence as fraught with mercantilist competition and
prone to large-scale violence, patterns that can offset or overwhelm the
conflict-dampening effects of economic interdependence. Yet we resist
the tendency to reify these patterns into immutable laws of the global
political economy that are destined to recur in the interactions of the
United States and China (and India) in the balance of this century. Nor
do we think that the presence of these patterns implies that cooperative
(bilateral and multilateral) solutions are bound to be fruitless. Rather,
we view the explication of historical patterns as opportunities for social,
or more aptly, strategic learning that can lessen the probability that the
deadly dynamics of great-power interactions characteristic of prior centuries will be repeated.

The clearest implication to emerge from a historical-structural review is that sustained scientific and technological innovation and the resulting capacity to generate transformative technologies and leading sectors is an essential way to protect national interests amidst the turbulence associated with great-power emergence and transition. As evidenced by the information technology–spurred revitalization of the United States in the 1990s, the flexibility and innovation of the US economy can translate into the ability to maintain its position as the world's lead economy. Failure to innovate on a virtually continuous basis in the twenty-first century will mean that the United States will be faced with ongoing losses of market shares and employment to hard-charging, low-cost challengers, such as China and India, as they converge on the industries associated with the last cluster of technological innovations. Technological competition, therefore, is what makes economic interdependence complicated in transitional settings. At best, it means economic interdependence is likely to have mixed effects. While there may well be conflict-pacifying processes that are operative at the dyadic level, there are also likely to be increased competition and tensions both at the dyadic level and systemically. It is difficult to say which set of effects is more likely to be predominant. However, in the past, it would seem that competition and tensions have prevailed over the desire to prevent interruptions of commerce.

If the democratic consideration seems irrelevant and economic interdependence seems to be a weak reed to depend on as a constraint against transitional conflict escalation, what of the third leg of the Kantian tripod? Can international organizations compensate for the shakiness of the other two legs? We see international organizations as not irrelevant but unlikely to play much of a constraining role in a transitional conflict. We turn to an elaboration of this question in the next section.

International Governmental Organizations (IGOs) and Peace

A previous section briefly summarized liberal expectations about how the trinity of Kantian variables operates collectively to constrain conflict. We now turn to consideration of more specific questions concerning IGOs' conflict-dampening effects, in general and in the particular contexts posed by systemic transitions. The liberal prescription is for established system leaders to engage ascending challengers and to accommodate their expanding regional or global interests in hopes of socializing them peacefully into the existing order. System leaders that are characterized by democratic regimes are viewed as more accommodating. Ascending states that are democratic are also thought to be more likely to internalize prevailing norms and thus also more susceptible to socialization. Such engagement (or binding or accommodation) strategies are contrasted with the containment (or balancing or confrontational) strategies typically associated with realism.[63]

Another form of engagement involves international institutions, specifically IGOs, that is, institutions whose members are territorial states. Since IGOs are thought to function as "an organizing process of conflict management at the supranational level," engagement via IGO membership is expected to dampen conflict. But does participation in IGOs actually reduce the risk of militarized conflict?[64] Has Inis Claude's claim that, "[i]n the realm of organizations, the essential criterion of legitimacy is relevance to the prevention of war," been corroborated?[65] Or do many (most?) IGOs lack both legitimacy and relevance to war prevention? Before reviewing the empirical evidence that bears on these questions, we first examine the various causal mechanisms that have been adduced to account for the expectation that IGOs are likely to exert pacifying effects.

Causal Mechanisms: How and Why IGOs Are Expected to Have Pacifying Effects

Several literatures can be brought to bear on the question of whether and how IGOs are likely to affect the prospects for US-China transition conflict. One relevant line of research involves tracking whether and how an ascending China is being engaged (or contained) in IGOs and other locations and the extent to which it has internalized (and complied with) IGOs' prevailing principles and norms of behavior. Another is concerned with historical patterns in how and with what strategies established powers have responded to challengers.[66] Yet another is the growing literature focusing on quantitative tests of IGOs' impact on conflict and cooperation.

Several problems arise in attempting to summarize and pull together these diverse strands. One is that while generalizations of IGO effects may be derived in some fashion from the empirical record of all states, small and large, weak and powerful, there is little reason to think they are also relevant to the specific circumstances of system leaders and ascending challengers during transitions at the top of the global hierarchy. A second problem, as will be demonstrated in the balance of this section, is an overabundance of causal mechanisms claimed to bring about the antici-pated effects on cooperation and/or conflict. Another difficulty is the in-consistency of dependent variables. Some researchers test whether mem-bership and participation in IGOs prevent, reduce, or ameliorate conflict; others expect IGO membership to facilitate compliance with rules and norms,[67] or to encourage cooperative behavior; and still others posit two or more of these salutary effects. Bruce Russett and John Oneal, for ex-ample, are clearly interested in the conflict-suppression question, asking "whether dense networks of ... IGOs also reduce the incidence of mili-tarized disputes."[68] Russett and Oneal go further to identify as many as six different "functions" performed by IGOs that can serve to promote peaceful relations among states:[69]

1. Use of coercion to maintain or restore peace
2. Mediating, adjudicating, or arbitrating disputes
3. Conveying information and reducing transaction costs
4. Altering states' conception of their interests in the direction of being more inclusive and longer term, and linking issues so as to promote trade-offs and side payments that can help to reach cooperative agreements
5. Encouraging formation of, and socialization to, shared norms which, in turn, create common interests and facilitate cooperation
6. Generating narratives of mutual identification

Most of these functions are explicitly about facilitating cooperation, but two of the posited functions bear directly on conflict prevention or management (numbers 1 and 2). The first of these presupposes IGOs "act-ing in a quasi-supranational capacity to enforce established agreements by military action," a capacity that Russett and Oneal acknowledge "most international organizations [are] rarely able to exercise."[70] Also note that while all six are plausible in application to most IGO members, it strains the imagination to envision circumstances in which an IGO, say the UN, would attempt to coerce China or the United States to main-tain or restore peace (number 1 above). Aside from both being perma-nent, veto-equipped members of the United Nations Security Council, the council was never intended or empowered to intervene in such situations. As Ian Hurd points out, "[t]he power that the council wields over the strong comes not from its ability to block their military adventures ... but rather ... by raising the costs of unilateral action."[71] Nor is it likely that (as in number 2 above) China or the United States would agree to be bound by the results of IGO arbitration of a security dispute (though some sort of mediation is conceivable).

Alastair Johnston and Paul Evans are interested in how engagement strategies have affected the frequency of China's participation in multilateral security organizations and the quality of that participation, and whether its participation spills over into Chinese behavior outside those IGOs. Toward those ends, they stipulate five "causal processes that might link participation with these different levels of outcomes":

1. China is compelled to develop the organizational and bureaucratic expertise to handle the complexity of IGO issues, thus creating an "emergent constituency" of experts that has an interest in continued participation.
2. These experts develop linkages with state and nonstate experts in other countries through which flow information, ideas, and interests.
3. Participation helps China develop a reputation for credibility, trustworthiness, and cooperation.
4. Participation exposes China to "backpatting" and opprobrium in response to its positive and negative behaviors, respectively.
5. Participation in IGOs leads to constraints on action.[72]

All five of these causal mechanisms involve cooperation in security IGOs, but only number 5, "constraints on action," might describe *direct* suppression of conflict. It can be plausibly hypothesized, however, that the greater the cooperation (of the sort represented by numbers 1–4.) the lower the probability of conflict (transition or otherwise). Researchers should be explicit about whether they are invoking this *indirect* causal mechanism and/or more direct variants. Even allowing for the possibility that generic cooperation can indirectly suppress conflict even if it is not intended first and foremost for that purpose, it is necessary to be clear about exactly which kinds of cooperation are being invoked. Is cooperation under the auspices of economic, environmental, human rights, or security IGOs equally likely to dampen conflict? Or is there significant variation among these? And, if any type of cooperation will do, how much is necessary to produce pacifying effects? We should also avoid creating or leaving the impression that cooperation and conflict simply occupy opposite ends of the same dependent-variable scale.[73]

Taking into account how IGO-sponsored cooperation in nonsecurity as well as security issue areas might help to suppress conflict certainly complicates the IGO leg of the Kantian tripod. Consider the array of goals and mechanisms that Margaret Pearson offers to explain how economic

IGOs promote cooperation. First, five "subgoals" fit within an overall engagement strategy intended to cope with China as a rising power:

1. "[T]o transform a country's preferences by erecting a set of positive incentives and building a domestic constituency for further integration into the global economy."
2. Serve as an acknowledgment that it is legitimate for a rising world power to have "a place at the table."
3. Provide information on a country's economic regime to the multilateral institutions.
4. Facilitate access by the global economic institution and its members to the market opportunities offered by the rising power.
5. Enmesh a country in the regime so that it is costly for the country either to breach its norms or to defect from the regime, thereby limiting its ability to disrupt the system.[74]

Pearson then adds another four "mechanisms" by which IGOs gain influence over members through "entanglement" with the latter's domestic political processes:

1. Domestic policy makers learn new ideas.
2. These ideas are as used to provide leverage in domestic politics.
3. IGOs gain a foothold in a country's bureaucracy.
4. IGO's establish positive and negative incentives for compliance.[75]

How then to summarize this assortment of hypothesized causal mechanisms?[76]

Those commonalities that can be found across this profusion of categories, connections, and incentives to join IGOs are almost all concerned with how IGOs facilitate cooperation: Pearson's "goals" and "mechanisms" overlap substantially with Johnston and Evans's "causal processes"—despite the difference in issue areas (trade and security, respectively)—and with several of Russett and Oneal's more generic "functions" that address IGO cooperation. Among the authors and categories examined, only Russett and Oneal offer hypotheses that directly link IGOs to conflict prevention, management, or termination. The argument that IGOs exert pacifying effects can be salvaged, in a manner consistent with Kantian reasoning, by postulating that webs of IGO cooperation serve to reduce the likelihood of conflict among member states. Expectations that shared IGO memberships might dampen or prevent conflict associated with a US-China transition must rest on this *indirect* kind of causal mechanism, as the probability that direct mechanisms such as IGO coercion will be operative verge on zero.

There are other challenges to drawing sound inferences about how the IGO-conflict linkage operates. As argued persuasively by Steve Chan, one obstacle to modeling the pacifying influence of IGOs is the likely presence of "selection effects." We must allow for the possibility that some states join IGOs because of a "generic disposition" to comply with international norms.[77] Put differently, those states that are more inclined to settle disputes by peaceful means are also more likely to join (i.e., self-select) IGOs. To the extent that this statement is valid, IGO membership is no longer simply an independent variable hypothesized to reduce the propensity to use militarized means. Instead, IGO membership is determined endogenously via reverse causation by underlying conflict propensities. Much the same argument can be made regarding "common interests": "Presumably, states join the same IGOs ... because they have a common stake in matters falling within these organizations' jurisdiction. It seems ... obvious, that states with such common interests are less likely to have militarized disputes with each other."[78] IGOs may still have value-added effects, that is, subsequent and independent pacifying effects that are not simply manifestations of preexisting generic predispositions and common interests. For example, drawing on the earlier discussion, IGOs might produce pacifying effects by providing a forum for negotiation or deliberation or by socializing members to adopt peaceful norms. The research design task is to devise tests that enable estimates of subsequent and independent effects to be sorted out from selection effects, as well as separate estimates of direct and indirect effects.

Whether the IGO portion of the liberal tripod is regarded as conceptually messy or theoretically persuasive is less important to many analysts than its empirical effectiveness. Do measures of IGO membership perform in a manner consistent with the expectations of pacific effects generated by the Kantian research program? The results, considered as a whole, are at best mixed, perhaps even more so than those concerning the pacifying effects of economic interdependence.[79] We cannot explore all the permutations here, but suffice it to say the findings are less than robust across different time periods, samples, conceptualizations of both dependent and independent variables, operational definitions, and methods of testing.[80] In some cases, the findings provide support for the Kantian argument.[81] In a number of others, however, the results are mixed, weak, and insignificant or, in some cases, contrary to hypothesized expectations.[82]

In sum, theory and research on the connection between IGOs and mitigation of conflict have not yet yielded robust, unequivocal results. At this early juncture—early in this line of research and early in the putative US-China transition process—the quantitative literature is not yet sufficiently refined to instruct how IGOs might help to ensure a peaceful, or at least minimally conflictual, transition. More recent research has yielded some qualified positive results by further specifying the IGO variable. For example, Charles Boehmer, Erik Gartzke, and Timothy Nordstrom report that more institutionalized IGOs reduce the risks of militarized disputes.[83] And Jon Pevehouse and Bruce Russett find that IGOs whose membership is most "densely democratic" are more successful in reducing conflict.[84] These results suggest that empirical progress may hinge on further differentiating among IGOs to discover which among them positively influence conflict reduction and which do not. The lists of possible causal mechanisms reviewed above provide a number of clues as to how the IGO variable might be further refined.

Should We Discount the IGO-Conflict Reduction Connection?

This section first reviews some general theoretical reasons to be skeptical about the pacifying effects of IGOs and then turns to more China-specific ones. We view IGOs as especially afflicted by problems of limited influence and the decay of institutional orders.

Organizational Mortality and Decay

Bruce Russett and John Oneal acknowledge that IGOs do not live forever.[85] The implication is that organizations tend to possess finite institutional life cycles. Yet there is more at stake than simply a few marginal organizations that come and go. Richard Cupitt, Rodney Whitlock, and Lynn Richards Whitlock confirm that IGOs are not immortal.[86] Along with Michael Wallace and J. David Singer, they find that in an examination of nearly one thousand organizations created since 1865, there is a pronounced tendency for new IGOs to emerge in the aftermath of intense major power warfare and to die "before or during eras of global conflict."[87] Some 30 percent of the organizations created between 1865 and 1990, moreover, have disappeared. Nor does it take more than a century for this much organizational death to occur. Cheryl Shanks, Harold

Jacobson, and Jeffrey Kaplan find that 32 percent of the IGOs functioning in 1981 were no longer in operation in 1992.[88]

IGOs not only do not live forever but also do not come and go randomly. They are strongly linked with periods of regional and global crisis. Presumably, institutions that have lost their functional purpose or supporters die off at a higher rate in highly conflictual periods. New institutions are created by the victors of global wars as part of their postwar order-building activities. IGOs help institutionalize the new status quo and are expected to act as agents in sustaining the new order.

Most discussions of Kantian dynamics proceed as if the evolution of the main variables is somehow self-organizing. Yet it is victors in global war that are most likely to create new IGOs. Waves of technological change—that not coincidentally tend to be pioneered in the lead economy, that is, that of the principal victor—foster increased economic interdependence at least among more developed states. Early technological pioneers also found it easier to democratize than did latecomers.[89] These same technological pioneers worked to promote systemic norms favoring democracy over other forms of political organization (i.e., aristocracy, fascism, and communism) and were forced to fight intensive wars to defend themselves against autocracies attempting to catch up with the technological leaders.[90] Although the track record of democratic system leaders is less than perfect in regards to the types of political regimes they accept as clients, there is at least intermittent encouragement of greater democratization, both by system leaders, their closest allies, and the IGOs that they have created.[91]

Thus, democratization, economic interdependence, and IGOs do not emerge spontaneously. Nor are they subject to immaculate conception. They emerge within a political-economic context in which elite states create structures to preserve their transactions and hierarchical status. As such, they are linked to the ascendancy and decline of those elite actors. The stronger the ascendancy, the more clout and funding the new organizations are likely to possess. The more precipitous the decline of the global elite power structure, the less clout and funding the now older IGOs are likely to possess. IGOs not only do not live forever but also are likely to have trajectories that resemble life cycles. Even when organizations do not die, they can still fade from political relevance as they become less well suited to the changing environment in which they are expected to operate. Nonrelevancy translates into institutional impotence. One of the ironies of arguments advocating the Kantian dynamic's effectiveness is that they currently depend in part on IGOs that emerged in the aftermath of the last global war. Whether they will be around or sufficiently powerful to help head off a future global war is less than a sure thing.

Disjunctions between Institutions and Power Distributions

A line of realist reasoning sees IGOs and their norms, rules, and procedures as merely derivative of the distribution of power across states.[92] Without independent capacities, IGOs lack agency and are of marginal importance in the mitigation of conflict. It follows that, if changes in power distributions are not matched by corresponding adjustments in the allocation of authority and influence in IGOs—that is, when IGOs are no longer reflective of state power—they are doomed to ineffectiveness and irrelevance. Thus Michael Glennon attributes the inability of the UN Security Council to block the US invasion of Iraq (or, depending on one's perspective, the inability of the United States to gain council approval of the invasion) to shifts in the post–Cold War period toward a unipolar distribution of power that is incongruent with the reflective-of-post–World War II distribution of authority in the UN Security Council: "The upshot was a Security Council that reflected the real world's power structure with the accuracy of a fun-house mirror—and performed accordingly."[93] Put differently, we should not expect IGOs to prevent, manage, or resolve adequately conflicts associated with systemic transitions since such transitions mark the very moment that IGOs are least effective.[94]

For the same reasons, we should also expect IGOs to be generally declining in influence or effectiveness as (or if) a transition period looms. To the extent that periods of transition and uncertainty increase the probability of "outlaws," "rogue," or "pariah" states—because systemic hierarchy is being loosened as the relative power of the formerly lead states declines—we might also expect IGOs to have the least effects on these states engaged in behavior perceived to be unacceptable. The historical record is that it is the pariahs that are most likely to leave IGOs.[95]

There is, however, one caveat to this type of speculation that nevertheless also works against the Kantian expectations. It is a fact that IGOs membership is most dense in Western Europe and North America).[96] The constraints of organizational density—that is, where international engagement is greatest—should be most effective precisely where future transition threats are least likely to emerge. Put another way, to the extent

IGOs tend to be regional in scope and that future transition problems are likely to be interregional in character, the Kantian argument rests on only a fraction of the IGOs that might be relevant.

Disjunctions between IGO Problem-Solving Capacities and the Range of Functional Problems in Need of Solution

At the time that the UN, IMF, World Bank, General Agreement on Tariffs and Trade (GATT), and other IGOs were created, their charge, in the aggregate, was to create a global political economy that would avoid a recurrence of the 1930s depression and of global war. Since environmental damage, secure access to energy supplies, and global pandemics such as HIV/AIDS, among other functional problems, were not yet manifest, problem-solving IGOs were not constructed. Now that these problems are manifest, neither the creation of robust new institutions nor the adaptation of existing ones has been forthcoming in sufficient supply.

The Bretton Woods institutions provide interesting cases in point as they have repeatedly adapted their roles and missions to changes in their operating environment: from facilitating postwar reconstruction to helping newly independent developing countries, to assisting in the transition of former communist countries, and to poverty reduction among the least developed countries. The IMF was able to reinvent itself after it lost its exchange-rate management role with the demise of the fixed exchange-rate system in the early 1970s. Following its controversial and widely criticized role in dealing with the East Asian financial crisis, however, the IMF is having great difficulty adapting its role to a world economy in which private capital flows are vastly greater than public flows, financial flows dwarf the value of trade flows, and most crises in need of bailouts involve the capital account rather than the current account. An increasing number of emergent market economies and developing countries are paying off IMF loans early, forgoing access to IMF resources altogether, and relying instead on capital markets. With the number of its borrowers, the amounts it is owed, and its income from interest payments dwindling, the IMF is said to be experiencing a credibility crisis, a legitimacy crisis, a financial crisis, and even an existential crisis. If existing IGOs are unable or unwilling to adjust their functional capacities to solve new problems and if states are unable or unwilling to create new IGOs empowered to do so, then IGOs are hardly likely candidates to ameliorate transitional conflicts.

China-Specific Reasons

General problems aside, is there something about its past behavior or innate characteristics that lead us to be circumspect about claims that China's participation in IGOs will result in either more cooperation and/or less conflict over the course of the looming transition? Michel Oksenberg and Elizabeth Economy identify eight "deeply ingrained strategies and tactics" that guide Chinese behavior in eight case studies:

1. "[R]etaining flexibility ... and avoiding enduring commitments and entangling alignments."
2. "[F]ree riding and seeking influence without shouldering responsibility, acquiescing to [IGO] policies that manifestly serve China's interest while expressing reservations about the policies. Then extracting side-payments for acquiescing"
3. "[M]aking compliance with [China's] objectives the litmus test of whether the interlocutor wants 'good' or 'friendly' relations with China, and placing the burden of maintaining 'good' relations on the other side."
4. "Mobilizing support for China's position among developing countries."
5. "Taking advantage of the ambiguities in the norms of international regimes.
6. "Adopting an aggrieved posture, capturing the moral high ground, and placing the interlocutor—whether a country, a regional organization or an international regime—on the defensive, claiming it owes China special consideration because of past injustices."
7. "Maintaining secrecy and opacity."
8. "Entering into agreements knowing China lacks the institutions to implement them ... as part of an effort to entice the international regime to assist the nation in acquiring the necessary institutional capacity."[97]

These behaviors toward and in IGOs hardly represent a warm embrace, but there is no reason to think that any of them are uniquely Chinese; many seem common, especially among sovereignty-conscious developing countries. The combination and frequency with which these tactics and strategies are deployed may be more distinctively Chinese, but none suggest that Chinese participation in either conflict resolution or meaningful cooperation under IGO auspices is impossible or even improbable. The case study literature so far supports this conclusion. For example, Robert Lawrence's analysis of the early phases of China's participation in the WTO "concludes that China's trade policies are broadly supportive of a rules based multilateral trading order and its behavior at the WTO is that of a status quo power rather than one seeking major systemic changes."[98] On the basis of his survey of China's participation in a number of economic and security IGOs, David Lampton concluded that "Beijing's post–cold war record has been mixed but on the whole encouraging inasmuch as the trend has been toward greater multilateral participation, more frequent compliance, and a closer fit between the institutional structures and personnel of the world community and China's domestic apparatus.[99] Ann Kent's case studies of security, economic, environmental, and human rights IGOs lead to a similar conclusion: "In general, China complies with the rules of international organizations and treaties and its compliance has usually improved over time."[100] While sharing this literature's cautious optimism, we also must concede that there is also little to suggest that China is especially susceptible to successful engagement via IGOs.[101]

To sum up, the third leg of the Kantian tripod advances the general hypothesis that international institutions serve to reduce conflict and/or promote cooperation. The number of causal mechanisms that are claimed to link IGOs to these outcomes are numerous. The hypothesis, which dovetails with engagement strategies for coping with ascending powers, enjoys quite limited and mixed empirical corroboration. Moreover, there are several reasons to discount the prospects that IGOs will dampen conflict, especially the distinctive category of conflicts associated with systemic transitions.

The Nuclear Constraint

The main problem with questions about the effects of nuclear deterrence is that there are very definite limits to just how far we can pursue this question empirically. In the abstract, it may seem quite straightforward and obvious that it is suicidal to initiate a nuclear attack against a foe that has the capability of responding in a similar way. The probable destructiveness of such an exchange should work to deter most leaders. There are strong statements to that effect in the literature.[102] Yet that did not stop the United States and the Soviet Union from not only preparing for a massive exchange of nuclear missiles but also accepting, to some degree, the very real possibility of such an exchange occurring. Even so, the most serious problem for analysis of nuclear deterrence is an empirical one. We are fortunate in having little in the way of concrete observations of the phenomenon in question. Atomic bombs were dropped on Hiroshima and Nagasaki in 1945 and nothing like that has occurred since. States with nuclear weapons have rattled their respective sabers. The US-Soviet Cold War experienced a close call in the 1962 Cuban missile crisis. There were other crises in which escalation might have taken place but did not. States with nuclear weapons have come very close to escalating to warfare and backed off—as in the 1969 Sino-Soviet clash. States with nuclear weapons have now even gone to war—as demonstrated in the 1999 Indo-Pakistani Kargil War, without using their nuclear arsenals. All this means that we lack variance on the dependent variable of nuclear escalation. Without it, there are strong handicaps in exploring the empirical question of whether nuclear weapons can be counted on to deter warfare.

Still, there is sufficient variance on different types of nuclear arsenals and differential escalation patterns that allows for modeling questions about nuclear deterrence.[103] The evidence to date, not surprisingly, supports the premise that nuclear powers are unlikely to go to war with one another.[104] At the same time, nuclear weapons do not deter crisis escalation and, in fact, nuclear powers, compared to nonnuclear powers, are more likely to escalate their disputes.[105] Even more troubling is the instability-stability paradox argument that accepts the likelihood that a full-fledged war will be deterred but that one or both powers may be tempted to use nonnuclear capabilities knowing that the other side's response will likely be restrained.[106] As T. V. Paul suggests, the Kargil War may have been just such a case.[107]

In asymmetrical situations, with only one side possessing nuclear capabilities, the nuclear power is more likely to win disputes, which, if nothing else, reinforces the desirability of possessing nuclear weapons.[108] Whether nuclear weapons make some difference in extended situations in which a third party seeks to protect country A from being attacked by country B remains disputed, but it is quite possible than nonnuclear weapons matter more than nuclear ones do.[109]

Thus, the evidence is mixed. The absence of a nuclear war so far means that the evidence must support the premise that an unrestrained war is unlikely. But perhaps there have been other reasons for the absence of full wars between the United States and the Soviet Union, China and the Soviet Union, or India and Pakistan.[110] We really do not know and are forced to either accept the belief that deterrence works or to remain agnostic. The latter position seems more prudent at this juncture. The evidence supporting the crisis propensity of nuclear powers and the logic of the stability-instability paradox suggest that someone may try to employ nuclear weapons, even if only of the tactical variety, given the right incentive. There is also, of course, the possibility of error or accident, just as there may be some proclivity to think that a reliance on conventional weapon superiority in a local theater may suffice to win the day.

None of these considerations preclude a deterrence effect for nuclear weapons. They only mean that such an effect is more difficult to assess than many might think. It is far from a sure thing. Even if industrialized states seem to be moving away from an inclination to fight wars of any kind with other industrialized states, we cannot be sure how far down that road we will have come as we approach the midpoint of the twenty-first century.[111]

Nuclear deterrence is no better "proven" in East Asia than anywhere else. Nuclear proliferation proceeds with six states (China, the United States, Russia, India, Pakistan, and North Korea) in the larger Asian theater armed with variable numbers of nuclear weapons. Other Asian states could join these ranks. Yet one should presume that China's nuclear inventory will continue to expand and become more capable of reaching distant targets, both on land and at sea. Whether these improvements contribute to the likelihood of deterrence working as anticipated or not remains to be watched.

Conclusions

The Kantian triangle of democracy, economic interdependence, and international organizations presumably will continue to grow in strength, albeit unevenly. The number of democracies in the world may expand, although some of the upward expansion in numbers seems to have leveled off. Economic interdependence in the China-US dyad, in particular, but also in Asia and in the world at large, continues to stay high. US's trade with China has become increasingly significant, while China's trade with the United States has remained highly significant for China as well, albeit declining somewhat in the past decade. At the same time, China holds at least $1.6 trillion in US Treasury notes and therefore has strong incentives to keep the US economy healthy.[112] The number of IGOs has not diminished but neither has the relative weaknesses of the UN and other institutions in playing significant roles in peace-making situations in Asia and elsewhere.

Our view all along has not been that the Kantian peace is illusory. These are very real processes that both represent and reflect equally real changes in how states deal with each other. Our question, however, is how applicable they might be to transitional dynamics at the global level and in East Asia in particular. Assuming China remains authoritarian, democratic peace effects are negated in the China-US dyad. Assuming major IGOs are incapable of intervening in a fight between the strongest states in the international system, the pacific effects of IGOs are likely also to be negated. Economic interdependence, we have argued in chapter 5, is a coin with two sides. On the one side, "Chinamerica" prevails and might be expect to continue prevailing.[113] China and the United States are highly intertwined in terms of trade, investment, and debt. Both sides have much to lose if these processes are seriously interrupted. Both sides have incentives, therefore, to avoid serious interruptions. But the other side of the coin is that these two states are increasingly industrial competitors. As long as China remains a staging area for the inexpensive assembly of commodities desired by foreign firms, the competition is less apparent. As China moves into more high-tech areas of production, the competition becomes more obvious. So do the resentments of the late-development actors attempting to catch up and the pioneers who are being eclipsed by upstarts.

The list of US complaints about Chinese trade practices is long and classical: export dumping; import restraints through inspections, tariffs and quotas; government subsidies for selected types of production; government procurement preferences for domestic firms; copyright piracy; restrictions on the exports of selected raw materials, policies that favor indigenous innovation in high technology; and currency undervaluation.[114] Chinese trading partners usually complain about Chinese practices more so than the other way around, but that too may be changing.[115] It is not that there are complaints about unfair trading practices. Rather, the problem is that increasing complaints about trading unfairness are apt to contribute to perceptions that an economic competitor is an enemy, thereby reinforcing general rivalry perceptions and antagonisms. At least they have done so in the past and there seems little reason to expect that their effect will have been transformed somehow in the twenty-first century.

Moreover, it will not be just trade over which China and the United States will perceive commercial threats. The markets for solar energy, hybrid and electrical automobiles, and water desalination equipment—to name a few of the newly emerging industries—will experience expanding markets. If China is not competitive in these industries, its economic threat to the United States will be substantially less than it might be

otherwise. But, on the contrary, China is likely to be an important producer of new technologies. To the extent that China and the United States
are or become intense competitors in sectors on the technological frontier, one can expect that the likelihood of viewing the other as a threat is
more likely to increase than it is to decrease.

We all hope that nuclear deterrence will do its job. If it does, it may
suffice to ward off an intense transitional conflict. But it does seem more
hope than "proven" fact. Accidents, wild cards, local theater advantages,
the stability-instability paradox, or even the extremely high stakes involved may work against the hope becoming fact. Yet, even if it does not
work totally or suffice, we should be able to anticipate that the costs of a
nuclear exchange would constrain the probability of a US-China conflict
escalation to some extent. To what extent remains the question.

It may also be that the Kantian dynamics will prove to be just the pan-
acea the world system needs to avoid a transitional conflict in the twenty-
first century. But there are also good reasons for healthy skepticism. The
constraining effects of the Kantian dynamics may be less strong than
needed should a transition showdown loom in the future. In turn, this
weaker effect may be due to the emergent nature of the Kantian dynamics. They constitute relatively novel phenomena from a long-run perspective. IGOs, especially, have not been on the world scene even as long as
democracies have. We cannot expect them to operate at full strength in
their early stages of development.

Just how long it may take for the Kantian processes to operate at full
strength may vary from one leg of the tripod to another. Ultimately, the
democratic peace, whatever its origins, is precarious as long as there are
strong autocracies that do not behave in accordance with joint democracy
expectations, especially if one is the challenger in a systemic transition.[116]
It may also be that democratization will ultimately prove to have been
a red herring. Some parts of the world definitely appear to be moving
toward greater pacificity. Whether it is due to Kantian dynamics or other
types of dynamics remains to be seen.

Economic interdependence, on the other hand, can increase almost
without limitation and still lead to more conflict, rather than less, if we
are right about its negative implications for competition among the most
powerful adversaries. The importance of IGOs among the three legs of
the Kantian tripod may be the easiest to downplay. The set of existing organizations are probably not up to the task of managing transitional conflict. And, the ones we need—which would comprise an organizational

field that renders the traditional state fitness trial-by-strength obsolete—
are apt to be a while longer in coming. This much is acknowledged by
Russett and Oneal, who argue that until a full-strength Kantian system
is up and running, "[t]wo complementary strategies—one realist and one
Kantian—can together manage the rising power of China."[117] Accordingly, they prescribe that the United States and its allies should maintain
a "preponderance of power for as long as possible" for purposes of deterrence, as a kind of bridge to a Kantian world order.

In the interim, we are faced with some prospects for transitional dynamics that will gain momentum later in the twenty-first century. It would
certainly be advantageous if the Kantian dynamics were in place and operating at full strength when they are most needed. Yet it may be that
even if they are operating at full strength, something that we judge to be
most unlikely, the dynamics will still not suffice to head off an intensive
conflict between a challenger and declining incumbent system leader. A
great deal is at stake in acquiring and defending systemic leadership. The
costs of losing leadership are quite significant. So, too, are the benefits associated with attaining some degree of control over the world's political
economy. That is one major reason why states have continued to fight
over this positional prize, one that is unlike anything else at risk in interstate relationships.

With very strong factors promoting conflict, the constraints will need
to be equally strong, if not greater. Whether the Kantian dynamics (and
other conceivable constraints such as the problems associated with em-
ploying nuclear weapons) will be up to the task, of course, remains to be
seen. Our suspicion is that the contribution of IGOs to constraining transitional conflicts in particular (at least in the first half of the twenty-first
century) will be slight or marginal. Nor is it a sure thing that the "democratic peace" or the net effects of economic interdependence can pick up
the slack. They all share at least one common denominator. Kantian dynamics work best within the set of countries least likely to challenge the
status quo. The applicability of Kantian dynamics to authoritarian challengers that may choose to sever ties of economic interdependence and to
withdraw from relatively weak IGOs is highly debatable. The question remains whether the constraining effects of Kantian dynamics will outweigh
the highly charged, conflict-inducing effects that pull in the other direction in transition situations. As we have shown, even Russett and Oneal
seem to have some reservations on this issue.

Weak Conflict Constraints and Weak Conflict Inducements: The "More of the Same" and "Pax Americana II" Scenarios

In the next few chapters, we present a series of five scenarios that represent the four possible intersections of our conflict and constraint drivers. In chapter 2, we specified a 2 × 2 matrix of factors facilitating conflict and constraints on conflict. The result is a four-celled matrix with each cell representing a unique mix of the two categorical variables. One or more scenarios need to be constructed for each of the four cells identified in figure 2.1. The "need to be constructed" requires stressing. Specifying matrix cells does not magically yield one and only one possible scenario. On the contrary, each scenario must be constructed within the parameters established by the combination of the chosen variables. Therefore, infinitely varying stories might be told within each cell configuration. But we have no need to tell infinitely varying scenarios. What we need are broadly representative story lines that work within the theoretical frame indicated by each cell's combination of parameters.

Without these parameters, we are simply telling stories.[1] It is possible that we could end up with similar stories to those constructed within the varying parameters but how would we know if we had "covered the waterfront"? Indeed, most scenarios are single stories and we can either take them or leave them, as demonstrated in chapter 3. Occasionally, analysts will offer multiple scenarios from which to choose. But how do we know that the multiple set that is offered is reasonably comprehensive of the alternative possibilities? The 2×2 matrix forces the analyst to develop story lines in all four matrix cells—as opposed to focusing randomly or concentrating on one or two of the four on the basis of unstated preferences or bets about the future.

Starting in the upper left-hand cell, a combination of weak conflict facilitators and weak constraints yields two possibilities—a situation in which things stay roughly as they are today (termed "More of the Same") or, alternatively, a reversal of the transition dynamic due to a resurgence in US relative strength ("Pax Americana II"), which reverses the relative decline and halts the movement toward transition. In the upper right-hand cell of figure 2.1, strong conflict facilitators are combined with weak constraints, leading to a transitional war (chapter 8). In the lower right-hand cell, strong conflict facilitators are paired with strong constraints. The scenario in this chapter (chapter 9) leads to a Chinese transition and world order ("Pax Sinica") attained relatively peacefully. Finally, the lower left-hand cell in figure 2.1 links weak conflict facilitators with strong constraints. A liberal peace scenario (chapter 10) seems most appropriate for this corner of the theoretical matrix.

These five scenarios represent alternative futures, with a pronounced emphasis on a possible US-China structural transition and some of the contingencies that might be associated with such a phenomenon. Do they exhaust all conceivable outcomes?—certainly not. But they are intended to be reasonably comprehensive in running the gamut of the most conceivable possibilities, given our theoretical priors. Either US relative decline and Chinese ascent will persist or they will not. Either leadership transition conflict will be encouraged or constrained. Four general, possible outcomes (unconstrained but limited transition conflict, unconstrained transition conflict, constrained transition conflict, or strong constraints but limited transition conflict) emerge.

We supply two variants on the first of the four possibilities in this chapter. Symmetry considerations would suggest a preference that each possible cell created by our confrontation of the two categorical variables (conflict facilitators and constraints) should lead to a single scenario per cell. But, in reality, multiple scenarios per cell are conceivable. All it would take is a few wild cards interspersed here and there to alter the outcomes fundamentally. But our mission is not one of advancing every possible scenario. Nor are we interested in showing how selected contingencies might alter outcomes.

Our task is to develop representative story lines that fit each of the four cells in figure 2.1. One way to assess whether we have succeeded or failed in accomplishing this goal is to ask whether any of the scenarios that we put forward are more likely to fit in a different cell than the one we suggest. In the asymmetrical cells, the stories that we develop do not seem strained (at least to us). Strong conflict–weak constraint suggests a coercive challenge effort. Weak conflict–strong constraint suggests relatively peaceful evolution. The symmetrical cells are more open-ended. Strong conflict–strong constraint could lead to a variety of outcomes. Our representative scenario has China emerging as the system leader without needing to win a war to attain that position thanks to the effects of various constraints. We might have had the United States or even a united Europe coming out on top, but this seemed to us less likely in a context of strong conflict facilitators *and* constraints. For instance, a united Europe might emerge at the top of the global hierarchy after China and the United States had inflicted some serious damage on each other, but then what role would one ascribe to the strong constraints? If the constraints are sufficiently strong, even strong conflict tendencies could be suppressed. But the strong conflict tendencies/facilitators presume some movement toward a China-US transition. If so, Chinese ascent might be able to take advantage of the constraints and avoid a transitional war.

At the same time, significant movement toward transition and US success seems unlikely in a context of strong constraints. Yet American success is imaginable if movement toward transition stopped and reduced the effects of conflict facilitators. The most likely way to achieve this type of situation involves a revival of the US technological lead. We might have developed a story line that had this wild-card outcome in the strong conflict facilitator–constraint cell, but it seemed more straightforward to place this conceivable trajectory in the diagonally opposite weak conflict facilitator–constraint cell. In this story, conflict facilitators are weak because the foundations for US systemic leadership are renewed.

Yet that leaves "homeless" what many observers might think of as the most likely scenario—a situation in which conflict facilitators and constraints remain more or less as they exist today. Neither facilitators nor constraints are currently nonexistent. But it is certainly conceivable that neither will escalate beyond the levels of inducements to conflict and constraint that are observed at the present time. Thus, we felt the need for two scenarios in the upper left-hand cell (weak conflict facilitators–weak conflict constraints).

Finally, we note that the scenarios are not completely independent of one another. Some events will show up in more than one story line, but not always with the same effect. For instance, we have crises breaking out over the possession of islands in the East China Sea in two scenarios. In one case, the Chinese side blinks first and retreats. In the other, the US side essentially capitulates. We think these alternative outcomes are equally plausible given the theoretical structures of the scenarios. In part for this reason, our use of the same crisis in two scenarios with different outcomes is entirely noncoincidental.

The "More of the Same" Scenario

The first scenario plot line resembles its title—"more of the same." But, of course, there is no great likelihood that we would all agree on what more of the same might mean. Therefore, some clarifying preamble seems highly appropriate. In the second decade of the twenty-first century, we are past the peak of the US's relative position in the world system's hierarchy. Economically, a number of observers might nominate 1973 as marking the end of a period of high economic growth rates due to the postwar wave of new technology (for instance, as manifested in jet airplanes and semiconductors). The same year marked the retreat from Vietnam and foreshadowed the advent of the oil price shocks. The heady days of Cold War triumphalism and unipolarity have only obscured the high watermark of the early 1970s.

Yet it does not really matter to our analysis that we agree on a specific peak for the incumbent system leader. What has become increasingly apparent to many observers is that the US position is and has been in relative decline. Relative decline, it must be emphasized repeatedly, is not the same thing as absolute decline. Relative decline only means that the lead the United States once held over other major powers has diminished. The United States profited from World War II, while its rivals were devastated by it. Yet that was only one source of the lead the United States enjoyed through the 1960s. Its economy was also the most technologically advanced. Its multinational corporations dominated the business world. It was the primary source of investment capital. Recovery from the war, investment, and adaptations of the new technology enabled some other economies to catch up. Non-US multinational corporations have thrived. Where once US capital was the primary source of international loans, it is now the primary beneficiary of international lending. In many respects, the United States retains the lead economy status just as the dollar still

TABLE 7.1. **Structure of the "More of the Same" scenario**

Scenario components	Specific emphases
Principal driver	Slow rate of US relative decline
Predetermined elements	Emphases on multinational activity, polarity, regionalization, international organization effectiveness, world economic growth, and climate/environmental deterioration
Critical uncertainties	Interaction of overwhelming Chinese domestic problems
Wild cards	Not applicable

serves as the primary world currency. It has managed to hang on to leads in information technology hardware and software. But its leads overall are no longer as commanding as they once were. The system leader no longer dominates the generation of new leading sectors to the extent that it did previously. That is what relative decline means. As leaders decline relatively, the prospects of other states catching up and passing them by becomes more probable.

Yet if the United States is currently in relative decline, it has been a fairly slow paced decline.[2] Something similar happened to Britain if we mark its economic peak in the 1840s. It was not surpassed (by the United States) before some point near the end of the nineteenth century. Fairly slow-paced decline could well continue through much of the first half of the twenty-first century, barring very rapid gains by other economies and some kind of economic collapse within the US economy. "More of the same" then translates into a continued, slow, relative decline of the US lead for the next several decades. In this alternative future, the US lead eventually will disappear but only after a quite protracted process of decay.

Table 7.1 summarizes the structure of this scenario. The principal driver is the slow pace of relative decline. The predetermined elements are multiple. Most trends already well established continue in the same direction. The US share of multinational activity continues to decline. Tendencies toward multipolarity and regionalization become more pronounced, as do climate and environmental problems. The world economy continues to be characterized by slow growth. International organizations do not disappear but their ability to function shows little improvement.

One of the major reasons for slow growth and slow US relative decline in this scenario is the abrupt slowing of economic growth in China caused by a number of problems ranging from resource shortages through inequality to an aging population. All of the problems had been manifested early on and one could argue that the growth-thwarting implications are a straightforward extrapolation. But it probably makes more sense to view these problems as critical uncertainties. Although the various domestic weaknesses of China are reasonably well established, it was by no means clear that they would interact in such a way as to derail the runaway growth of the Chinese economy. No wild cards are featured in this scenario.

*   *   *

- Economists have speculated about how long fast-growing economies can be expected to maintain annual growth rates in the vicinity of 10 percent per annum. Empirical evidence had been generated early in this century that it is possible for some late-developing economies to take advantage of specializing in inexpensive manufacturing. Spectacular productivity gains can be made for a while as agricultural workers are shifted into factory jobs. But this structural shift is not infinite in length. Pressures build up to work against continuing productivity gains. The labor pool begins to shrink, wages improve, and less-productive service demands increase. Ultimately, the late-developing economy needs to become less dependent on borrowed and purchased technology and begin developing its own. Other factors include an aging population, rising inflation, and a devalued currency. If this proves difficult to do, a noticeable slowdown in economic growth can be anticipated. Based on an analysis of earlier slowdowns in economic history, one prediction in 2011 suggested that the Chinese slowdown would commence in the early 2020s when the Chinese economy had achieved a gross domestic product (GDP) per capita equal to 58 percent of the lead economy's average income and when 23 percent of the Chinese economy was devoted to manufacturing activities. Remarkably, the prediction was borne out by the beginning of a marked slowdown in Chinese economic growth that began in 2023. Slower economic growth certainly did not eliminate China as a potential contender for the world system's lead economy position but it did dampen considerably the rate at which the Chinese position seemed to be catching up and possibly passing the United States economy.
- The trend in the distribution of leading multinational corporations has been toward a declining number of US firms and an increasing number of European and, to a lesser extent, Asian firms. This trend has continued into the 2020s and 2030s, with the qualification that the number of top firms is roughly divided among the three regions. That is, the Europeans have more or less held their own, whereas US firms have declined in number and Asian firms have increased in number. Secondly, the new leading Asian firms are increasingly

more likely to be Chinese than they are to be Japanese in nationality. While the geographical dispersal of these firms' activities continues to be multinational, there is some increasing tendency toward regionalization—with Asian firms operating primarily in Asia, European firms in Europe, and US firms in the Americas. New industries have emerged slowly and their emergence appears to be concentrated geographically but not all in one place. Solar energy, for instance, is dominated by Chinese firms. Electric vehicles are produced primarily in Japan and North America. European firms are less likely to be found in the new industry ranks, but US and Chinese/Japanese firms tend to be about equally likely to develop novel products and new ways to manufacture products more efficiently.

• The late-twentieth and early twenty-first centuries were characterized by an unusual development: the world economy was becoming increasingly multipolar while the distribution of military power appeared to become decisively unipolar after the end of the Cold War. That disjuncture proved to be something of a mirage. The world proceeded to become even more multipolar in the distribution of wealth, especially with the rise of China and India. Military unipolarity was quite temporary as the US's military-technological lead was allowed to slip away slowly and gradually. This was accomplished in part by US budget cuts and the tendency to rest on the laurels of its weapons platform. Bombers aged, the number of carriers in operation dwindled, and the space program was more or less put on hold.

Other states, including China, Russia, Japan, India, and Europe, continued to expand their space programs. China, Russia, and India worked on producing their own carriers (smaller models than the American heavy carriers). Bombers were not especially favored by military procurement budgets, but nuclear and ballistic missile submarines were. Russian building resumed. Chinese efforts were redoubled, but with uneven and halting success, in attempts to overcome their problems with building and operating both carriers and submarine-launched ballistic missile submarines. The Indians were relatively more successful, and the Europeans increasingly unified their naval operations, especially in terms of joint operations of carriers and submarine fleets. By 2025, the United States still retained its monopoly in heavy aircraft carriers, although the number of ships were half the number in operation in 2010. Other states continued to build lighter aircraft carriers, which certainly did not equal the aircraft carrying capability of the heavy carriers, but two tendencies helped to level the maritime playing field. US heavy carriers rarely carried full complements of planes that detracted from the numerical advantage of the heavy carriers over lighter versions. A second trend involved increased reliance on small unmanned drones of varying sizes, which were gradually replacing the reliance on fighter planes based at sea. The drones that could be launched from land were not as dependent on carriers serving as floating bases as were the more conventional fighters. SLBM capabilities at sea were moving toward a more equal distribution among the five main competitors, as was the distribution of nuclear-attack submarines. All in all, by the 2030s, the distribution of global-reach capabilities was definitely approaching equality among the major powers.

- Consistent with the tendencies for multinational corporations to concentrate in their home regions, the five major powers increasingly focused their political-military capabilities on behavior aimed at optimizing local security and stability. The one exception has been the United States, which retains commitments to East Asia and the Middle East. In East Asia, the natural continental-maritime divide of eastern Eurasia provided a geographical frame for politics. US commitments to Taiwan, Japan, South Korea, Australia/New Zealand, and Thailand were extended to Indonesia, Singapore, and India. This maritime "rim-land" confronted a Chinese-centric group of continental states—North Korea, Pakistan and the other "Stans," Laos, Cambodia, Myanmar, and, intermittently, Russia. Within this constellation, Taiwan was becoming increasingly integrated with the mainland Chinese economy and Vietnam was a most reluctant ally of China but was hardly in a position to do much about it. Other than occasional clashes, however, this constellation remained fairly static—not unlike the North Atlantic Treaty Organization (NATO)–Warsaw Pact of the peak Cold War days. With the Taiwan issue largely defused, only North Korean antics provided occasions for interbloc confrontations. Even these, however, were relatively muted because North Korean threats seemed increasingly hollow (even as or perhaps because their nuclear inventory was expanding).

- Nothing much changed in terms of the operations of the major international institutions. The United Nations (UN) remained underfunded and lacking in other types of independent capabilities. Peacekeeping/making operations remain its principal mission, but its peacekeeping forces continue to come from poorly equipped, third-world contingents, and there is little that can be accomplished in complex, large-scale, intrastate turmoil. Attempts to reform the UN Security Council voting structure always run afoul of Chinese vetoes of plans to give either India or Japan veto powers, or even a permanent seat.

- Once the Afghan operation wound down, NATO refrained from further out-of-area missions due to their considerable unpopularity in Europe. Once Russia was permitted to join, even the most enthusiastic supporters began to lose interest, especially in Eastern Europe. The alliance continues to exist but seems unlikely to commit itself to any collective undertaking. The various economic problems of the weaker economies in the EU keep that collectivity engaged in bailing-out activities, which thus far has prevented the EU from becoming a more integrated enterprise. There is some discussion of spinning off a core group of the most-affluent EU states and letting the less-affluent peripheral states fend for themselves. The Shanghai Cooperative Organization persists but exists largely to justify Chinese involvement in Central Asia.

- Relatively slow-growth rates have prevailed over three decades. The older, more-affluent states remain relatively affluent, but their economic growth rates remain anemic. It was once hoped that the BRICs (Brazil, Russia, India, and China) would become a new driver of world economic growth, but that hope withered after each BRIC encountered limits to continued rapid growth. China seemed the best bet, but its cumulative problems with separatist revolts in the west and southwest, the absence of water in the northern plain, massive migration from rural areas into urban areas that are ill equipped to absorb the new residents, a shrinking working force due to the graying of its population, extensive environmental deterioration, and the loss of manufacturing jobs to competitors with lower wages, brought its growth almost to a grinding halt in comparison to the very fast growth experienced early in this century. The Chinese economy continues to develop but seems unlikely to ever realize the dream of becoming the system's lead economy. In many respects, Chinese decision makers prefer slower growth rates because it allows them to better manage the widespread domestic impacts of economic growth.

- Russia's growth was always predicated on selling its raw materials, which means that its economic growth is dependent on the growth of demand for its gold, gas, and petroleum. Slow economic growth throughout the planet has therefore limited Russian growth, despite the increased agrarian output in Siberia, thanks to the melting of the once-frozen tundra. Indian growth potential is always there, but somehow is also always stymied by serious infrastructural problems that are never addressed adequately. As in China, India has also suffered from the overwhelming problems associated with rural migration to huge and overpopulated cities. Brazil's petroleum discoveries proved exaggerated. The loss of control over most of the major cities to gangs operating out of the slums has created an awkward bifurcation of law and order. The Brazilian government controls some rural areas and suburbs but has surrendered control over the largest cities. Little control was ever exercised over the Amazon interior, which continues to be leveled for cattle raising and other agrarian activities.

- Global-warming problems have continued unabated. Melting ice in the Arctic and Antarctic has contributed to rising sea levels. A number of small islands in the South Pacific have disappeared. About a third of Bangladesh is often underwater and has become uninhabitable, causing major refugee problems for both Bangladesh and neighboring India. Miami's population was forced to

move north to already crowded central Florida as the Keys were lost to rising
water levels. Manhattan only survived by erecting a dike system that rivaled
anything ever contemplated in the Netherlands, another state that is hard
pressed to hold off the North Sea. New Orleans might have had similar problems, but it was abandoned after the hurricanes of 2019, a series of storms unprecedented in their ferocity, destroyed the levee infrastructure for controlling
water levels.

• Food problems have been encountered as the traditional growing areas have
succumbed to heat and aridity. Much of the American Midwest now copes with
heat levels once associated with Texas and Arizona. Canadian grain output, on
the other hand, has doubled. Major water problems in the American Southwest
and in some of the world's most heavily populated river valleys in Egypt and
India have created a variety of new problems. In Egypt and India, the problems
are more about interstate quarrels over control of rivers that flow through multiple states. The Egyptian-Ethiopian war of 2023 quickly diffused to involve
Sudan, Southern Sudan, Chad, Eritrea, Djibouti, and Tanzania. India and
Pakistan engage in nearly constant guerrilla warfare and terrorist attacks. In
general, much of the water that flows into South and Southeast Asia originates
in Chinese-controlled territory. To address their own rapidly declining water
supply in central China, China has attempted various schemes to divert Tibetan
rivers for consumption in northern Chinese areas. While not always successful,
the diversion of water to the north means that there is less water flowing south.
Increased frictions between China and India and Vietnam have been one of the
results, but the downriver states find that there is little that they could do about
it, short of declaring war on their powerful northern neighbor. Problems associated with the Colorado River in the American Southwest, on the other hand,
were resolved to some extent by the US-coerced appropriation of Canadian
water and the viaduct built to channel Canadian water to California and Arizona. The viaduct, too, is subject to occasional attacks from Canadian national-
ist groups.

• China makes periodic attempts to control traffic through the South China Sea
and to exert control over atolls claimed by Vietnam and the Philippines. These
clashes flare up and then dissipate in large part because no one has yet determined how to extract petroleum from the area.

                              *   *   *

In general, new problems emerge and some old ones become more
acute. However, the scenario premise is that none of these developments

alter the structure of world politics. There remains considerable ambiguity about which state (and economy) is in the lead. In other words, no headway toward structural transition has occurred.

The "Pax Americana II" Scenario

Our first scenario depicted a world not changing very quickly but one in which US relative decline—the structural driver—continued slowly. The second scenario turns this storyline on its head and imagines a restoration of US systemic leadership predicated on a renaissance in technological innovation that boosts its economy ahead of everyone else. The main structural driver has definitely sped up. This type of development has happened once before. Britain led in global affairs in the eighteenth century based on its predominance in Asian and American commerce, as well as its first defeat of the French in combat during 1688–1713. The late-eighteenth-century Industrial Revolution gave it systemic leadership, with the help of the French Revolution/Napoleonic Wars, in the nineteenth century. That the British managed to repeat, despite or because of the switch from commercial to industrial preeminence, does not mean that the United States will also have a second century to call its own. It only means it has not been impossible to come back for a second leadership term. At present, the United States' economy retains many dimensions of leadership in technology developed in the twentieth century. It is not far-fetched to imagine breathtaking US breakthroughs in nanotechnology and biotechnology, just as it already has made earlier ones in information technology. These breakthroughs could reposition the US economy on the twenty-first-century's production frontier. If it did, the US lead on potential challengers, including China, would be lengthened. That might not preclude conflict with China, but it could make transitional conflict far less likely. Remove US relative decline from the equation and the primary structural driver diminishes accordingly. In such a context, it should not matter too much whether constraining drivers are operative or not.

Table 7.2 summarizes this scenario's frame. The primary driver is again relative decline, but the emphasis is no longer on its very slow pace but on its surprising reversal. US relative decline diminishes as the United States regains its technological and global-reach leadership. Whereas the "More of the Same" scenario featured multiple predetermined elements, this storyline is built around multiple critical uncertainties. The most cen-

TABLE 7.2. **Structure of the "Pax Americana II" scenario**

Scenario components	Specific emphases
Principal driver	Reversal of US relative decline
Predetermined elements	None since this scenario depends on a reversal of the main trends
Critical uncertainties	Leadership in technological innovation, US immigration policy, US share of multinational activity, and centrality of US dollar
Wild cards	Diaoyu crisis, Korea, Saudi Arabia, Central Asia, South Asia, and Sudan

tral one is the US lead in nonpetroleum-fueled automobile and nano/bio-technologies, which, in turn, is partially related to a change in immigration policies that reinforces renewed economic innovation. The revival of US multinational activity and the central financial role of the US dollar are byproducts. So, too, is the limited revitalization of key international organizations.

There are a large number of wild cards in this scenario, but none block the United States' return to systemic leadership. An early Chinese lead in space leadership is thwarted by a coalition of Indian-Japanese and US efforts. A 2025 Diaoyu crisis is won by Japan and the United States. Chinese foreign-policy activity does not disappear, but its involvement in Korea and Central Asia do not escalate to major power confrontations. Similarly, US military interventions in Saudi Arabia, South Asia, and northeast Africa manage to evade greater complexities in terms of the international politics involved. US systemic leadership is manifested particularly in the policing of the new Arctic commercial route.

*   *   *

- For the first time (2024), China has dominated in the number of Olympic gold medals awarded at the Singapore games. In the summer games, only basketball has proven elusive and remained an American preserve. However, China is preparing a team with an average height of seven feet that should prove formidable in the 2028 Mumbai games.
- After a long drought, the 2034 Nobel prizes in physics and chemistry were won once again by scientists affiliated with US institutions.
- In 2035, Harvard, Stanford, MIT, and Cal Tech retained their rank among the top five research universities in the world. Foreign graduate students matriculating in American universities continue to outnumber the numbers attending all other universities. While the research reputations of these institutions has

remained strong for decades, the 2031 Immigration Act giving preference to immigrants to the United States who possess US graduate degrees in the hard sciences has also contributed to US universities remaining highly desirable.

- As of 2040, half the world's population now speaks English as one of its languages. Throughout the more advanced industrial states, the language had become a standard offering from kindergarten on.

- In 2020, only twenty of the world's fifty largest corporations had US headquarters and ownership. By 2030, the number had expanded to twenty-four. In 2050, forty of the world's fifty largest corporations were American owned. A number of different stories are associated with this phenomenal rebirth of American multinationals.

- The United States managed to hang on to its early lead in computer software design and production. Another major story is associated with American auto manufacture. At various points in the first fifteen years of the twenty-first century, Detroit was dismissed as an unlikely place to launch a rebirth of the American automobile industry. In 2009, China even passed the United States to become the world's leading auto market. But the near failure of General Motors and Chrysler in the 2008 economic crisis served as a major shock and wake-up call to work on innovations in vehicle propulsion alternatives. Initially, hybrids combining gasoline-powered engines with electric batteries predominated. But these gave way to fully electric vehicles as smaller and more reliable batteries were developed. Another breakthrough occurred in the development of hydrogen engines, which were considerably more efficient and created less pollution. By 2030 two-thirds of the world's automobiles relied on electricity, hydrogen, or some form of hybrid propulsion. Many of these automobiles were produced and sold by Ford-Tessla and General Motors–Chrysler-Fiat companies. American factories also quickly seized the lead in automobile production because the new vehicles necessary to optimize the use of the novel types of propulsion could be built by robots, thereby leveling some of the production costs. These leads in battery and automobile development could be maintained as long as American manufacturers could stay several years ahead of their competitors. A welcome byproduct of these developments was the rapid decline of the world's demand for petroleum.

- More fundamentally, though, the interaction of nanotechnology and biotechnology gave the US economy the lead in the development of new medicines and artificial replacements for damaged limbs and organs. One of the main problems in computer design—so many chips were positioned on boards that only some of them could be used at any given time due to heat buildup—was resolved by miniaturization so profound that it was unimaginable a decade before it was developed. Food production was revolutionized, as were the design and manufacture of computing and communication equipment and robotics. Ultimately, new types of miniaturized batteries were developed that could be used to power electronic equipment and even vehicles. Military weapons were also dramatically altered, making human-delivered firepower much less critical. In sum, the scale and scope of the changes in products and manufacturing techniques were akin to the adoption of the assembly line in the early twentieth century. One illustration is that all automobiles and computers built before 2020 were rendered effectively obsolete by 2030. Naturally, all the old vehicles and work stations did not disappear over night, but strong pressures to replace them were put in play. Moreover, the new techniques diffused throughout the US economy, giving it or, more accurately, restoring the technological lead it had enjoyed in the middle of the twentieth century.

- The US dollar had long been the lynchpin of the international monetary system in providing a common medium for exchange. Instabilities in its value and a growing lack of confidence in the future productivity of the US economy saw it fade as the world's principal currency in the second half of the 2010s. Initially, a basket of different currencies was employed—mixing dollars, Euros, and yen. Gradually, though, the US dollar resumed its role as the world currency. By 2045, there was no longer any doubt about its staying power.

- In 2010, a Chinese trawler was seized by the Japanese Coast Guard after the trawler collided with patrol boats in the Senkaku Islands (Diaoyu Islands from the Chinese perspective). The Chinese have claimed these islands, located about midway between Japan and China (and a hundred miles or so north of Taiwan) on the basis of records demonstrating Chinese discovery dating from the fifteenth century. The Japanese had occupied the islands in 1895 during the war with China and held them until 1945. Temporarily occupied by the United States to 1972, control of the islands reverted to Japan. Since the islands are not mentioned by name in the Potsdam Declaration and the treaty that formalized Japan's surrender in 1945, China has asserted that the islands should have been returned to Chinese control. Japan's response has been that the islands have always been an extension of the Ryukyu chain and therefore natural possessions of Japan—as opposed to relatively recent conquests of war. The islands themselves might not seem worthy of dispute, but their possession has major implications for who has the right to exploit oil and natural gas deposits in the East China Sea.

Fifteen years later, Japan's Coast Guard seizes vessels belonging to Shell Oil Company, which claimed it had a lease arranged with China to explore and exploit oil deposits in the general Diaoyu area. As the Coast Guard patrol boats were taking the company vessels in tow, a Chinese destroyer arrived and delivered an ultimatum to the Japanese Coast Guard boats: either release the company vessels or face destruction. The two Japanese boats attempted to contact their headquarters for instructions but were unable to make contact because their signals were being jammed by the Chinese warship. Without instructions, the Japanese boats continued to make way for their home port with the commercial vessels in tow. Both boats were destroyed by missiles fired from the destroyer. The Chinese warship remained in the area to protect the operations of the oil exploration vessels.

A Japanese destroyer was dispatched to learn the fate of the missing Coast Guard boats. Spotting the remaining debris, the Japanese destroyer hailed the Chinese destroyer and demanded to know what it was doing in Japanese waters and whether it was responsible for the missing Coast Guard boats. The captain of the Chinese ship responded briefly that the Japanese destroyer was in Chinese waters and should immediately leave the area. The response was accompanied by a warning shot literally across the bow of the Japanese destroyer. Believing his ship was under attack, the captain of the Japanese destroyer ordered return fire on the Chinese destroyer. Both ships engaged in a brief and inconclusive battle that managed to do enough damage to both ships to take them out of commission. Other ships were dispatched to the battle zone by the Japanese and Chinese naval commands. The new ships arrived but did not continue the battle. Instead, both sides towed their damaged destroyers back to their home ports for repair and taking care of the wounded survivors. Japanese and Chinese warships, however, remained in the battle area, confronting their opponents while their governments deliberated how to resolve the maritime crisis.

The Chinese government asserted its right to control of the Diaoyu Islands. The Japanese government denied the claim and called on the Chinese warships to leave the vicinity of the Senkaku Islands. The Chinese response was one of flat rejection of the ultimatum. The time had come, it was announced, to put an end to the false maritime claims of Japan. From this point on, the Diaoyu Islands were now Chinese territory and would be defended with whatever force was required. More Japanese ships were sent toward the Senkaku confrontation zone. The Chinese government ordered a general alert of its military forces and warned Tokyo that further naval interference with Chinese operations in the Diaoyu Island area would result in the use of all China's military arsenal, including its nuclear missiles.

Japan had begun work on developing its own nuclear missile force but had not yet developed enough weapons to survive the first strike. For too long,

Japan had depended on the American nuclear umbrella. Naturally, the Japanese government had maintained close contact with US decision makers as the crisis unfolded. Confronted with what might or might not be a Chinese nuclear bluff, Japan requested the intervention and protection of its US ally.

American decision makers were divided on how best to respond. Were they willing to risk a nuclear war over the Senkaku/Diaoyu islands? How would the Chinese respond to an American demand that the Chinese back away from their confrontation with Japan? Would the Chinese believe that the United States was prepared to go to war over relatively insignificant islands, albeit with major energy-resource implications? If the Chinese called the American bluff, would they retaliate by punishing the US economy in some way? An interruption of trade seemed unlikely since that would cost the Chinese as much as the Americans, but there were other possibilities involving boycotts of investment in United States or the financing of US debt.

On the second day of US deliberations, China complicated the problem by announcing that it had decided to begin balancing its own investment portfolio by converting some of its large holding of US treasury bills into gold for at least the short term. That also implied that China could not be relied on to purchase more US governmental debt in the near future. While the financial implications could prove to be quite serious, it is less well known that Japanese investors own almost as much US public debt as do the Chinese.

A further complication was a sharp increase in cyberattacks on both Japanese and US governmental computer systems. Most of the attacks seemed to be originating at IP numbers located in Guangdong Province, but it was not clear whether they were being initiated by governmental hackers or patriotic hackers seeking a way to privately express their displeasure at Japanese and US hostility.

After three days of internal debate, the US president informed the Chinese prime minister that, in the US opinion, it would be most prudent to withdraw its demands. In other words, the United States was prepared to go to war with China in defense of what it regarded as the territorial integrity of its close ally, Japan. Considering their options, Chinese decision makers reluctantly and bitterly capitulated to the resolve demonstrated by Japan and the United States. Their naval flotilla was withdrawn from what were now officially called the Senkaku Islands by most of the world.

- The China National Space Administration (CNSA) announced in 2015 that it had successfully established a small orbiting laboratory in space. In the same year, phase three of the Chinese lunar exploration project was completed. Lunar soil samples were collected by an unmanned vehicle and returned to Earth.

In 2017, Shenzou 11 was successfully launched from Jiuquan Satellite Launch Center with a Long March 5E propulsion vehicle carrying a crew to the Chinese space laboratory (Tiangong [Heavenly Palace] 1). Although subject to rotation, the crew was expected to remain in space permanently.

For two years, 2020–22, China was the only state with a presence in space. The old International Space Station with US, Russian, Japanese, and other states participation had been closed in 2019, a year ahead of schedule.

In 2022, the Chinese monopoly in space was challenged by a Japanese-American joint effort. Jaxa (the Japan Aerospace Exploration Agency) and NASA announced that it too had established a "manned" lunar base using robots exclusively. American and Japanese astronauts were expected to follow within a year or two.

The Chinese lunar exploration project had been delayed by technical problems. It had announced plans for an observatory and base on the Moon as early as 2020. The Japanese-American successes galvanized the Chinese space program into frenetic, around-the-clock activity. A Long March 7F rocket was rushed into action to place a small group of taikonauts on the Moon in August.

In December, Jaxa announced that its robotic lunar base was no longer responding to messages. It requested CNSA assistance in determining the nature of the problem. A small group of Chinese taikonauts made the journey to the nearby Japanese-American base but reported that it had seemingly vanished. Markings on the lunar landscape indicated that something like a base had existed, but no other sign of the robots or the base could be found. There were indications of a number of small meteors in the area. CNSA speculated that perhaps the base had been the victim of one or more meteors.

In February 2023, India joined the Japanese-American effort by establishing a new lunar base, named Sriharikota 2 after the island that the Satish Dhawan Space Centre used for launching its space vehicles. Robots were replaced by a crew of Indian, Japanese, and American astronauts. The brief Chinese lead in space was effectively nullified by the combined space effort. In the future, continued cooperation among the three states would give their unified space programs an unbeatable edge. In turn, the weaponization of space was averted for at least two generations.

- By 2027, the increasingly erratic nature of the North Korean ruling family had begun to jeopardize national security in both Koreas. Widespread concern that nuclear missiles might be launched on a personal whim encouraged plans to eliminate the risk. In 2029, a Chinese-backed military coup removed the family from power in a single night. No resistance was encountered from any military units. Not surprisingly, there was no popular resistance either. However, the new military regime proved no more successful at dealing with drought, famine, and declining productivity than the earlier regime. Secret unification negotiations with the Republic of Korea were initiated. The sticking point was what to do with the huge North Korean military establishment. By 2031, an agreement was reached in which all North Korean officers and senior enlisted men were guaranteed to at least maintain their ranks in a unified Korean military until retirement. A unified Korea meant an end to the demilitarized zone and the need for the presence of US troops, which were withdrawn to bases in Japan. China and the newly unified Korea drew closer initially in terms of economic interactions and, later, in terms of policy coordination.

- Fighting within the Saudi royal family over succession to the monarchy ballooned into a civil war. Different royal factions controlled the Army and National Guard and these forces, which were roughly equally armed, ended up on opposing sides. Neither side seemed to be winning, which might not have mattered all that much outside the Saudi Peninsula except that Saudi oil production had ground to a halt. Increases in production in Iran, Iraq, Kuwait, and Venezuela could not make up the losses since they simply did not have the capacity and what they did have was diminishing in terms of what could be readily extracted. The only solution for regaining access to Saudi oil involved a military intervention by outside forces with sufficient firepower to stop the local fighting. Troops, primarily from the United States, but with smaller contingents from Japan, China, and the European Union, were assembled and supported by US logistics in the Indian Ocean and Persian Gulf. Ships from the US Sixth and Seventh Fleets, provided the main naval support for the operation. Fortunately, the intervention coincided with a general trend toward decline in the demand for petroleum so that the conflict in the peninsula no longer threatened to bring the world economy to a halt.

- The Secretariat of the Shanghai Cooperation Organization (SCO), located in Beijing, triumphantly announced in June 2025 that half the members of the Association of Southeast Asian Nations (ASEAN) had formally decided to apply for full membership in SCO. Vietnam, Thailand, and Indonesia refused to accede to the SCO. Pakistan quickly announced that it, too, would apply for membership after the SCO proclaimed that it was interested in developing a new security architecture for all of Asia.

- The Islamic Movement of Turkestan (IMT), which promotes an Islamic Caliphate throughout Central Asia, has gained followers in the past decade. Its appeal is based partly on the popular disgruntlement with repressive regimes in each of the Central Asian states and partly on its growing reputation for successful raids. In 2028 it managed to shut down the Saman-Depe gas pipeline between Turkmenistan and China for six weeks. The IMT followed up this feat with attacks on the Atasu-Alashankou oil pipeline in Kazakhstan. Oil flows to China were interrupted for almost three weeks. Chinese dependence on energy resources from Central Asia had expanded in the 2020s. By 2030, it accounted for about 35 percent of China's energy supply. To make matters worse, the IMT successes were making inroads into Uyghur discontent in Xinjiang. If one of the Central Asian states bordering Xinjiang fell to the IMT, the support for a Uyghur rebellion would be difficult to resist. In 2031 the Turkmenistan regime collapsed and was replaced by a coalition in which IMT personnel figured prominently. The regime in Kazakhstan appeared to be wobbling.

Chinese decision makers were confronted with a double threat—a loss of vital energy resources and an incitement to Uyghur revolt. The response was to call for a SCO military intervention into Kazakhstan in response to what was described as clear American subversion throughout Central Asia but especially in Kazakhstan. Although the SCO now has twelve members, the main brunt of the intervention was executed by Russian troops entering from the north and Chinese troops coming in across Kazakhstan's eastern border. The eventual outcome was the division of the state into two de facto states: Northeastern and Southeastern Kazakhstan. China's potentially turbulent Kazakhstan frontier largely disappeared as a consequence, even if China did increase the number of Uighurs within its population. Tajikistan shortly thereafter requested SCO protection from internal subversion. Three Chinese army bases were established at critical points within Tajikistan in response to the request for assistance.

- The Taiwan issue became less and less prominent. The commercial connections between the island and mainland expanded to the point at which any thought of interruption simply became unthinkable by both sides. As a consequence, Taiwanese independence became a dead political issue in Taiwanese elections for all except the population that had always resided on the island. Taiwanese elites wanted assurances that the mainland government would not intervene in commerce and investment. The mainland initially offered a trade arrangement that more or less guaranteed the economic status quo indefinitely. Non-intervention in political matters proved to be a trickier question, but the tendency within China had been one of moving toward allowing greater autonomy for areas of strong economic productivity—as in Guangdong and Hong Kong. Elections and multiple parties were tolerated for what was now a provincial government. Even so, the Guomingdang Party invariably won and took on the dimensions of a branch office of the Communist Party.

- Partially in response to the American refusal to pay its dues for several years after its major debt crisis, in 2020, the UN threatened to downgrade its presence in New York and upgrade its activities in Geneva. The threat worked to refocus

US commitment to the UN. Back dues were paid and Manhattan remained the center of UN activities.

A Chinese economist had become a standard feature of the International Monetary Fund (IMF) upper management since 2011. Even though a Brazilian and an Indonesian had broken the Europeans' lock on the Executive Director position, no Chinese nationals had yet been selected for this highly sought position. Perhaps even more importantly, successive reforms of the IMF-weighted voting system had trimmed the US share of the total votes to below 15 percent, thereby stripping the United States of its veto on those decisions requiring an 85 percent supermajority.

A Chinese-led initiative to reform the structure of the Security Council was unsuccessful but stimulated a reconsideration of which states should be considered to be most critical. The United States and Russia retained their slots, along with China. Britain and France lost theirs but were replaced by an EU seat. Japan, Brazil, India, and South Africa were added to make an eight-member council. All the new members, as well as the old ones, were given a veto on the use of military force. Otherwise, majority rule would be decisive. Thirteen additional states, roughly reflecting regional representation, joined the council on a nonpermanent, rotating fashion and without any veto powers. In many respects, this new council resembled the G20, which continued to meet and discuss predominantly economic issues without actually committing to doing anything about the problems that were considered.

- Pakistani infiltration into western Kashmir catches India off guard once again (this time, in 2033). Indian forces are rushed northward to deal with the invading force, which is being rapidly reinforced by the movement of Pakistani troops into Kashmir. A second Indian battle group is assembling in the Thar Desert for a counterinvasion. Pakistani troops in Kashmir are just beginning to retreat when a massive Chinese military intervention coming through Aksai Chin catches the Indian forces in Kashmir by surprise. A large number of casualties forces the Indian troops to retreat, while the Indian forces in the Thar Desert are redirected toward the Kashmiri front. Chinese troops have also moved into Arunachal Pradesh. US troops move in to reinforce the Indian position in the Kashmir area. After some intense fighting, the Indian-US forces regain control over most of the Kashmiri territory that had been held by India before the Chinese intervention. The Indian government is forced to concede the loss of Arunachal Pradesh. While Indian forces are arrayed against their Chinese-Pakistani counterparts along the borders in multiple theaters, the likelihood of renewed fighting seems slim until or unless Indian logistical capabilities are enhanced substantially.

- The third attempt by North Sudan to reconquer South Sudan in the past twenty years is making considerable headway, particularly since North Sudan is now federated with Egypt in the third United Arab Republic (UAR). The invasion forces are mainly North Sudanese, but their offensive power is augmented by Libyan and Syrian troops. But this attempt is also interrupting oil supplies to Europe and China. Initially, the United States sent in advisers, but it becomes quite apparent that more involvement will be necessary to repel the invasion from the north. Three brigades are airlifted into Juba and two hundred tanks are off-loaded at the Port of Djibouti. However, it will take a week for the tanks to reach the front lines traveling through Ethiopia. A large contingent of Egyptian troops is rushed to the battlefield in an effort to complete the invasion before the US tanks arrive. The United States called on its Israeli ally to open a new front in the Sinai/Suez theater. Israeli tanks were soon crossing the Nile River and approaching Cairo. The UAR call for truce negotiations led to a negotiated cease-fire and, ultimately, a withdrawal of UAR troops from South Sudan. It was decided that a sizeable number of US/EU troops would need to remain along the border between the two Sudans to act as a trip-wire deterrent against a potential fourth attack from the north.

- The Arctic route had become a critical trade conduit between Europe and Asia by 2035, thanks to the melting of polar ice. To augment Canadian resources and to ensure the predictable movement of trade through Arctic waters, US naval bases were created in Prudhoe Bay and Churchill in Canada. The US Eighth Fleet, headquartered at Kodiak, has as its mission the suppression of piracy and pirates using Canadian and Greenland bases from interfering with Arctic commerce. Essentially, this was the same model used in the late 2020s to finally bring an end to Somali piracy in Indian Ocean waters—also carried out primarily by US naval vessels operating out of the home port of Diego Garcia—once the involvements in Iraq and Afghanistan had wound down.

- By midcentury, the US lead in technological innovation and global reach is well established. Any prospect of a transitional conflict with China has been averted by the improbability of a concerted challenge to a much less vulnerable system leader. The Diaoyu crisis in 2025 was a bellwether. Once the Chinese backed down, they proved reluctant to risk a subsequent crisis. The world is not a peaceful place, as manifested in the series of interventions in the Global South, but is reasonably prosperous, at least in the Global North and parts of the South, buoyed by new technological production involving automobiles no longer propelled by gasoline engines and bio/nanotechnologies that have transformed once again the basic nature of manufacturing.

Weak Conflict Constraints and Strong Conflict Inducements: The "Transition War" Scenario

A third world war sometime in the twenty-first century, quite naturally, is a prime concern of observers of transition dynamics, if for no
other reason because they have occurred before with some frequency and
increasing lethality. Yet it is only one possible outcome of several and certainly may not be the most likely alternative future. At the same time, it
would definitely be a mistake to rule out a transition war between China
and the United States. We doubt that the scenarios in chapter 3 provide
good clues as to how such a war might break out, but it is possible to construct a storyline that might make such an outcome plausible. Table 8.1
outlines what we have in mind. It features the primary driver of relative
decline, but, in this case, no one else is a clear beneficiary of the US positional loss. Technological innovation is dispersed, contrary to the pattern
displayed by previous tendencies.

The linear extrapolations that are linked to predetermined elements
in this scenario are several: continued Chinese economic growth, naval
buildup, space program progress, climate deterioration, increasing scarcity
of energy resources and water (especially in terms of rivers originating in
Tibet), increasingly polarized major power rivalry, and the intensification
of several different rivalries at different levels of status. There are two
kinds of critical uncertainties in this story. One has to do with the pace of
change. How fast are the Chinese expanding economically or at sea? How
quickly is the environment deteriorating? What is the rate of loss of access to adequate or even minimal water supply? Presumably, the faster is

TABLE 8.1. **Structure of the "Transition War" scenario**

Scenario components	Specific emphases
Principal driver	Continued US relative decline but no new Chinese concentration yet
Predetermined elements	Multipolarization, water and petroleum scarcities aggravated by climate change, multiple rivalries intensify, slow economic growth, UN paralysis, and limited economic interdependence constraints
Critical uncertainties	Extent of intensification of multiple rivalries, nuclear deterrence, US withdrawal from eastern Asia, extent of Chinese dissatisfaction, and US threat perception
Wild cards	South China Sea, Korea, Naxalites in India, Nigerian civil war, Moon bases, Saudi civil war, Diaoyu Islands, Sino-Indian border

the pace, the more unsettling are the implications for actors attempting to cope with their increasing problems. The other type of critical uncertainty has to do with the many wild cards (civil wars, external interventions, bilateral clashes, and even wars) in this scenario. Each one has some potential to escalate into something more serious with greater scope. Most of the crises do not escalate into something more dangerous until the scenario that we have constructed gets to one that ultimately does.

*   *   *

• Technological innovation continues apace but, unlike in the past, is no longer geographically concentrated. That is, centers of intensive technological research and application are dispersed around the globe in a number of different technological hubs. The United States retains its long-held lead in software development, medicine, and the management of environmental problems. China has moved ahead in computer hardware, space, and robotics. India is threatening the US lead in software development. Both India and China have specialized in producing world cars that are inexpensive to purchase and run. The competition between India and China is particularly acute, because both states are attempting to move their economies from a less-developed status to an industrialized status. Although China has a definite head start on India, the timing of the competition and the nature of economic development means that both states need to develop competencies and competitiveness in many of the same industries, such as computers and other types of consumer electronics. They also need to export these similar products to similar markets. Conflict is nearly preordained by this combination of overlapping production and export markets. South Korea, Japan, and Germany continue to lead in luxury automobiles, but demand for these expensive vehicles that run on large batteries is declining. Nanotechnology remains a largely Japanese specialization. South Korea and Japan specialize in the production of consumer electronics. Israel and Abu Dhabi nearly monopolize the lead in the production of saltwater conversion devices for which demand is booming, despite the high expense of the conversion processes.

- In general, world economic growth is positive through the 2010s and 2020s, with China continuing to post large gains in economic growth.

- Domestic opposition to US forces armed with nuclear weapons in Japan encourages the US to reposition its Pacific forces in Hawai'i, Guam, and Singapore by 2018. US protection of Japan continues, but a less visible US presence and the dimming of popular memories of World War II encourage increased defensive preparations by Japan, especially at sea and in the air. Japan's own secret nuclear weapons program is accelerated. A fleet of twenty-five nuclear-powered attack submarines begins construction. Some of the planned submarines appear to be configured to be able to fire ballistic missiles. The Japanese government insists vehemently that this is not the case.

- A popular referendum held in Taiwan on the desirability of unification with the mainland was defeated by a substantial margin in 2016. Voters rejected once again a special status similar to those enjoyed by Hong Kong and Macao. China and Taiwan have tacitly agreed to discontinue further negotiations on political integration. As long as Taiwanese decision makers continue to refrain from openly voicing preferences for the independence of Taiwan, mainland China will attend to other, more pressing problems.

- The rivalry between the United States and China is explicitly acknowledged by both Washington and Beijing after an unarmed US intelligence trawler operating in the South China Sea is seized by Chinese naval vessels in 2019. Beijing announces that the South China Sea is hereafter closed to the military vessels of enemy states. The United States, in response, demands the release of the trawler and its crew and denounces as illegal the assertion that the South China Sea is a Chinese "lake." At the same time, US naval surface vessels are ordered to steer clear of waters claimed by its principal rival until or unless contrary orders are issued. The trawler crew was eventually released after a year of detention. The fate of the trawler is unknown. Hereafter, however, the United States relied less and less on surface vessels to gather intelligence information in the South China Sea. Submarines and military satellites, on the other hand, are used more frequently, if less overtly to gather similar information.

- Two years after the final withdrawal of NATO/US forces from Afghanistan in 2018, the breakaway Islamic Republic of Pashtunistan was created, encompassing significant portions of western Pakistan and southern Afghanistan. Conflict with what remained of the older states of Afghanistan and Pakistan continues but is characterized mainly by the intermittent infiltration of Pashtun irregulars into the two adjacent states. Speculation that Pakistan may lose control over its nuclear weapons increases.

- A unified Korea emerges in 2022 after a disgruntled son of Kim Jong-il brought an automatic weapon to an elite event in Pyongyang and proceeded to spray the room in which about fifty of the most powerful individuals in North Korea had congregated to celebrate the Chinese new year. The attacker (Kim Jong-chul, who had been passed over in an earlier succession by a younger brother who was supported by the army when Kim Jong-il died after a third stroke, was killed in the ensuing firefight with bodyguards but not before a dozen or so of the elite had been killed, including Kim Jong-un, Kim Jong-il's successor. The surviving elite could not agree on a succession formula. China intervened militarily to preempt the potential outbreak of a civil war between opposing factions in the military. But China had no desire to maintain an occupation of North Korean territory for long, particularly once it had secured control of North Korea's nuclear weapons. The eventual solution was to broker a unified Korea in which all North and South Korean military officers maintained their ranks and privileges in the newly expanded armed forces. Economic reunification programs increasingly absorbed Korean energies and attention not unlike the unification of Germany had some thirty years before.

- Russia and China formalize their tacit strategic alliance with a mutual defense pact in 2025, informally targeted against the United States. Chinese naval development proceeds at a pace exceeding the Soviet Union's naval buildup in the 1970s and 1980s. By 2025, China possesses two smaller aircraft carriers at sea and three heavier types building and expected to be commissioned by 2035. Its submarine force has doubled from its 2010 size, with an emphasis on nuclear attack submarines replacing older, diesel-powered models. After several decades of frustration in developing a sea-based capability, China's nuclear ballistic missile submarines are now operative and expanding in number. Two new submarines, either of the submarine-launched ballistic missile (SLBM) or SSN (nuclear-powered submarines) variety, are built and launched each year. Chinese naval bases have been built on the coasts of Pakistan and Myanmar. Negotiations continue with Southern Somalia for the first Chinese base in Africa. Chinese strategic doctrine has expanded its former focus on projecting naval force to the two-island chain perimeter that had prevailed prior to the mid-2020s to the more ambitious conception of acting as a major player throughout the Pacific and Indian Oceans, and eventually beyond.

- Flooding from important rivers originating in Tibet (the Mekong in Thailand, Laos, Myanmar, Cambodia, and Vietnam; the Salween in Myanmar and Thailand; the Yellow and Yangtze in China; and the Tsangpo/Brahamputra in India), which, induced by extensive glacial melting due to global warming, has been controlled by quickly constructed Chinese dams and the creation of an international riparian regime encompassing parts of South and Southeast Asia in addition to China (formally ratified by 2027).

- Rebellious Naxalite activity has escalated throughout the "Red Corridor" (a large area in eastern India stretching from Nepal down to Tamil Nadu with something of a gap in the Orissa region) overwhelming local police efforts to control, let alone suppress it. In contrast to earlier episodes, some type of central coordination of the Maoist rebels appears to be operative by 2028. The Indian Army has been called in to deal with the insurgents, but its efforts are handicapped by the need to maintain order in West Bengal given the large influx of Bangladeshi refugees escaping permanently inundated parts of Bangladesh. Other parts of India are also finding it difficult to cope with refugees from submerged islands in the Indian Ocean caused by rising sea levels.

- A widespread civil war in Nigeria commences as three states in different parts of the country attempt to secede more or less simultaneously in late 2029. The fighting becomes increasingly confused as tribal, ethnic, religious, and geographical loyalties are tested. Refugees are sent streaming into adjacent countries. Nigerian oil production virtually grinds to a halt due to attempts by multiple domestic groups to seize this source of wealth. Since Nigerian oil is important to both the United States and China, troops from both states are landed in different parts of the country in an attempt to salvage oil-extraction efforts. For the most part, the two forces are able to maintain sufficient distance from each other to avoid any friction. However, neither external actor is very successful in coercively reviving the flow of oil

- Disputes about sovereignty and oil extraction in the South China Sea remained low key through the 2020s largely because of the continued absence of an overt US naval presence and Chinese cooperation with the various stakeholders (mainly Vietnam and the Philippines) who established a condominium to extract petroleum and share the proceeds, albeit asymmetrically. In 2030, a change in regime in Vietnam brought to power a more nationalistic faction, and one prepared to challenge China over the fairness of the asymmetric profit sharing in oil revenues from the Spratly Island area. Vietnam quickly encouraged the beginning (or, really a renewal) of a US naval presence at Cam Ranh Bay. A few Indian and Japanese naval vessels had also begun to make port visits there.

- Rising sea levels along the East Asian coastline, as well as elsewhere, are forcing internal migration away from coastal areas in eastern China. New cities are being built hastily and older inland cities are expanding to accommodate the large influx of migrants. However, a sizeable number of refugees are moving to the north in and around Russian-controlled Siberia. This area continues to be underpopulated, at least by Russians, even though global warming has greatly improved the region's agricultural productivity. Land-hungry Chinese have been infiltrating the area for decades, but the pace of infiltration has been accelerated by the new pressures from coastal refugees.
- China establishes the first self-sustaining base on the Moon in 2030. An earlier US effort had to be abandoned when suitable technology for creating and maintaining a livable environment could not be developed. Concerns about the possibility of China taking the lead in basing laser weapons in space increase.
- India and Japan solidified several decades of increasing cooperation on security issues by signing a mutual defense pact in 2031. Both states are cooperating in expanding their naval forces to deal with anticipated problems in the South and East China Seas and the Indian Ocean. While not mentioned in the treaty, the implied target of the pact is China. Both states have agreed to expand their naval forces and engage in annual fleet exercises alternating each year between locations designated within the Indian and Pacific Oceans. Both states are on good terms with the United States but prefer to keep the incumbent system leader officially at arms length in order to play down the "containment of China" implications of the India-Japan alliance. Nonetheless, the high level of interaction and cooperation among the three states, particularly on maritime defense issues, suggests a close alignment unofficially. A few months after the initial signing of the Indo-Japanese pact, Indonesia requested that it be allowed to join.
- A good portion of the initial flooding of the main rivers originating in Tibet was contained by the Chinese dams constructed in the 2020s. An extended period of drought, in conjunction with rivers (that are no longer fed by glaciers that have for all practical purposes melted) are reduced to mere trickles of water that are now even more contaminated than they had been when fresh water was introduced seasonally. These climate problems complicate further the problems associated with Chinese diversion of Tibetan water to northern China. Widespread distress results by 2031 in an increasingly water-scarce Southeast Asia and parts of South Asia. Protests and demands for a larger share of the water controlled by China are heard in a number of southern Asian capitals.
- Singapore and Malaysia have a border clash over the control of water in southern Malaysia on which Singapore is highly dependent. This leads to a brief

ground war (2032) in which Singapore is able to establish some control over the Malaysian state of Johor before US and Chinese diplomatic efforts are able to bring an end to the fighting. The new border remains highly tense, with Malaysian decision makers vowing to recover their lost territory once they have improved the status of their armed forces. The friction between the two states tends to be aggravated by their respective alignments with the United States (Singapore) and China (Malaysia).

- Civil war in Saudi Arabia breaks out with the death of King Sultan (June 2033) and a disputed succession process. Members of the Saud royal family can be found on both sides of the conflict, which pits more secular elites against more fundamentalist Islamists. The regular armed forces and the National Guard, which, historically, have been maintained at roughly equivalent capabilities, align on opposite sides, with the National Guard supporting the more fundamentalist side. The risk to the world's oil supply leads to a large US military intervention, which is able to reduce the amount of fighting but not keep oil flowing at previous levels. A third of the Saudi oil-well infrastructure was destroyed in the initial fighting. Restoration efforts followed, protected by a sizeable US occupying force. While a good number of US armed forces are preoccupied in the Saudi peninsula, Turkey moved forces into now independent Kurdistan in order to suppress PKK (the Kurdish Worker's Party) bases. Turkey is able to occupy the main cities and seize most of Kurdistan's oil wells but is finding it as difficult to control Kurdish resistance centered in the mountains as Baghdad-centered political authorities once learned. Shi'ite Iraq, with Iranian assistance moved as soon as it learned the Turkish intervention was underway to seize (Kirkuk or Mosul). Turkish occupation forces are confronting Iraqi forces uneasily on the new border. Syrian armed forces have been placed on alert and also moved toward what had once been northern Iraq. Both Iraq and Syria have complained for years about inequities in their share of river water flowing from Turkish-controlled sources. Water conflicts had already led to three occasions on which a Syrian-Turkish war might have broken out. Iraq has also begun to revive its claims to Kuwait, although its efforts have so far remained verbal.
- Domestic pressures on Chinese decision-making elites have increased with climate change–induced problems, including rising average temperatures, widespread water shortages, expanding desertification, Uighur and Tibetan unrest, agricultural productivity losses, and refugees from the east coast fleeing flooded cities. A new "China Can Say No" faction stressing the need for more aggressive policy actions takes control within the Chinese Communist Party. Decades of commitment to policies emphasizing internal economic development and

external benevolence, originally inspired by Deng Xiaoping, are overturned to deal with what appears to be a major looming domestic political-economic crisis that could destabilize China thoroughly and tear apart the Party's control in the process. The new faction in power vows in 2034 to address the domestic policy problems aggressively and put Chinese needs first even if it harms the interests of its neighbors. China, it is argued, is now strong enough to no longer need an extended period of external peace to bolster its internal development. If increased external conflict is the price to pay for resolving serious domestic problems, so be it. The very survival of the Chinese Communist Party and China itself is at stake. More enemies abroad may even help China stay united in the face of environmental deterioration, water and energy scarcities, and multiple Eurasian competitors.

- War between Venezuela and Colombia begins in 2035 after Colombian decision makers reach the conclusion that it is the only recourse for suppressing Venezuelan safe havens for Colombian rebels. The Colombian invasion is initially successful but slows down after increased regular and irregular resistance is encountered. Russian support for Venezuela is matched by support for Colombia on the part of a hard-pressed United States that is heavily committed in the Saudi peninsula. Both major powers have bases in their respective ally's country, although the Russian base is primarily naval-servicing submarines while the US bases have focused on training counterinsurgency operations and drug-interdiction efforts.

- Reductions in world oil supply, already dwindling after peaking in 2020, are seriously aggravated by 2035 due to ongoing conflicts in Saudi Arabia, Iraq, Nigeria, and Venezuela. World economic growth slows discernibly, easily matching the global economic recession in the century's first decade. The search for alternatives to dependence on petroleum as one of several principal energy sources is being accelerated. Reactions to the slowing pace of economic growth are seen in increasing barriers to trade. India accuses China of dumping (selling at prices lower than production costs in order to drive out competitors) textiles and computers in Indian markets in which Indian products had controlled the major market share. India increases its tariffs on these Chinese products. China responds by demanding that Indian automobile producers accept a quota on the export of their world car models to Chinese markets. Japan, the European Union, and the United States follow suit with their own increased tariffs on both selected Indian and Chinese goods. Russia, still dependent on marketing its natural resources, had earlier started expanding its protectionist barriers to give its own industries a chance to compete with more advanced goods produced elsewhere.

- Negotiations among the member states of the riparian regime encompassing rivers with sources in Tibet have reached an impasse in August 2037. States downstream from the Tibetan dams are demanding a larger share of the now limited waters. Their agricultural economies and general welfare hinge on more water in their main rivers. A significantly increased supply to the south, however, would require China to reduce the amount of water being sent to northern China, which is also suffering from a major water deficiency. China refuses to consider taking any actions that would jeopardize the vitality of its north. The head Indian delegate to the negotiations states publicly that China is forcing the other members of the riparian regime to take some sort of drastic action to save their societies from further extreme hardships caused by the lack of water. An Indian Foreign Ministry note to its Chinese counterpart saying something similar is rejected as an unacceptable request. Regrettably, no Chinese water can be spared for non-Chinese consumption at this time of rising temperatures and widespread drought. Only if more water should somehow become available in the future would the Chinese government reconsider its position. Further consultation among the non-Chinese member of the regime leads to the conclusion that there is little to be done other than lodging a complaint in the United Nations Security Council. The complaint is made, but no action can be taken in view of the anticipated Chinese veto.
- Simultaneous surprise commando attacks on three of the five Tibetan dams disrupt the ability of the dams to control water flow without damaging the integrity of the dam structures themselves. Most of the commandos are evacuated successfully, but a few are captured. Interrogation reveals that the commando attacks were carried out by forces from the Indian army. The Chinese have already responded with great outrage over what they call unprovoked attacks by unknown forces. Once the identity of the attackers is revealed, Chinese decision makers decide some type of punishment is in order for what it describes as an act of war. The reasoning in Beijing is that the punishment can be carried out at a subnuclear level as long as both sides persist in not escalating to a nuclear exchange. Chinese decision makers calculate that India will choose to rely solely on conventional weaponry, just as it has in previous Indo-Pakistani clashes. If India can be beaten decisively and quickly, moreover, the odds are that China can avoid a two-front war. Japan will hesitate since it is outgunned at sea by the close-at-hand Chinese navy. No third party support, without escalating to a nuclear confrontation, can be anticipated in the first week of the crisis because no US forces of consequence are stationed near an Asian theater. Given the other problems with which the United States is attempting to cope and the high economic costs of conflict with China, there should be ample reasons to anticipate American hesitation, and perhaps stalling, as well.

Chinese ground forces move into the disputed area of Arunachal Pradesh. Simultaneously, Pakistani regulars move into Kashmir. The Indian army suddenly finds itself under attack on two additional fronts to its interior counterinsurgency operations against Maoist insurgents operating in a number of Indian states. One of two Indian carriers operating in the Indian Ocean near the Malaccan Straits is quickly sunk by a Chinese submarine not actually authorized to sink any Indian vessels. Indian ships still maneuvering with Japanese ships in the Pacific come under air attack. One Indian destroyer is sunk, but five Chinese planes are shot down. A nearby Japanese destroyer, struck inadvertently by a Chinese missile in the confusing air-sea battle, sinks with all hands.

India, under attack from China and Pakistan, mobilizes for war and invokes the Indian-Japanese defense pact. Somewhat reluctantly, Japan agrees to honor its commitment. Japan, in turn, appeals for assistance from the United States in terms of the now old US commitment, which was never renounced, to defend Japanese territory dating back to the 1950s. The US dilemma is that it has no troops and few ships or planes to spare given its holding operation in Saudi Arabia and escalating assistance to Colombia. Even if that were not the case, it has limited assets left in place in the general Asian theater and it remains unclear whether Japan is threatened directly. The choice is stark: either disavow the commitment to defend Japan or offer nuclear protection in a context that might otherwise remain conventional. The US response is not immediately forthcoming while an internal debate proceeds in Washington. Some argue that the US has no choice but to remind China of Japan's nuclear umbrella provided by the United States. The high degree of dependence on Chinese products and investments in American markets and vice versa suggests extreme caution in antagonizing China, let alone contemplating damaging the Chinese economy (and that of the US) by warfare. A third position is that the United States is simply stretched too thin to act in a meaningful way. A compromise response ultimately emerges. The United States announces that it will honor its treaty commitment to defend Japan and will respond in kind to any form of physical threat to the main Japanese islands. The private rationale is that this will buy time for everyone to back away from their extreme positions and, if nothing else, put the onus of escalation to the nuclear level primarily on the initiator of conflict. What remains of the diminished Seventh Fleet—now about one-third of its original size—is ordered to move toward Japan from its homeport of Honolulu. Needless to say, it will take some time for it to reach Japanese waters.

Indian forces find themselves fighting on three separate fronts. Chinese ground forces have launched a massive attack on the northeast border. Indian forces in that sector are outnumbered and reeling in a somewhat disorganized fashion from the scale of the attack. Indian counterinsurgency operations in the Red Corridor are failing to cope with what appear to be unusually well-coordinated attacks by Maoist rebels in a number of different places. Control over some states (Bihar and Andhra Pradesh) is lost very quickly, and Indian forces are being forced to retreat in several other states. On the third front in Kashmir, Indian forces initially handle the Pakistani attack with customary ease, but their problems are suddenly aggravated by Chinese forces entering the fray. Control over Kashmir is slipping away as Indian forces find themselves retreating on this front as well.

- In the East China Sea, considerable ship movement is underway as the respective main Chinese and Japanese fleets mobilize, but no additional fighting has been reported. Taiwanese forces are placed on full alert, but no announcement is issued in Taipei. Taiwanese vulnerability is accentuated by its proximity to the maritime area being contested by China and Japan. If Taiwan takes a side that ends up losing, its own future could be short-lived. For different reasons, Korea has also remained silent as events unfold around it. Korean decision makers realize that they have too much to lose if they offend China. Although the Korean army is quite large, it is not well armed. Most available government money has been devoted to northern economic reconstruction efforts. The nuclear weapons built in the north were lost when the Chinese intervened in 2022 and managed to seize all the warheads and then remove them from Korean territory.

- Back-channel negotiations with the Russian Federation, which has expanded to reincorporate most of Central Asia, proceed. Japanese and US signals have been sent to Moscow probing Russian intentions. It is pointed out that Russia has much to gain by defecting from its treaty commitment to China. Most specifically, it has an opportunity to reclaim control over its Siberian Far East that has been slipping away as more Chinese immigrants move into the area. Its subordinate position to China could also be altered. A coalition including the United States, Japan, India, and Russia would force China to reconsider its aggressiveness and back down from challenging the status quo. Russian decision makers are reportedly tempted by the opportunity but are reluctant to act prematurely. Japan and India seem to be losing, and there is little incentive to join a losing cause.

After four days of fighting, China has gained effective control over Arunachal Pradesh, and Chinese-Pakistani forces control most of Kashmir. In both sectors, the invading forces have stopped their forward movement and are focusing on consolidating their territorial control. A communiqué from Beijing announces that its punishment of Indian aggression has been completed successfully. Kashmir and south Tibet (Arunachal Pradesh) have been taken away from Indian control permanently. The former will become part of Pakistan and the latter state will be restored as a part of China and its Tibetan province. Further Indian aggression will be met with additional punishment and possibly the breakup of the Indian state into a number of smaller states. The Indian government is initially stunned by its sudden losses. No response is made to the Beijing communiqué as Indian decision makers disagree over the appropriate response. Indian military forces are regrouping however for a possible attempt to renew combat in one or both sectors. In the Indian Ocean, Indian antisubmarine warfare (ASW) operations force a Chinese submarine to surface. Since the crew's ability to breathe has been damaged by depth charges, the submarine is unable to fight as it ascends and is captured by an Indian flotilla. A second communiqué from Beijing is released. If the Chinese submarine is not released immediately, India can expect to lose more territory as its punishment is expanded to encompass the state of Assam. New Delhi replies that a state of war is still in progress and the submarine and its crew will be treated as prisoners of war. Chinese forces move into Assam and encounter little effective resistance. Additional Indian forces are attempting to reach Assam but are hampered by the Bangladeshi inundation from rising sea levels and panicked refugees fleeing the advancing Chinese forces.

*   *   *

We stop the scenario at this cliff-hanging point. Indian forces have been damaged and the state of India is in disarray, but Indian decision makers have not conceded and appear ready to fight on. Japan and China appear to be squaring off for a naval duel in the East China Sea. The United States is hard pressed to offer much support but is sending a fleet across half the Pacific toward Japan. Russia is sitting on the fence possibly waiting to exploit an opportunity to weaken Chinese pressures on its Far East. India might choose to surrender or accept a cease-fire. Japan might blink and back down from the naval confrontation. The US forces might arrive too late to play much of a role. Russia may well stay on the fence. That is to say, we think the transition war has begun. It is not our task to describe how it works out. The multiple probabilities at play may suggest some likelihood of further fighting and probably escalation in terms of the weaponry used. All the major actors might be damaged as a consequence. On the other hand, if no further fighting takes place, Chinese primacy may have been won by default. But our only mission is to develop a plausible story about how such a war might commence in the late 2030s.

CHAPTER NINE

Strong Conflict Constraints and Strong Conflict Inducements: The "Pax Sinica" Scenario

W e take many dimensions of our current international system for granted. Yet how might things have changed if the Allies had lost World War II? A German-Italian-Japanese victory would have led initially to a regionally compartmentalized world. Berlin would have controlled Europe and had extensive influence throughout Africa. Tokyo would have dominated East and Central/South Asia. The Soviet Union probably would have been divided between the two main Axis partners. The Americas would have remained outside this Eurasian compartmentalization, although surely influence and more would have been contested in the southern zone of the Americas. If there were international organizations, they would not have resembled the ones we currently have—no United Nations, no International Monetary Fund, and no World Court. There would be no world currency and probably only limited trade and investment across spheres of influence. Voluntary migration would not occur, although forced migrations might. Perpetual skirmishing would have put the Cold War to shame. It seems doubtful that the system would have been able to maintain some degree of structural stability. But it is conceivable that the distribution of atomic/nuclear weapons might have contributed some sense of stable equilibrium and preference for maintaining the status quo.

The point is that the current international system is due in some respects to the concentration of technological innovation in the US economy and the related victory in 1945 by the coalition in which the

TABLE 9.1. **Structure of the "Pax Sinica" scenario**

Scenario components	Specific emphases
Principal driver	Continued US relative decline and supplantment by Chinese lead in technological innovation and global reach
Predetermined elements	Economic interdependence and nuclear deterrence
Critical uncertainties	International organizations reform and revitalization
Wild cards	Diaoyu crisis, Saudi civil war, Central Asian intervention, Kashmir, and Sudan

United States was preeminent. Substitute all the systemic features that are traceable to the United States with a Chinese flavor and you have a Chinese-centric world system. Something like that could emerge from a Chinese victory in a transition war, as in the preceding chapter, but it could also emerge in the absence of a transition war. The latter possibility is the storyline in this chapter's scenario.

The more abstract structure of the Pax Sinica scenario is specified in table 9.1. The primary driver is once again US relative decline—but this time the pace is very fast and Chinese ascendance is rapid. The predetermined elements include extrapolating Chinese gains in a large number of spheres of activity (e.g., sports, entertainment, science, education, language, culture, space, multinational business, investment, and auto production) into predominance in a fairly short period of time. Movement up the technological ladder generates a secondary driver in terms of a changing geopolitical orientation. China is increasingly committed to the idea that controlling sea routes is necessary to safeguard its energy source flows and exports. A greatly expanded navy and naval presence in the Pacific, the Indian Ocean, and the Arctic is the result.

One of the main critical uncertainties is the Chinese success in solving its economic problems by creating new technology to address them. Environmental problems, health problems, and water scarcity create enormous incentives for radical economic innovations. Simply having the incentives does not mean anyone will take advantage of the opportunities created by the problems. In this Pax Sinica scenario, the Chinese are successful exploiters just like the English used damp coal mines to develop steam engines several hundred years earlier. But there is a second major critical uncertainty associated with the outcome of the Diaoyu crisis. In this story line, the United States backs down after it realizes the potential costs associated with defending Japan are too great. A combination of economic interdependence and nuclear deterrence appears to encourage the US capitulation. There are a number of wild cards (Saudi Arabia, Central Asia, Taiwan, Korea, South Asia, and Africa) but none generate serious problems for the predominance of China.

*   *   *

- For the first time, China has dominated in the number of Olympic gold medals awarded at the 2024 Singapore games. In the summer games, only basketball has proven elusive.
- Hengdian World Studios, sometimes called "Chinawood" had already set the world record for the production of the most movies and television dramas by 2005. Multiple sequels to *Crouching Tiger, Hidden Dragon* and *Hero* and the availability of inexpensive extras and governmental cooperation helped consolidate the centrality of Chinawood and its gradual supplantment of increasingly impoverished Hollywood. Hollywood had found it increasingly difficult to make movies in southern California and to raise money for films that did not focus on action themes. More investment money was readily available in China. Action films—that did not depend on dialogue or complex plots—could be made anywhere and sold throughout the world gravitated to Chinese studios. Chinese studios, in turn, became somewhat less wedded to large cast stories about ancient Chinese combat. The old "chop-socky" movies of the 1960s with heroes armed with magical powers and able to spring over houses and fight in the air curiously proved to have universal appeal and were revived with even more dramatic technical effects. *Kung Fu Panda 17* set new records for the first weekend box-office receipts.
- The 2034 Nobel prizes in physics and chemistry were won once again by Chinese scientists. This represents the fifth year in a row that Chinese scholars had taken these awards.
- As of 2035, Beijing University, Hong Kong University, and Tsinghua University are now ranked among the top five research universities in the world. Harvard and Stanford in the United States are ranked third and fifth, respectively. Chinese universities, long exporters of students to other parts of the world, now import many more students than they export. Foreign students matriculating in Chinese universities outnumber those attending non-Chinese universities.
- As of 2040, half the world's population now speaks Mandarin Chinese. Anyone engaged in business needs to have some competence in this difficult language. Throughout the more advanced industrial states, the language had become a standard offering from kindergarten on.

- Fashion observers have remarked that shirts with mandarin collars are now pretty much universal—only a few marginalized teenagers insist on wearing button-down shirts and ties as a symbol of adolescent rebellion. Some Iranians claim that they began this fashion trend, but most informed analysts attribute it to the predominance of China in economic production and exports of commodities, styles, and media by the early 2040s.

- The Chinese New Year is now (2050) celebrated everywhere as a formal holiday. Although China had accepted the Gregorian calendar in 1929, the traditional Chinese lunar calendar has replaced the old and obsolescent calendar associated with the West. A new year usually starts on the second new moon after the winter solstice. The practice of Western astrology is now banned in sixty-two countries.

- In 2020, only tem of the world's fifty largest corporations had Chinese headquarters and ownership. By 2030, the number had expanded to twenty-four. In 2050, forty of the world's fifty largest corporations were Chinese. A number of different stories are associated with this phenomenal growth of Chinese multinationals.

- One of the stories involves overcoming initial fragmentation and tradition. China initially possessed a large population addicted to smoking. Its rapid industrialization seriously damaged the Chinese environment. But these twin-policy problems has a bright side. Chinese policy makers and scientists possessed strong motivations for tackling these problems as concerns with extremely high priority. The environmental degradation encouraged the development of alternative energies and machines that could use them. The health problems linked to smoking led finally to a cure for many types of cancer after rising numbers of Chinese began to die prematurely in the late 2020s. China became the leader in alternative energies, medical research, and drug production.

- China had a growing market for pharmaceuticals but also had too many small firms competing for small shares of the local market. In 2004, there were an estimated five thousand or more firms. This number was reduced to three thousand five hundred in 2011. But it required governmental intervention and the coincidental advances in developing new drugs for AIDs and cancer that brought about the consolidation of Chinese pharmaceutical production. By 2028, three firms—Zensun, Wuxi Pharmatech, and Shijiazhuang Pharma Group—controlled 80 percent of the Chinese market. With this huge market base and the new drug products, they were able to expand throughout the world. By 2040, the three firms controlled 45 percent of the world's pharmaceutical market.

- Another major story is associated with Chinese auto manufacture. China had bypassed Japan as early as 2006 as the second largest auto market. In 2009, China passed the United States to become the world's leading auto market. The scale of the enterprise was important but so were the innovations in propulsion of automobiles. The first breakthrough occurred in the development of hydrogen engines that were considerably more efficient and created less pollution. By 2030 one-third of the world's automobiles relied on hydrogen or some form of hybrid propulsion. Many of these automobiles were produced and sold by ChangAn Auto Company. The second breakthrough was achieved when Chinese researchers took advantage of their lead in battery development to be the first to create a new, small, and relatively inexpensive battery that propels autos with a weekly recharging. Chinese factories also quickly seized the lead in automobile production, because new vehicles had to be designed to optimize the use of the novel batteries. These leads in battery and automobile development could be maintained as long as Chinese manufacturers stay several years ahead of their competitors. Selective alliances with Volkswagen, Peugeot, and Chrysler allowed Dongfeng Motor Corporation (DMC) and Great Wall Motors (GWM) to develop control of worldwide market shares not seen since the heydays of General Motors. Many of DMC and GWMs' competitors, saddled with suddenly obsolete vehicles, simply went out of business. A byproduct of this development was the rapid decline of the world's demand for petroleum.
- A third variation on the theme took place at the huge desalination plant project constructed for the Tianjin-Binhai development zone, initially using Israeli technology. The main obstacle to seawater desalination was its cost. As long as regular water could be pumped from rivers or aquifers, consumers were reluctant to pay the added cost of treated water. But as the northern plain of China grew increasingly dry, Beijing's survival as an urban center increasingly depended on coastal seawater that had been converted to drinking water. The huge scale of the operation cut costs further as it encouraged improved technology that could then be sold around the world to the one-fifth of the world's population that did not have access to potable water.
- China finally seized the lead in software design and production from India by 2029, despite the Indian head start and decisive lead a decade before.
- In 2036, Chinese advances in nanotechnology had proceeded to the point that computer chips were too small to be observed by the human eye and powerful computers were roughly the size of late-twentieth-century hand calculators. With this advance, all personal and a good number of corporate and governmental computers had been rendered obsolete. China was not the only source

of the new computers but controlled about 85 percent of the production (carried out in Laos and Cambodia).

- Agricultural research carried out at the China National Center of Biotechnology Development located in Beijing led to a new way to triple rice and grain production by bioengineering seed DNA structures. The innovation was immediately put to use in China and Southeast Asia, leading to bumper crops and surplus food production throughout eastern Asia.

- Still another route to multinational success were the large holdings of surplus cash earned in marketing profitable commodities. Chinese investors were able to purchase selected Western firms and franchises as their owners encountered financial problems. In this fashion, for instance, Walmart, Starbucks, McDonalds, and even the Disney theme parks were purchased by Chinese investors.

- Up to about 2015, China's naval strategy was focused on Taiwan, Japan, and the South China Sea area for its transit traffic and its potential oil and gas resources. Three fleets, accordingly, were stationed in the Taiwan Strait, the Yellow Sea, and the South China Sea. These waters are referred to as the "Near Seas." By 2030, the "string of pearls"–basing network had been extended into the Indian Ocean. Bases of different sizes and functions were situated at or under construction at Sittwe (Myanmar), Chittagong (Bangladesh), Hambantota (Sri Lanka), Gwadar (Pakistan), and Aden (South Yemen). Some 80 percent of China's oil imports moved through the Straits of Malacca so that protecting this route had become increasingly important. Any serious interruption of the flow could bring the Chinese economy to a standstill. A fourth Indian Ocean fleet was stationed primarily at Gwadar. In 2038, work had finally begun on a canal through the Kra Isthmus, which would permit shipping to avoid altogether the potential choke point at the Strait of Malacca. Most of the construction for the canal was being done by Chinese firms.

The expansion of the Chinese navy's (PLAN) activities was accompanied by a more ambitious reach into the Pacific as well. No longer were the Near Seas to claim first priority. Whereas the earlier, semicoastal strategy had been bounded by the first island chain (the Ryukyus, Taiwan, and Kuriles), PLAN increasingly focused on the second island chain (Bonin, Guam, Indonesia, and Mariannas) after 2025.

Changes in ship inventories were also associated with these strategic shifts. By 2020, two smaller aircraft carriers had been commissioned. In 2025 and 2030, respectively, the first two heavy carriers had completed their sea trials and were assigned to what had now become the Pacific (combining the initial three fleets) and Indian Ocean fleets. Two more were being constructed and expected to be completed in 2035 and 2040. It was unclear whether others were planned or under construction. In the days of preoccupation with Taiwan, China had acquired a number of fairly quiet diesel attack submarines. In the 2030s, the diesel ships were being assigned to noncombat duties and being replaced at the rate of about 1.5 submarine/year by nuclear attack submarines (Shang and Xia classes). Despite a long history of problems with ballistic missile submarines (SSBN) dating back to the 1980s, the Jin class of SSBN had proven fairly reliable. Twenty-four in all had been constructed and assigned to patrol throughout the Pacific and Indian Oceans by 2035. Chinese sea-launched missiles could now hit most targets in the United States.

In comparison, the US fleet had dwindled in size by 2030 to about 50 percent of its strength at the beginning of the millennium. China and the United States were about equal in the number of nuclear attack submarines and SSBNs. The carrier fleet was down to six, but the broader reach of the US navy meant that no more than one carrier was ever in the Pacific at one time. In 2030, China had both of its heavy carriers operating in the Pacific. A decade later there were three (the other one was assigned to the Indian Ocean theater).

• The China National Space Administration (CNSA) announced in 2015 that it had successfully established a small orbiting laboratory in space. In the same year, phase three of the Chinese lunar exploration project was completed. Lunar soil samples were collected by an unmanned vehicle and returned to Earth.

In 2017, Shenzou 11 was successfully launched from Jiuquan Satellite Launch Center with a Long March 5E propulsion vehicle carrying a crew to the Chinese space laboratory (Tiangong [Heavenly Palace] 1). Although subject to rotation, the crew was expected to remain in space permanently.

For two years, 2020–22, China was the only state with a presence in space. The old International Space Station with US, Russian, Japanese, and other states participation had been closed 2019, a year ahead of schedule.

In 2022, the Chinese monopoly in space was challenged simultaneously by India and Japan. A manned lunar mission to the Moon, Chardrayaan-3, was established successfully in March—following up unmanned missions to the Moon and the Sun in 2014 and 2016, respectively. The Indian Space Research Organization announced that it intended to send a satellite to Mars in 2025.

Selene 4 successfully landed on the Moon in June of 2022. Jaxa (the Japan Aerospace Exploration Agency) announced that it too had established a "manned" lunar base using robots exclusively. Japanese astronauts were expected to follow within a year or two. However, financial problems might require putting off that stage for several more years.

The Chinese lunar exploration project had been delayed by technical problems. It had announced plans for an observatory and base on the Moon as early as 2020. The Indian and Japanese successes galvanized the Chinese space program into frenetic, around-the-clock activity. A Long March 7F rocket was rushed into action to place a small group of taikonauts on the Moon in August.

In December, Jaxa announced that its robotic lunar base was no longer responding to messages. It requested CNSA assistance in determining what the nature of the problem. A small group of Chinese taikonauts made the journey to the nearby Japanese base but reported that it had seemingly vanished. Markings on the lunar landscape indicated that something like a base had existed, but no other sign of the robots or the base could be found. There were indications of a number of small meteors in the area. CNSA speculated that perhaps the base had been the victim of one or more meteors.

In February 2023, a mysterious explosion destroyed the Indian lunar base, named Sriharikota 2 after the island that the Satish Dhawan Space Centre used for launching its space vehicles. A rescue party from the Chinese lunar base reported that no there were no survivors and that the base was not inhabitable without extensive reconstruction. The brief challenge to the Chinese space monopoly had been brought to a premature end by a couple of apparent coincidences that worked in the Chinese favor.

- Fighting within the Saudi royal family over succession to the monarchy ballooned into a civil war. Different royal factions controlled the army and National Guard. Thus, these forces, which were roughly equally armed, ended on opposing sides. Neither side seemed to be winning, which might not have mattered all that much outside the Saudi Peninsula except that Saudi oil production had ground to a halt. Increases in production in Iran, Iraq, and Kuwait could not make up the losses since they simply did not have the capacity and what they did have was diminishing in terms of what could be readily extracted. The only solution for regaining access to Saudi oil involved a military intervention by outside forces with sufficient firepower to stop the local fighting. Troops primarily from China, but with smaller contingents from Japan, the United States, and the European Union, were assembled and supported by Chinese logistics in the Indian Ocean and Persian Gulf. The Chinese Tenth Fleet, headquartered at Aden, provided the main naval support for the operation.

- In 2010, a Chinese trawler was seized by the Japanese Coast Guard after the trawler collided with patrol boats in the Senkaku Islands (Diaoyu Islands from the Chinese perspective). The Chinese have claimed these islands, located about midway between Japan and China (and a hundred miles or so north of Taiwan) on the basis of records demonstrating Chinese discovery dating from the fifteenth century. The Japanese had occupied the islands in 1895 during the war with China and held them until 1945. Temporarily occupied by the United States to 1972, control of the islands reverted to Japan. Since the islands are not mentioned by name in the Potsdam Declaration and the treaty that formalized Japan's surrender in 1945, China has asserted that the islands should have been returned to Chinese control. Japan's response has been that the islands have always been an extension of the Ryukyu chain and therefore natural possessions of Japan—as opposed to relatively recent conquests of war. The islands themselves might not seem worthy of dispute, but their possession has major implications for who has the right to exploit oil and natural gas deposits in the East China Sea.

Fifteen years later, Japan's Coast Guard seizes vessels belonging to Shell Oil Company, which claimed it had a lease arranged with China to explore and exploit oil deposits in the general Diaoyu area. As the Coast Guard patrol boats were taking the company vessels in tow, a Chinese destroyer arrived and delivered an ultimatum to the Japanese Coast Guard boats. Either release the company vessels or face destruction. The two Japanese boats attempted to contact their headquarters for instructions but were unable to make contact because their signals were being jammed by the Chinese warship. Without instructions, the Japanese boats continued to make way for their homeport with the commercial vessels in tow. Both boats were destroyed by missiles fired from the destroyer. The Chinese warship remained in the area to protect the operations of the oil exploration vessels.

A Japanese destroyer was dispatched to learn the fate of the missing Coast Guard boats. Spotting the remaining debris, the Japanese destroyer hailed the Chinese destroyer and demanded to know what it was doing in Japanese waters and whether it was responsible for the missing Coast Guard boats. The captain of the Chinese ship responded briefly that the Japanese destroyer was in Chinese waters and should immediately leave the area. The response was accompanied by a warning shot literally across the bow of the Japanese destroyer. Believing his ship was under attack, the captain of the Japanese destroyer ordered return fire on the Chinese destroyer. Both ships engaged in a brief and inconclusive battle that managed to do enough damage to both ships to take them out of commission. Other ships were dispatched to the battle zone by the Japanese and Chinese naval commands. The new ships arrived but did not continue the battle. Instead, both sides towed their damaged destroyers back to their homeports for repair and taking care of the wounded survivors. Japanese and Chinese warships, however, remained in the battle area, confronting their opponents while their governments deliberated how to resolve the maritime crisis.

The Chinese government asserted its right to control of the Diaoyu Islands.

The Japanese government denied the claim and called on the Chinese warships to leave the vicinity of the Senkaku Islands. The Chinese response was one of flat rejection of the ultimatum. The time had come, it was announced, to put an end to the false maritime claims of Japan. From this point on, the Diaoyu Islands were now Chinese territory and would be defended with whatever force was required. More Japanese ships were sent toward the Senkaku confrontation zone. The Chinese government ordered a general alert of its military forces and warned Tokyo that further naval interference with Chinese operations in the Diaoyu Island area would result in the use of all China's military arsenal, including its nuclear missiles.

Japan had begun work on developing its own nuclear missile force but had not yet developed enough weapons to survive the first strike. For too long, Japan had depended on the American nuclear umbrella. Naturally, the Japanese government had maintained close contact with US decision makers as the crisis unfolded. Confronted with what might or might not be a Chinese nuclear bluff, Japan requested the intervention and protection of its US ally.

American decision makers were divided on how best to respond. Were they willing to risk a nuclear war over the Senkaku/Diaoyu Islands? How would the Chinese respond to an American demand that the Chinese back away from their confrontation with Japan? Would the Chinese believe that the United States was prepared to go to war over relatively insignificant islands, albeit with major energy-resource implications? If the Chinese called the American bluff, would they retaliate by punishing the US economy in some way? An interruption of trade seemed unlikely since that would cost the Chinese as much as the Americans, but there were other possibilities involving boycotts of investment in United States or the financing of US debt.

On the second day of US deliberations, China complicated the problem by announcing that it had decided to begin balancing its own investment portfolio by converting some of its large holding of US treasury bills into gold for at least the short time. That also implied that China could not be relied on to purchase more US governmental debt in the near future. While the financial implications could prove to be quite serious, it is less well known that Japanese investors own almost as much US public debt as do the Chinese.

A further complication was a sharp increase in cyberattacks on both Japanese and US governmental computer systems. Most of the attacks seemed to be originating at IP numbers located in Guangdong Province, but it was not clear whether they were being initiated by governmental hackers or patriotic hackers seeking a way to privately express their displeasure at Japanese and US hostility.

After three days of internal debate, the US president informed the Japanese prime minister that, in the US opinion, it would be most prudent to capitulate to the Chinese demands. In other words, the United States was not prepared to go to war with China in defense of what it regarded as the territorial integrity of its close ally, Japan. Considering their options, Japanese decision makers reluctantly and bitterly capitulated. The Senkaku Islands were now the Diaoyu islands.

- By the end of 2031, Chinese naval bases had been created in Myanmar, Bangladesh, Pakistan, Cambodia, Vietnam, Philippines, Tanzania, Madagascar, Aden in the newly independent South Yemen, and some South Pacific islands. These bases provided an effective armature for projecting naval power from the Pacific to eastern Africa.

- The Secretariat of the Shanghai Cooperation Organization (SCO) triumphantly announced from Beijing in June 2025 that the Association of Southeast Asian Nations (ASEAN) had formally decided to apply for full membership in SCO. The SCO terms for full membership essentially meant dismantling ASEAN. Each state that was formerly a member of ASEAN would simply become an individual member of SCO, although all members of ASEAN would be permitted to join as a bloc. Vietnam had attempted to put off this move but was outvoted. At the same time, Vietnam realized that it was in no position to go it alone. Pakistan quickly announced that it, too, would apply for membership after the SCO proclaimed that it was interested in developing a new security architecture for all of Asia. A subsequent Indian request for an associate membership was declined.

- The Islamic Movement of Turkestan (IMT), which promotes an Islamic Caliphate throughout Central Asia, has gained followers in the past decade. Its appeal is based partly on the popular disgruntlement with repressive regimes in each of the Central Asian states and partly on its growing reputation for successful raids. In 2028 it managed to shut down the Saman-Depe gas pipeline between Turkmenistan and China for six weeks. It followed up this feat with attacks on the Atasu-Alashankou oil pipeline in Kazakhstan. The flow to China was interrupted for almost three weeks. Chinese dependence on energy resources from Central Asia had expanded in the 2020s. By 2030, it accounted for about 35 percent of China's energy supply. To make matters worse, the IMT successes were making inroads into Uyghur discontent in Xinjiang. If one of the Central Asian states bordering Xinjiang fell to the IMT, the support for a Uyghur rebellion would be difficult to resist. In 2031 the Turkmenistan regime collapsed and was replaced by a coalition in which IMT personnel figured prominently. The regime in Kazakhstan appeared to be wobbling.

Chinese decision makers were confronted with a double threat—a loss of vital energy resources and an incitement to Uyghur revolt. The response was to call for a SCO military intervention into Kazakhstan in response to clear American subversion throughout Central Asia but especially in Kazakhstan. Although the SCO now has fifteen members, the main brunt of the intervention was executed by Russian troops entering from the north and Chinese troops coming in across Kazakhstan's eastern border. The eventual outcome was the division of the state into two de facto states: Northeastern and Southeastern Kazakhstan. China's potentially turbulent Kazakhstan frontier largely disappeared as a consequence, even if China did increase the number of Uighurs within its population. Tajikistan shortly thereafter requested SCO protection from internal subversion. Three Chinese army bases were established at critical points within Tajikistan in response to the request for assistance.

- The Taiwan issue became less and less overt. The commercial connections between the island and mainland expanded to the point at which any thought of interruption simply became unthinkable by both sides. As a consequence, Taiwanese independence became a dead political issue in Taiwanese elections for all except the population that had always resided on the island. Taiwanese elites wanted assurances that the mainland government would not intervene in commerce and investment. The mainland initially offered a trade arrangement that more or less guaranteed the economic status quo indefinitely. Nonintervention in political matters proved to be a trickier question but the tendency within China had been one of moving toward allowing greater autonomy for areas of strong economic productivity—as in Guangdong and Hong Kong. Elections and multiple parties were tolerated for what was now a provincial government. Even so, the Guomingdang Party invariably won and took on the dimensions of a branch office of the Communist Party.

- By 2027, the increasingly erratic nature of the North Korean ruling family had begun to jeopardize national security. Widespread concern that nuclear missiles might be launched on a personal whim encouraged plans to eliminate the risk. In 2029, a Chinese-backed military coup removed the family from power in a single night. No resistance was encountered from any military units. Not surprisingly, there was no popular resistance either. However, the new military regime proved no more successful at dealing with drought, famine, and declining productivity than the earlier regime. Secret unification negotiations with the Republic of Korea were initiated. The sticking point was what to do with the huge North Korean military establishment. By 2031, an agreement was worked out in which all North Korean officers and senior enlisted men were guaranteed to at least maintain their ranks in a unified Korean military until retirement. A unified Korea meant an end to the demilitarized zone and the need for the presence of US troops, which were withdrawn to bases in Japan.

- Partially in response to the American refusal to pay its dues for several years after its major debt crisis, in 2020, the UN downgraded its presence in New York and upgraded its activities in Geneva. Thereafter, General Assembly and Security Council deliberations were carried out exclusively in Switzerland.

- A Chinese economist had become a standard feature of the International Monetary Fund (IMF) upper-management personnel as early as 2011. The first Chinese head of the IMF was appointed in 2023. Since that point in time, it was assumed that the preferences of the Chinese government would be privileged in selecting the head of the IMF. This was by no means a symbolic sop to the BRIC (Brazil, Russia, India, and China) countries' rising economic significance. By the 2020s, Chinese reserves had become the leading source of funding for IMF lending.

- A Chinese-led initiative to reform the structure of the United Nations (UN) Security Council was successful. The United States and Russia retained their slots, along with China. Britain and France lost theirs but were replaced by an European Union seat. Brazil, India, and South Africa were added to make a permanent seven-member council. Eight other states joined the council as nonpermanent members serving five-year terms. No state retained or possessed a veto power. Majority rule would be decisive. Since China was the one state most likely to receive support from three other states, Chinese-constructed majorities usually prevailed.

- The US dollar had long been the lynchpin of the international monetary system in providing a common medium for exchange. Instabilities in its value and a growing lack of confidence in the future productivity of the US economy saw it fade as the world's principal currency. Initially, a basket of different currencies was employed—mixing dollars, Euros, and yen. Gradually, though, the Chinese renminbi or yuan became the world's key currency. By 2045, there was no longer any doubt about its staying power.

- In 2030, Pakistani infiltration into western Kashmir catches India off guard. Indian forces are rushed northward to deal with the invading force, which is being rapidly reinforced by the movement of Pakistani troops into Kashmir. A second Indian battle group is assembling in the Thar Desert for a counterinvasion. Pakistani troops in Kashmir are just beginning to retreat when a massive Chinese military intervention coming through Aksai Chin catches the Indian forces in Kashmir by surprise. A large number of casualties forces the Indian troops to retreat while the Indian forces in the Thar Desert are redirected toward the Kashmiri front. Chinese troops have also moved into Arunachal Pradesh. The Indian government is forced to concede the loss of Kashmir, now occupied by Pakistani and Chinese troops and Arunachal Pradesh. While Indian forces are arrayed against their Chinese-Pakistani counterparts along the borders in multiple theaters, the likelihood of renewed fighting seems slim until or unless Indian logistical capabilities are enhanced substantially.

- The third attempt by North Sudan to reconquer South Sudan in the past twenty years is making considerable headway, particularly since North Sudan is now federated with Egypt in the third United Arab Republic (UAR). The invasion forces are mainly North Sudanese, but their offensive power is augmented by Libyan and Syrian troops. But this attempt is also interrupting oil supplies to China. Initially, China sends in advisers, but it becomes quite apparent that more involvement will be necessary to repel the invasion from the north. Three brigades are airlifted into Juba and two hundred tanks are off-loaded at the Port of Djibouti. However, it will take a week for the tanks to reach the front lines traveling through Ethiopia. A large contingent of Egyptian troops is rushed to the battlefield in an effort to complete the invasion before the Chinese tanks arrive. China calls on its Israeli ally to open a new front in Sinai/Suez theater. Israeli tanks are soon crossing the Nile River and approaching Cairo. The UAR calls for truce negotiations that negotiate a cease-fire and, ultimately, a withdrawal of UAR troops from South Sudan. It is decided that a sizeable number of Chinese troops will need to remain along the border between the two Sudans to act as a trip-wire deterrent against a potential fourth attack from the north.

- The Arctic route had become a critical trade conduit between Europe and Asia by 2035, thanks to the melting of polar ice. By 2040, problems had emerged in Canada's northern territories, due to its forbidding winter climate, limited population, and long maritime border. US naval forces, in any event, had their hands full dealing with problems in the Caribbean and Gulf of Mexico. To ensure the predictable movement of trade through Arctic waters, Chinese naval bases were created in Wonson and Ulsan in Korea and a joint Canadian/ Chinese base was established in Churchill in Canada. The Chinese Sixth Fleet, headquartered at Ulsan, has as its mission to suppress piracy and pirates using Canadian bases from interfering with Arctic commerce. Essentially, this was the same model used in the late 2020s to finally bring an end to Somali piracy in Indian Ocean waters—also carried out primarily by Chinese naval vessels operating out of the home port of Aden.

*　　*　　*

By midcentury, the Chinese lead in technological innovation and global reach is well established. Any prospect of a transitional conflict with the

United States has been averted by the improbability of a weakened former leader taking on a newly emerged system leader with few overt vulnerabilities. The Diaoyu crisis in 2025 was a bellwether. Once the United
States backed down, they proved reluctant to risk a subsequent crisis. The
world is not a peaceful place, as manifested in the series of interventions
in the Global South, but is reasonably prosperous, at least in the Global
North and parts of the South, buoyed by new technological production
involving automobiles no longer propelled by gasoline engines and bio/
nanotechnologies that have transformed once again the basic nature of
manufacture. By the late 2040s, the new technological regime was firmly
in place within most of the more advanced economies.

CHAPTER TEN

Strong Conflict Constraints and Weak Conflict Inducements: The "Liberal Peace" Scenario

O ur last scenario combines weak conflict facilitators and strong constraints. Entitled the "liberal peace" scenario, it emphasizes continued relative decline on the part of the United States, but not to the point that China surpasses its position on all fronts or achieves hegemony as in the previous chapter. The dollar remains the world currency, but China becomes the leading source for manufacturing and investment capital. Given the title, it should not be too surprising that the secondary drivers—economic interdependence, international organizations, and nuclear deterrence—figure prominently.

We might have entitled this scenario "Kant muddles through." Although we construe this scenario as liberal or Kantian, it is certainly not a "textbook" representation of how liberal ideas might be manifest. The potential impact of joint democracy—the core of liberal democratic peace theory—is diminished significantly by China's continued rejection of most precepts of Western democracy. International governmental organizations (IGOs) are useful in limited ways but do not operate quite as liberal theory maintains. Already existing IGOs that do not advance Chinese interests are marginalized, and new organizations are crafted to better serve the ascendant challenger's purposes. Only economic interdependence functions somewhat as liberals expected. Although dense US-China economic ties generate no small measure of economic conflict, they always fall short of escalation to military conflict.

China is able to selectively reconfigure a number of international insti-

TABLE 10.1. **Structure of the "Liberal Peace" scenario**

Scenario components	Specific emphases
Principal driver	Continued and gradual US decline; gradual Chinese movement toward trade and financial leadership
Predetermined elements	Nuclear deterrence presumed, halting economic growth, and protectionism
Critical uncertainties	Escalation in competitive support for client states, reinvigoration of international institutions at regional level, and popularity of authoritarian capitalism
Wild cards	None

tutions, including the World Trade Organization (WTO), the United Nations (UN), and some Asian organizations. Economic interdependence is manifested most obviously in terms of the financial interdependence binding the United States and China. The very large US public debt held by China limits US financial independence but also restrains Chinese actions lest China act in such a way that it harms its own wealth position. Nuclear deterrence appears to work as well as it did during the Cold War, even though no "smoking gun" occurs that would permit us to be sure of its impact. Table 10.1 lists a few prominent wild cards—Chinese intervention into Myanmar and US intervention into Indonesia—that could have been transformed into broader conflicts but did not. There is no central systemic crisis featuring the two major adversaries in this storyline.

The predetermined elements in this scenario include continued Chinese economic growth and its corollary of China's leading financial position as a source of capital. The critical uncertainties focus on whether or to what extent China will choose to work with older institutions, make its domestic financial operations more transparent, and develop a mutual understanding with the United States that financial interdependence is an important binder for both parties. Even though it does not appear explicitly, the possibility that a confrontation between China and the United States could escalate to nuclear levels remains a possibility throughout the storyline.

* * *

- By the first decade of the new millennium, the main contours of systemic transition were shaping up. An ascending China seemed a good bet to eventually challenge the United States as system leader. China itself was frequently compared to challengers in previous transitions (as in the cases of Germany and Japan in the twentieth century), and there was much speculation about whether enough "learning" had taken place to navigate the anticipated transition without another economic depression and transition war. One major difference between the Great Depression of the 1930s and the global recession of 2007–15 was that during the earlier period there was little or nothing by way of an institutional framework to shore up the world trading system and to adjudicate the mounting number of trade and exchange-rate disputes. Absent such a multilateral framework there was no means to prevent the major trading states from resorting to the kinds of protectionist trade policies and competitive currency devaluations that only served to exacerbate their collective circumstances. Without means to check the proliferation of these "beggar thy neighbor policies," there was no way to arrest the slide down the proverbial "slippery slope of protectionism."

- In the early twenty-first century enough of a trade regime was in place to avoid the slippery slope. To be sure, the WTO Doha Round of trade talks continued to flounder well short of completion—an outcome China helped bring about— and no comprehensive substitute ever arose. The trade regime was under stress as global trade volumes shrank during the low points of the recession and recovered only slowly in many locales. Leaders in China, Japan, Europe, and to a lesser extent the United States, as well as others north and south of the equator, often resorted to protectionist measures, usually to cope with domestic political exigencies. Antidumping cases increased; safeguard and escape clauses were invoked more frequently; allowable tariffs were stretched to the breaking point; and nontariff barriers were again a showcase for bureaucratic creativity. China's large trade surpluses (as well as those of other Asian countries relying on export-led growth strategies) remained controversial and were widely criticized in the United States and elsewhere as the result of "currency manipulation."

The WTO's main purpose evolved toward piecemeal dispute resolution, while moving further away from its original role as a multilateral platform for negotiating uniform, liberalizing trade agreements. Further complicating this variegated, particularistic landscape were decades of bilateral and regional preferential trade agreements (PTAs), some facilitating trade and others merely diverting it. Eventually, the gradual, intermittent appreciation of the Chinese yuan, the gradual moderation of China's trade surpluses, and the fact that others were unable to exert much influence on China's commercial and exchange-rate policies defused the controversy over exchange rates, trade surpluses, and reserves.

The trade regime seemed to serve as a kind of firewall that prevented trade conflicts from escalating to systemic conflagrations. Member states tended to retreat from the protectionist brink as they were reluctant to be seen as undermining the WTO or as abandoning it altogether. The global trading system, though shaky, held. China had become the world's largest exporting country in 2009 and the world's largest trading nation by 2015, but it did not quickly leap to assume the role of system leader. Instead, China was quite content with the latitude of maneuver afforded by the patchwork nature of the trading system. A major step for China was its recognition in 2012 as a "market economy," a WTO status that delimited the use of trade barriers, especially antidumping measures, by its trading partners, and was therefore worth billions to Chinese exporters. Its sheer economic size, large internal markets, and export dynamism enabled China to look after Chinese interests without much regard for establishing or maintaining global principles and rules.

- Other changes in the institutional landscape either moved the operation of existing international organizations in directions congenial to Chinese interests or influenced the formation of new institutions in the same directions. By 2020 Beijing had assembled a coalition of developing countries—a great many of them in Africa—and emerging market economies (Brazil, Turkey, Iran, and Venezuela) that could be trusted to vote with China in more and more global multilateral fora. At the UN, for example, China enjoyed more support for and less direct criticism of Chinese positions on human rights.

- Another institutional tack deployed by China was to strengthen Asian institutions at the expense of Western-influenced, global multilateral predecessors that been created largely under American auspices in the second half of the twentieth century. Accordingly, the Association of Southeast Asian Nations (ASEAN)–China free-trade agreement and the ASEAN 10 + 3 (China, South Korea, and Japan), both of which excluded the United States, were given more emphasis while the more liberally oriented Asia-Pacific Economic Cooperation was left to wither on the vine. This reordering of regional institutions also served as a means to marginalize Japan's role. For several decades around the turn of the century, the pace of regional institution building was slowed by Japan-China competition. Japan hoped to institutionalize its leadership before China became much stronger, whereas China calculated that institution building could wait until its ascent vis-à-vis Japan was beyond challenge, at which time it could fashion regional institutions more to its liking.

- Like the United States in the 1920s, China had emerged as the world's foremost financial power, supplanting the United States in that position just as the United States had surpassed Britain some eight decades earlier. Also, like the

United States, however, China was slow to deploy its considerable financial resources for purposes of systemic leadership. One consideration that served to curb China's willingness to assume a more active systemic role was that any such leap would have to take place within existing international financial institutions (IFIs), especially the International Monetary Fund (IMF). China was dissatisfied with these institutions, viewing them as the obsolescent remnants of a now-fading US hegemony and as reflective of Western values, interests, and state-society relations. Increases in China's system maintenance activities were therefore contingent on thoroughgoing reform of existing global IFIs and a more prominent role for newer Asia-centered institutions. Once the international financial architecture was overhauled to China's satisfaction, a path was created to a more expansive systemic role.

- China's huge holdings of US assets never provided the kind of leverage over US policy that Chinese officials hoped for and that many policymakers and academics in the United States expected. The limitations of Chinese financial power stemmed from the fact that China's selling off of dollar assets to hurt the United States would have exacted significant costs from the Chinese as well— a kind of shooting itself in the foot as the value of China's dollar-denominated holdings plummeted. Thus, as Lawrence Summers put it back in 2002, the US-China relationship was tantamount to "mutually assured financial destruction." This limitation, to continue the nuclear metaphors, certainly applied to the so-called "nuclear option," that is, the large-scale dumping of these assets in world financial markets. But smaller scale and more subtle ways also existed for China to exert leverage on the United States: for example, slowing down the acquisition of more new debt or altering the composition of its holdings to include more euros or other reserve currencies. The Chinese government tried, with mixed results, these and other methods to bend US policies to its preferences. Suffice it to say that China attained a kind of veto power over various US interest-rate and exchange-rate decisions, but not without being constrained by the enormity of its own dollar holdings and the risk of devaluing them. The United States retained some leverage over China insofar as implicit threats to inflate its way out of its debt troubles would have the same depreciating effects on those holding dollars. Thus, the two main parties to the transition, at least for a time, remained entangled in what was a tenuous form of interdependence.

- Also woven into this fabric of interdependencies at the apex of the global political economy were ongoing frictions over the role of the dollar as the key currency. China and others were clearly dissatisfied with the US dollar's continuing role as the de facto key currency and the singular prerogatives this role conferred on the United States: for example, the ability to issue debt in its own

currency and to avoid being subject to balance of payment constraints. Moreover, there was widespread global sentiment that the United States had abused
its reserve currency role, and that its profligate management of this role and of
its national accounts had been responsible for triggering the great recession of
2007–15. More generally, the centrality of the dollar in the global monetary system enabled the United States to wage costly wars around the planet, to sustain
unparalleled military expenditures, and to project global reach capabilities, particularly in China's own Asian neighborhood.

There is a wide chasm, however, between criticizing the role of the dollar
and taking the concrete steps necessary to construct a workable alternative.
Back in 2009, China and Russia, as well as a UN commission had recommended
introducing a new "supranational" reserve currency based on Special Drawing
Rights (SDRs), a kind of "funny money" comprised of a basket of currencies
(the dollar, the euro, the pound, and the yen) and used by the IMF in transactions with its members. But with such limited uses, SDRs were not supported
by the kind of market infrastructure needed for a reserve currency, inter alia,
liquid private markets on which SDRs could be bought and sold; SDR bonds
issued and traded; and other hard currencies purchased. While there was an
understandable preference for a global monetary system that was not so teth-
ered to the economic fortunes of a single country, creating an SDR-based system was an unlikely option. Perhaps the SDR proposals could be best construed as a way of signaling dissatisfaction with the dollar-centric system and a
willingness, at least in principal, to contribute to more desirable arrangements.
To the surprise of many, the US dollar remained a more than viable alternative,
at least for the short- to medium-term as the dollar actually strengthened in
response to the 2007–15 crisis; no dollar crash ensued and; the dollar declined
only marginally as a component in the official currency reserves held by other
countries. It remained the world economy's last best "safe haven."

What about China? Why did the yuan (or renminbi) not become a primary
(if not dominant) reserve currency until the 2030s? Chinese leaders had originally (in 2009) set 2020 as the target date for both Shanghai and Beijing to
become international financial centers that would rival New York, Brussels,
and Tokyo as the most important nodes in the global financial system. For all
intents and purposes, the emergence of international financial centers is tantamount to the date Chinese leaders would like for the yuan to become an international reserve currency. Why did this take until the 2030s for this to mate-
rialize? The short answer is that fulfilling a reserve currency role required a
degree of openness and transparency to which China was not willing to fully
commit. One such commitment was to a floating, rather than pegged, currency.

As late as 2020—long after it had begun to encourage others to make international use of the yuan—China was still tinkering with a "managed peg," that is, small adjustments in the value of the yuan to maintain the competitiveness of its exporters, thus indicating the priority given to domestic rather than international objectives. Another necessary condition for reserve currency status was complete opening of its capital account, accompanied by deep and liquid financial markets readily accessible to the rest of the world. These two larger steps encompass a number of constituent changes that China was reluctant to undergo, but without which holding the yuan as a reserve currency was not a viable or attractive option.

In almost every instance making the array of changes associated with convertibility of the yuan and opening its current account would entail dismantling of the export-led growth model that had served it in such good stead for decades and which had enabled the degree of control exercised by the party/ state over China's particularistic forms of state capitalism. For one instance among many, despite longstanding WTO obligations to liberalize its financial system, the Chinese government maintained tight control over the banking system and its complex linkages to the state-owned enterprises (SOEs) that were so instrumental to the regime's directed lending and other tools of economic management. This unwillingness to jettison its controls over banking and other aspects of the financial system constituted a choice of domestic policy autonomy over the kinds of liberalization necessary for Shanghai and Beijing to serve as international financial centers. Like China, Asian countries overall have underdeveloped financial markets relative to their economic size and vitality. Their institutional and regulatory deficiencies held back the appearance of a regional reserve currency until one centered on the yuan emerged in the 2030s.

China's cautious, gradual steps in international money and finance may have had the salutary effects of reducing conflict with the incumbent system leader. It is easy to imagine how a more hurried bid by an ascending China to displace the United States and the role of the US dollar in the tightly linked international financial and monetary systems could have magnified dissatisfaction and perceptions of economic threat on both sides.

- One development that definitely raised threat perceptions in the United States was the growing presence of Sovereign Wealth Funds (SWFs), government-sponsored investment vehicles set up to invest in foreign assets. These had been around for a while, but their number and size increased markedly in the wake of the 1997–98 East Asian financial crisis. The worst-hit countries in that financial crisis—Thailand, Indonesia, and South Korea—were compelled to go to the IMF on bended knee to seek bailouts. The conditionalities required by the IMF were seen in the region as imposing humiliating sovereignty costs and as bad policies that served to prolong the crisis. There would be no next time according to regional leaders and no more seeking of the onerous "collective insurance" provided by the IMF. Instead regional countries (1) would begin construction of regional institutions (e.g., the "swap agreements" featured in the Chiang Mai Initiative) to provide a local and likely less demanding form of collective insurance and (2) would stockpile international reserve currencies as a form of "self insurance." Should financial crisis again strike the region, countries would seek to call in the swap agreements they had made and could fall back on the large reserves they had accumulated by means of the export-led growth policies mentioned above in connection with China. Thus arose the impetus for accumulating large stocks of reserves, which were held in US dollars and other US Treasury instruments.

Amidst fears (voiced at times by Chinese officials) of being overexposed to low-yield, dollar-based instruments that might lose their value, surplus countries in Asia and elsewhere turned to SWFs as a way diversify their holdings and to invest in more productive assets. The first SWF to engender controversy was the China National Offshore Oil Company (CNOOC), which launched a bid in 2005 to purchase a fairly small American oil company, Unocal, only to withdraw it in the face of a congressional backlash against the sale of American energy resources to a strategic competitor. The following year similar national security concerns derailed the purchase by Dubai Ports World, an SWF based in the United Arab Emirates, of a British company that provided security management for six ports on the east coast of the United States. While these and other SWFs's professed to be pursuing only profit motivations, there is no guarantee that someday they will not be put to strategic purposes.

Up to a point SWFs were regarded as a likely source of conflict between the United States and China, as well as others, and assumed to lead eventually to some sort of showdown between state-led capitalism and the market liberalism characteristic of the West. By 2020, however, the United States had discovered that making it easier for SWFs to acquire American assets (excepting those firms and dual-use products with direct military implications) had the effect of binding investors, especially China, more closely to the United States and increasing their stakes in American economic success. The SWFs were emblematic of the hybrid forms of capitalism, melding liberal and authoritarian features, characteristic of the twenty-first century. Ironically, this was a kind of pacific outcome that was not anticipated by liberals.

• Did democratization in China play any role in how the twenty-first-century systemic transition played out? The answer is yes, but not in the manner expected by Kantian theory. The first thing to note is that, though there was some political liberalization, China did not undergo enough meaningful political reforms to meet even the most flexible conceptions of democracy. Noticeably lacking was any kind of electoral reform that permitted popular participation, transparency, and institutionalized lines of accountability. Second, not only did China reject adoption of democratic reforms within its own polity but it also actively (though not always openly) worked to undermine democratization in other countries, especially in Asia. Indeed, it was precisely those points where China's antidemocratic efforts intersected with American democracy promotion efforts that the United States and China came closest to armed conflict.

The 1980s and 1990s witnessed China attempting some initial, if extremely cautious, steps away from entirely monolithic party rule, as in the case of term limits for delegates to the party congress and mandatory retirement. Some other, more significant reforms launched in the 1990s entailed institutionalization of leadership selection within the party and experimentation with village-level elections. The latter was confined to the lowest of the six levels comprising China's governmental hierarchy, with no connection or evolution to higher levels envisioned. Taken as evidence of the stirring of "democracy with Chinese characteristics," these limited reforms were combined with a naive (or at least premature) belief that China's emerging middle class would sooner or later seek political freedoms to match the economic freedoms they had already gained.

Other evidence of China's evolution toward a more democratic polity pointed to informal processes, in particular the emergence of "intraparty democracy," the appearance of two competing coalitions within the upper reaches of the Chinese Communist Party. One was an elitist coalition representing the coastal provinces in the southeast that had benefited most from economic growth, globalization, and engagement with the West. The other was more populist, represented by the inland, rural provinces, and pursued the interests of workers, farmers, and social equity. Together the two factions reflected regional and socioeconomic interests, suggested a way that these interests might be reconciled, and thus served to inject a measure of something approximating bipartisan competition into the party's decision processes. Intraparty coalitions, however, still lacked transparency and other trappings of democratic political systems and made no pretense of public participation. While the achievements of intraparty coalitions waxed and waned over the first three decades of the century, at no point did they become the pathway to a more fully democratic China.

Democracy talk inside and outside of China was plentiful until the global financial collapse and ensuing recession in 2007–15. By 2008 or so it had become evident that China had come out of the recession more quickly, thoroughly, and with stronger economic growth than other countries, particularly the United States and Europe. This contrast affirmed for Chinese leaders not only the belief that their hybrid form of authoritarian capitalism was viable but also that theirs' was demonstrably the superior model. The weaknesses and excesses of liberal democracy had been revealed. This new discourse also featured explicit rejection of Western-style democracy and its constituent practices. China had no need, it was officially pronounced, for a multiparty political system, elections without government-chosen candidates on the ballot, separation of powers, a bicameral legislature, an independent judiciary, or rule of law.

The foreign-policy implications of such a stance are easy to deduce. If China has honed a superior socioeconomic system, then Western pressures to democratize and observe human rights are but ways to try to destabilize China's highly successful juggernaut and should be vigorously rejected. So, too, should China oppose Western efforts to democratize other countries in Asia or countries in Africa and elsewhere that China relies on for raw materials and various minerals. An additional motivation to oppose democracy was that what appeared to be successful democratization in other regional states could lead ordinary Chinese to think that democracy also may be well suited to China, that democracy does not reduce to chaos, and that there is nothing about Asianness or Confucianism that is antithetical to democracy. It is in this context that China views democracy as a threat to attainment of its strategic interests and, emboldened by its economic and diplomatic successes and growing military prowess, expended considerable efforts to secure these interests by undermining fledgling democracies.

- In what amounted to a military intervention in 2019, Chinese troops entered Myanmar to protect the military regime from its internal foes and their foreign supporters, and the Chinese Navy confronted and chased away Indian naval forces. Three years later, US delivery of military equipment to the Indonesian military to help suppress anti–United States, pro-China insurgents engendered repeated contacts between US and Chinese ground and naval forces before the Chinese and their surrogates backed off. Far from serving as an emollient to low-level conflicts with states in its neighborhood, democratization instead was a recurrent source of such conflicts, not only in Indonesia but also in Nepal, Thailand, and Vietnam.

- Democratization, of course, was not the sole factor in Chinese-US frictions in the greater Asia region. Occasionally, US intelligence ships and planes operating in the South China Sea clashed with Chinese ships and air defenses. These types of skirmishes gradually declined in number largely due to the high risk of

military escalation associated with seizing foreign intelligence vessels in nominally open waters. Japanese and Chinese naval vessels fired on each other on
two separate occasions in the East China Sea. The primary issue there involved
contested claims to extensions of sovereignty over overlapping economic zones
with oil and gas deposits. Indian and Chinese land forces also fired on each
other several times along their disputed borders. Intermittent clashes between
North and South Korean naval forces continued to take place in the Yellow
Sea. Despite all the militarized dispute activity, none escalated beyond the initial fighting. The one partial exception involved a Chinese submarine forced to
surface near the western entrance of the Malaccan Straits by a joint Indian-US
antisubmarine flotilla. The submarine was not armed with ballistic missiles but
responded to the forced surfacing with machine gun fire. The Indo-US forces in
the area backed off awaiting orders on how to proceed. Two Chinese destroyers, based in southern Myanmar, began proceeding toward the conflict site, as
did a US carrier force that had been in the vicinity of Diego Garcia when the
incident began. Both sides also dispatched jet fighters to the confrontation
zone. An error by a Chinese pilot led to the destruction of two jets, one Chinese and one Indian, when one jet flew close to another and clipped its wing.
The incident's potential for further escalation was diverted by crisis negotiations among the Chinese, US, and Indian governments. China accepted an apology for the forced surfacing of one of its submarines, which was described as an
error by the joint flotilla practicing its antisubmarine warfare tactics. The Chinese submarine was allowed to leave the area and the vessels moving in the
direction of the clash were ordered to stand down.

• The collapse of the Soviet Union and its Cold War challenge to the US-led
post–World War II liberal order ended without transition war, an outcome that
was widely attributed to the mutual deterrence provided by both sides' possession of nuclear weapons. US and Soviet leaders were (thought to be) constrained from escalating lower-level conflicts for fear that they would pass the
nuclear threshold, with catastrophic results for all concerned. China figured
into this defining nuclear aspect of the Cold War, though on much smaller scale,
first aiming to deter the United States and then shifting emphasis to deterrence
of the Soviet Union. Later, in the context of China's challenge in the twenty-
first-century transition, nuclear deterrence was again adduced as a suppressive
force, perhaps even one robust enough to prevent a transition war. Although
the United States was the primary adversary to be deterred, China's deterrence
calculus was now complicated by the emergence of India as a large, nuclear
Asian country. Though nuclear threats were not likely what Kant would have
had in mind, we can tentatively add them to the Kantian lineup of liberal con-

straints. To what extent they may have been involved in the failure of the multiple militarized disputes to escalate remains subject to dispute.

- From the outset—its first nuclear test was conducted in 1964—China opted for a relatively small arsenal accompanied by a doctrine of "minimal deterrence." This meant maintaining a credible retaliatory (second strike) capability while accepting quantitative and qualitative inferiority. The emphasis was on survivability of enough retaliatory capability to give pause to potential attackers. During the Cold War, China's minimal deterrence posture (vis-à-vis the United States and the Soviet Union) not only stemmed in part from the lack of resources to invest in a large nuclear arsenal but also derived from its leaders' belief, perhaps making a virtue of necessity, that nuclear primacy translates into neither greater security nor useful foreign-policy leverage. Reinforcing its commitment to minimum deterrence, China in 1964 pledged "no first use" (NFU) of its new nuclear arsenal. Operationally, minimum deterrence translated into a mere eighteen intercontinental ballistic missiles (ICBMs) capable of reaching American soil. These ICBMs were not constantly fueled; instead they were fueled on an "as-needed" basis with the more volatile liquid rather than solid variety; they were located in fixed-position silos; warheads were stored separately and; they were not MIRVed, that is, there was only one warhead per missile. Modernization of this arsenal was embarked on in the 1980s but took some time to complete. China overall, in 2010 had three hundred–plus nuclear weapons, mostly of theater, rather than strategic range but critical nonetheless in light of the centrality of Taiwan in its security interests and the ability to reach US bases and troops in East Asia.

Meanwhile, for several decades after the end of the Cold War, the United States undertook to modernize its strategic nuclear (and conventional) arsenal. Modernization included improvements in the accuracy, miniaturization, and explosiveness of US nuclear weapons and delivery systems (ICBMs, SLBMs, stealthy, long-range bombers, and cruise missiles), as well as upgrading of conventional strategic capabilities, a step that would not break the "nuclear taboo." Unwilling to forego the significant advantages presumed to follow from nuclear superiority, the US strategic stance reflected the stereotypical power transition logic associated with declining system leaders looking over their shoulders at rapidly ascending challengers.

Partly in response to the pressure created by the ongoing US modernization, the concept of minimum deterrence gave way to a kind of extension, "limited deterrence," which allowed some military utility for nuclear weapons, more specifically, their possible use for nuclear warfighting and for intrawar deterrence (or escalation dominance). China thus played its part in the transition script by converting more of its mounting productive assets into military capacity, albeit mostly conventional. US leaders were loathe to give up whatever benefits they associated with one of the dwindling areas of US advantage—nuclear weapons. Their Chinese counterparts also took note that the United States had never ratified the Comprehensive Test Ban Treaty, indeed had put up obstacles to its implementation, and had abruptly withdrawn from the 1973 Anti–Ballistic Missile Treaty with Russia. Other arms reduction measures, mainly with Russia in the first two decades of the twenty-first century, while involving significant cuts, were interpreted in China as ensuring that US primacy versus China would be maintained.

These steps paved the way for research, development, and partial deployment of ballistic missile defense (BMD) systems which, when combined with the continued US technological push to retain something approximating nuclear primacy, fed Chinese fears that these qualitative changes would erode, and possibly negate altogether, the country's limited deterrent. China would be vulnerable to a disarming first strike or, short of that, to coercive diplomacy. American disclaimers that the BMD was intended to be a theater missile defense (TMD) variety to protect against so-called rogue states (e.g., Iran) rang hollow in light of the possibilities that an improved version might someday be converted to defense against the Chinese arsenal or extended to defend Japan, Korea, or, in the worst, most provocative case, Taiwan.

In these circumstances, China's leaders undertook measures to augment, modernize, and improve the survivability of its still relatively small deterrent forces: new, mobile, more accurate, MIRVed (after 2010) strategic missiles, along with creative use of decoys and other forms of strategic deception were deployed. Nonetheless, the rudiments of a minimum or limited deterrence strategy still seemed to be guiding China's nuclear strategy. Just as China during the Cold War had never sought to engage in a full-fledged arms race with the United States or the Soviet Union, so too in the first couple decades of the twenty-first century did it refrain from trying to match quantitatively or qualitatively the evolution of American nuclear hardware and doctrine. By 2025 China had built about 125 mobile ICBMs, with many deployed in caves or next to decoys, as well as a growing SLBM fleet. This force, China's leaders believed, would suffice for purposes of dissuading US leaders from seriously contemplating a disarming first strike. From 2020 to 2040, China's resource constraints had long since fallen by the wayside and China had assembled rather active ballistic missile and nuclear warhead programs featuring quantity, quality, and diversity.

• The twenty-first-century systemic transition unfolded in a manner consistent with this familiar deterrence narrative. Looking back at the period, our best efforts to determine if deterrence actually worked are of course plagued by the counterfactuality of the claim. As of 2040 there had been no equivalent of the US-Soviet Cuban Missile Crisis, no occasion when the strategic forces of either side had been placed on alert, and no known instance of coercive diplomacy involving explicit nuclear threats.

CHAPTER ELEVEN

Using the Scenarios in the Twenty-First Century

A re our scenarios plausible? We think so but that only means that what goes on in these future stories could in our opinion happen. Their ultimate plausibility remains to be worked out in the future. Yet we actually assume much less than might be apparent in our story construction. Things may well work out differently in Korea, Nigeria, or Saudi Arabia than our fiction suggests but the main developments do not require major stretches of the imagination. One example is the severity of climate problems experienced in two of the scenarios. Tables 11.1 and 11.2 sketch the expectations of a group who have thought about these problems and how they might play out in the future. If anything, we are probably not giving climate problems enough attention in our scenarios.

Conflict tendencies are portrayed as emerging in a world characterized by climate deterioration and increasing resource scarcities. In these cases, current developments that seem probable are projected. The melting of Himalayan glaciers, the flooding of parts of Southeast Asia, and increased aridity in parts of China and India may appear to be convenient to our stories. However, we borrow these elements from a recent scenario exercise in which analysts considered the security implications of expected, severe, and catastrophic climate changes.[1] The elements that we have borrowed from the "expected" scenario—the least extreme version—which anticipates some continued trend in global warming through the first half of the twenty-first century, as described in table 11.1.

Table 11.1 projects an increase in average temperatures of 1.3 degrees Celsius over the next thirty years. That should suffice to cause a number of problems outlined briefly in table 11.2. China will be impacted by

TABLE 11.1. **Projections of global average surface warming and sea level rise relative to 1990**

Climate scenario	Duration	Warming, degrees Celsius	Sea level, m
Expected	1990–2040	1.3	0.23
Severe	1990–2040	2.6	0.52
Catastrophic	1990–2100	5.6	2.00

Source: Based on Kurt M. Campbell, Jay Gulledge, John R. McNeill, John Podesta, Peter Ogden, Leon Furth, R. James Woolsey, Alexander T. J. Lennon, Julianne Smith, Richard Weitz, and Derek Mix, *The Age of Consequences: The Foreign Policy and National Security Implications of Global Climate Change* (Washington, DC; Center for Strategic and International Studies, November 2007), 41, http://csis.org/files/media/csis/pubs/071105_ageofconsequences.pdf.

TABLE 11.2. **Expected regional differentiations in climate-induced problems to 2040**

North America	Increasing water scarcity in the southwest and in Mexico and storms/rising sea levels in the Caribbean will put more stress on the United States to cope with climate-induced migration.
South Asia	Increased flooding and other damage from rising seas and rivers, melting glaciers, monsoons and tropical cyclones; India will struggle with increased climate-induced refugees from Bangladesh and islands in the Bay of Bengal.
Sub-Saharan Africa	Nigeria will experience increased drought, desertification, sea level rise, and consequent domestic turmoil and instability. East African agriculture will be devastated by increased flooding, soil erosion, and drought.
Europe	A surge of migration from Africa and South Asia will contribute further to the expansion of Muslim communities in the region, possibly leading to a nationalistic backlash and, conceivably, a slowing of European Union integration.
Middle East and North Africa	Water shortages and increasing population should be expected to increase tensions among those states most affected, but especially Arab-Israeli relations
China	Warming well above the global mean in Central Asia, the Tibetan Plateau, and the north; decreasing wheat, corn, and rice yields; expanding desertification in the west; shrinking of all or most major rivers; heat waves and droughts in northern China; water shortages in a majority of Chinese cities; increased internal migration due to drought and rising sea levels; increased Han-Uighur tensions

Source: Based on Kurt M. Campbell, Jay Gulledge, John R. McNeill, John Podesta, Peter Ogden, Leon Furth, R. James Woolsey, Alexander T. J. Lennon, Julianne Smith, Richard Weitz, and Derek Mix, *The Age of Consequences: The Foreign Policy and National Security Implications of Global Climate Change* (Washington, DC; Center for Strategic and International Studies, November 2007), 46–69, http://csis.org/files/media/csis/pubs/071105_ageofconsequences.pdf.

increasing aridity in the north and desertification in the west. Sea levels will rise along the east coast, perhaps sufficiently to force some evacuation from major cities. Tibetan glaciers will melt faster than they are now, possibly leading to increased flooding in East, South, and Southeast Asia. One of the peculiar attributes of Tibet is that it contains the headwaters for many of the world's major rivers, all of which depend on melting Himalayan snow. Should Tibetan glaciers melt as glaciers have melted in

Europe and Africa already, those waters could initially flood and then dry up to trickles. Again, this is not a device borrowed from the severe or catastrophic climate-security scenarios to assist our storytelling. It is a storytelling device for sure but is borrowed from the milder expected scenario.

As it happens, it seems the data on Tibetan melting rates were misread, thereby accelerating the timing of Himalayan glacier melting.[2] We could have adjusted our story accordingly but chose not to do so since what is described seems still within the parameters of possibility. The next course of action could now be to spend more time attempting to justify the plausibility of other facets of our stories, but, instead, we will assume their inherent plausibility and focus on the theoretical structures and implications of the fabricated narratives.[3]

The Scenarios

Five scenarios are sketched in chapters 7–10. We can summarize them briefly in verbal fashion and by developing tables that specify three types of drivers: structural, secondary, and constraining, as well as their scenario manifestations. It is these drivers that are most important in differentiating the alternative futures.

The first scenario was the "More of the Same" scenario. Just what "more of the same" might mean, of course, is an "eye of the beholder" phenomenon. Our take on the "same" focuses on the lack of concentration in economic innovation and military capability—two of our paramount drivers for transition situations. It is the concentration in economic innovation and military capability that declines relatively and can set up transition dynamics. If the system is quickly reconcentrating, with China as the main beneficiary, one could expect a different sort of outcome than if the system is not reconcentrating. Whether radical economic innovation is taking place is not made explicit, but, clearly, no single center for innovation is emerging. "More of the same" also has an expanding number of major powers, each with a respectable share of the expanding military-capability pool. A third structural facet is an increasing tendency toward regionalization with each major power dominating in a different part of the world.

The "more of the same" world is characterized by slow economic growth. One of the reasons for the slowdown in growth is that the BRIC countries (Brazil, Russia, India, and China; BRICs) have not come online as major drivers of the world economy, as had been hoped. Both of the two main BRICs, India and China, have run into domestic problems that have thwarted further expansion of their economies. Another major source of difficulties is mounting climate and environmental problems. The more affluent world is less affected by these selective calamities than are the more impoverished states, and south of the equator, environmental problems are being experienced unequally. States bordering on oceans and close to sea level in elevation, as well as places with water shortages are experiencing the most serious problems. In these respects, more of the same is really more of the same "squared." Current features of the world system are pushed into the future on a gradually deteriorating trajectory.

The second scenario presented in chapter 7 is a "Pax Americana II" story. As noted in chapter 4, it is possible for system leaders to repeat— or, at least, it has occurred once before in the case of Britain in the eighteenth and nineteenth centuries. We hasten to remind the reader that a system leader is not as powerful as an all-dominating hegemon. Historically, system leaders have only slowly grown stronger than their competitors. In earlier centuries, system leaders predominated in terms of economic innovation (but not in economic size) and global-reach/naval capabilities (again, not the same thing as the size of the armed forces). In this sense, Britain was the leading source of economic innovation in Atlantic and Asian-European commerce prior to the development of the Industrial Revolution late in the eighteenth century. Whether a future system leader can repeat in two industrial or postindustrial revolution eras remains to be seen.

What might we expect in a second Pax Americana? Martin Jacques has a useful list of the characteristics of what he refers to as "American global hegemony" in his book imagining a Sinocentric world might.[4] Most of his entries are quite useful for constructing a story about a resurgence of a US-centric world order, perhaps because near the top of his list are emphases on economic innovation and naval/space leadership. The Jacques list in table 11.3 will look familiar to anyone who has read the Pax Americana II scenario

A significant spurt of radical economic innovation puts the United States back into the world economy's driver's seat. The spurt is focused on biotechnological-nanotechnological developments that fundamentally alter the way in which economic life is conducted. New automobiles, increasingly less reliant on petroleum, and new computers, no longer handicapped by space and size limitations on how many chips can be placed on a board, signal the wholesale revamping of these key industries. Major advances in medicine and food production also contribute to this growth

TABLE 11.3. **Selected characteristics of United States global hegemony, according to Martin Jacques**

Characteristics
World's largest economy
One of world's highest gross domestic product per head
World's most technologically advanced economy and also most innovative, as exemplified by Silicon Valley
World's strongest military power, which, based on its maritime and air strength, enables it to exercise its influence in every region of the world
Its global power means that it is a key factor in the calculations and attitudes of more or less every country in the world. All countries, as a consequence, enjoy limited sovereignty.
International economic system was predominantly designed and shaped by it and its rules are still largely determined by it
Home to the best universities in the world and has long attracted some of the most able global talent
English has become the global lingua franca largely because of its power and appeal
Hollywood dominates the global film market and, to a rather lesser extent, that of television as well
Corporate brand names like Google, Microsoft, Coca-Cola, and Walmart tend to predominate over those of other nations
Not only by far the most important country in the world, its largest city is also, de facto, the world's capital
Its values often enjoy a preponderant global influence

Source: Based on Martin Jacques, *When China Rules the World: The End of the Western World and the Birth of a New Global Order* (New York: Penguin, 2009), 367.

wave. The return of surplus wealth facilitates a revitalization of the US Navy and the space program (with help from allies on the latter front). Some revitalization of the United Nations (UN) takes place.

In this scenario, the Diaoyu crisis in 2025, the twenty-first-century equivalent of the Cold War's 1962 Missile Crisis has the Chinese back down in the face of US resolve to protect Japan from a Chinese threat. Subsequent interventions in South Asia, Africa, and the Arctic indicate that the world has not necessarily become a highly peaceful place. Nor was the earlier Pax America I in the post-1945 era.

It seems worthwhile to break from the chapter order and move directly to the "Pax Sinica" scenario sketched in chapter 9. The reason is that our Pax Sinica story is the mirror image of Pax Americana II. In the Pax Sinica scenario, it is China that ushers in a surge of radical new technology. The Chinese version has some overlap with the US specialization, especially in terms of auto and food production innovations. Distinctive to the Chinese economy, however, are emphases on pharmaceuticals, desalination, and the surplus cash to purchase a large number of founding American multinationals. The acquisition of the leading technological edge allows China to overcome the problems that it has experienced in developing a competitive navy and also finances what becomes a monopoly in space. International organizations are selectively revitalized under Chinese auspices.

In Pax Sinica, the Chinese win the 2025 Diaoyu crisis. The United States decides not to risk nuclear war over Japan's claims to islands in the East China Sea. By and large, this decision signals a withdrawal of the United States from East Asia, although not the Pacific. Subsequent Chinese interventions in South Asia, Africa, and the Arctic tend to work in the Chinese favor.

Returning to the chapter order, in chapter 8, one manifestation of diminishing relative clout on the part of the United States is the emergence of new major powers and the development of a more explicit multipolar system than already exists. US retrenchment and a virtual withdrawal from Asia is another. Structural decay is accompanied by regional bipolarization (the pairing off of China-Russia and India-Japan), increased rivalry, and disputes over territorial claims. All three of these early indicators have been observed before. Bipolarization creates a local structure in which a conflict between any members of the opposing sides can be transmitted to the other members, or all the local major powers. Rivalry is neither necessary nor sufficient for the onset of warfare, but rivals have opposed each in about 75 percent of the last two centuries of warfare. But it is not just rivalry that is problematic. It is a field of rivalries operating simultaneously that creates opportunities for nonlinear and diffused escalations of conflict. Finally, territorial disputes have been singled out as the leading common denominator of war onsets in the nineteenth and twentieth centuries. States may be prepared to fight about other issues but appear to have a special propensity for fighting about space. In this particular case, fighting about space is clearly wrapped into fighting about relative position as well.

Conflict-constraining features, for the most part, hardly seem to matter in this scenario. Yet they are very much present. The problem is that they are present in very weak forms. China is portrayed as autocratic in the future as it is today. This means that one of the three legs of the Kantian tripod does not come into play. Since the antagonists are not democratic dyads, the democratic peace is not relevant. The antagonisms of multiple mixed pairs of democracies and an autocracy suggest a greater probability of conflict rather than a lessened one, if earlier history is any guide.

A second Kantian leg, international organizations (IGOs), is portrayed as having experienced some reform with new major powers admitted to the UN Security Council. One of the main liabilities of the U.N. however remains unchanged—the ability of one major power to block Security Council activity. But even if no veto existed, it is not clear what the UN could do to intervene once the Chinese decide that India must be punished for its transgression. One of the minor ironies of this scenario is that it was a UN team that first reported the probability of oil and gas in the vicinity of the Senkaku/Diaoyu Islands.

Economic interdependence is part of the scenario. Concerns about the costs of disrupting trade and investments play some role but are not seen as likely to be definitive in blocking any conflictual activity. The other side of interdependence, increasing competition in producing and marketing similar products, is also in evidence as a source of friction.

Nor are the prohibitive costs of a major nuclear exchange ignored. The general idea is that the horrors of a previous war are not necessarily enough to deter subnuclear warfare. The question then becomes whether the antagonists will find themselves with their backs to a wall and nuclear option seems the only conceivable way out.

Finally, chapter 10 depicts a liberal peace, ironically with a strong nonliberal, Chinese flavor. China becomes the world economy's leader in trade volume and as a source of capital, investment, and lending. But this does not mean that economic innovation and global reach capabilities are equally dominated by China. After experiencing another major global recession and considerable conflict over trading barriers, regional institutions prove critical in developing new ways to facilitate order in trade. While Chinese autocracy does loosen somewhat, China does not adopt democracy. Its authoritarian capitalism model, on the contrary, is increasingly seen as a viable alternative to the earlier favoritism shown for liberal democracy.

The liberal peace scenario is not entirely pacific either. There are some clashes, most noticeably between the United States and China over supporting client states in Southeast Asia. Generally, though, military conflict between major powers is not all that visible. This may or may not be due to nuclear deterrence, which is hard to gauge in the absence of a crisis threatening to escalate into nuclear war

Collectively, the scenarios can be deconstructed into three sets of basic parts. The "heavy lifting" is done by the primary structural drivers and the selected predetermined elements. Scenario plausibility is achieved in part by featuring elements that can be extrapolated from ongoing trends. That is, the stories are more plausible, the more we are able to see how the processes emphasized stem from present day developments. Two manifestations of decline are featured in table 11.4 along with some nine

TABLE 11.4. **Scenarios and elements**

Scenarios	More of the same (chapter 6)	Pax Americana II (chapter 6)	Transition War (chapter 7)	Pax Sinica (chapter 8)	Liberal peace (chapter 9)
Primary drivers					
Technological innovation deconcentration	Slow	Reversed	Yes	Yes	Yes
Global-reach capability deconcentration	Yes	Reversed	Yes	Yes	Yes
Predetermined elements					
Multipolarity and the rise of new major powers	Yes	Not emphasized	Yes	Not emphasized	Not emphasized
Bipolarization of major powers	No	No	Yes	No	No
Multiple, intensified rivalries	Not emphasized	Not emphasized	Yes	Not emphasized	Not emphasized
Major power crises	No	Yes	Yes	Yes	No
Climate problems/ increasing scarcities of energy resources and water	Yes	Yes	Yes	Yes	Yes
Challenger dissatisfaction	Diverted by local problems	Possibly but rendered less than relevant	Strong	No	Limited
Incumbent threat perception	Limited	No	Strong	Possibly but rendered less than relevant	Limited
Democratic peace	Not applicable	Not applicable	Not applicable	Not applicable	Not applicable
Economic interdependence	Not emphasized	Yes	Yes	Yes	Yes
International institutions	Not emphasized	Some	Not emphasized	Some	Yes
Nuclear deterrence	Maybe	Maybe	Not yet clear	Maybe	Untested

TABLE 11.5. **Predetermined elements and critical uncertainties**

Predetermined elements	Critical uncertainties
Multipolarity and the rise of new powers	Pace of new powers rise
Bipolarization of the major powers	Extent
Multiple rivalries	Intensification
Major power crises	Stakes and outcomes
Challenger dissatisfaction	Extent
Incumbent system leader threat perception	Extent
Democratic peace	Relevance?
Economic interdependence	Extent and dual nature as both facilitating and discouraging conflict
International institutions	Reform and revitalization?
Nuclear deterrence	Nuclear accidents/temptation to employ in limited fashion/full exchange

predetermined elements. The decline drivers are almost constants, even though they take on different values, in terms of their presence in the story line. The predetermined elements are more variable. The only two constants in this group are the presence of resource scarcities and the absence of a democratic peace effect. One could add nuclear deterrence to the list but its effects are highly conjectural. The others are sometimes there and sometimes not. As a consequence, each scenario represents a distinctive mix of primary and secondary drivers.

But other things could happen that would alter what we think is possible and probable at the present. This is where the "critical uncertainties" come into play. How or to what extent they are present varies across scenarios. The critical uncertainties shape the effects the predetermined elements have. Are they accelerating or diminishing? How quickly? Are they intensifying or staying about the same? Table 11.5 summarizes the "predetermined elements" and "critical uncertainties" built into the five scenarios of chapters 7–10.

Thus, we assume that there will be some degree of climate deterioration and increasing scarcities that could very well influence general rates of economic growth. Greater degrees of scarcity and slower growth should aggravate general conflict propensities. Climate deterioration could be much worse. Oil could become scarcer much more quickly just as alternative energy resources could come on line much more quickly. Presumably, the petroleum age is closing out just as steam gave way to petroleum in the nineteenth and early twentieth centuries. How quickly that occurs will depend on various considerations, such as consumer demand, the size of exploitable reserves, and the development of new energy resources. Water-supply problems in certain parts of the world, on the other hand, seem nearly inevitable. For that reason, water plays a bigger role in our scenario than does oil/natural gas, but increasing scarcity in both areas is thought to be likely.

Still, the most important feature in our stories is what happens to technological innovation and global-reach capabilities—the main manifestations of systemic leadership decline. Are they concentrated within one state as in the past? If so, which state is more likely to be the system leader? A reconcentrating incumbent has different implications than a concentrating challenger. At what pace is concentration (deconcentration) proceeding? Again, the implications are different for incumbents and challengers. But without relative decline of some sort, there is no transition story to tell.

Some type of multipolarity seems guaranteed but there are various possibilities. One could have multipolarity in which the major powers were becoming increasingly equal in capability. Or, the exact opposite could occur in which one major power was becoming increasingly predominant yet falling short of anything resembling unipolarity. New major powers seem highly likely, but at what pace is their emergence? How dissatisfied are they likely to be with the systemic status quo? We also need to ask to what extent are the major powers bipolarized? One basic cleavage which encourages states to align on one side or the other should be more conducive to conflict than circumstances in which there is no pattern to the alignment of the major powers. There is also the question of which major powers are rivals of one another and how intense are the rivalries. Intensifying multiple rivalries aggravate conflict propensities in nonlinear ways. Last but not least in this category are the major powers engaging in crises that could become showdown confrontations for transitional wars.

The constraint category encompasses four elements. The Kantian trio is pretty much a mixed bag of effects for transitional situations. There does not seem to be much reason to anticipate a democratic peace playing a strong role if the main opponents are not both democracies. International institutions currently are quite limited in what they can do to limit or reduce conflict propensities between major powers. What is the probability that substantial reform is in the offing?

Economic interdependence has a dual nature. It can render potential interruptions of commercial exchange very costly and thus discourage conflict. But it can also increase the incentives for conflict if the main protagonists find themselves quarreling over access to resources, barriers to trade, or the production and marketing of similar products. In this respect, economic interdependence is both a potential facilitating and constraining factor. Which effect will have more impact? What is the net impact likely to be?

We assume some strong reluctance to employ nuclear weapons, given the devastating implications of their use, but we cannot be sure that reluctance is sufficient to assume absolute nuclear deterrence. Accidents are possible. The instability paradox seems to have some support as well. That is that nuclear capability encourages the use of conventional weaponry in the sense that an attacker will believe that a nuclear-armed opponent will show restraint in responding in order to avoid the possibility of escalation to the level of a nuclear confrontation. Then there are possible temptations to use nuclear weapons in a limited fashion, either out of desperation or strategy. Should that happen, can we assume that a full-fledged exchange is still unlikely?

The third type of story feature is the wild card. Taiwan could declare its independence. North Korea could attack South Korea, or vice versa. Conflict could erupt again in the South China Sea. Russia could decide that it cannot permit the gradual loss of its Far East. Any of these potential occurrences could throw our scenarios completely off their fictional tracks. In developing the scenarios the way we did, our bet is that the wild cards, other than the ones that we employed, are simply that—occurrences with low probability or, at least, lower probability than some of the occurrences we are predicting as likely or possible. The main exception to this generalization is the 2025 Diaoyu crisis, which appears in two story lines, with variable outcomes. This particular wild card is central to the stories in which it appears and the outcome of the crisis makes considerable difference to how the two stories turn out.

The "So What" Question

Our position is that the forward-reasoning model idea is helpful, with considerable elaboration needed here and there, in constructing what we think are plausible scenarios. We do not predict that our scenarios will come to pass—only that they could happen and can give us valuable clues about the process by which the world system can transit from one side of a power transition to the other. Structuring the scenarios has been facilitated by the discipline imposed by considerations about drivers, predetermined elements, critical uncertainties, wild cards, and outcomes. It is always possible to tell a story about the future. Science fiction writers have been doing it for some time. But it is another thing altogether to attempt to harness future storytelling to social science interests—in this case, what does international relations theory tell us about something that might happen a generation or more down the road? That is what the forward-reasoning approach provides—an infrastructure for telling stories in a theoretical vein.

A related point is that it is possible to construct a war scenario without too much difficulty, allowing us to assess the pushing and pulling effects of variables likely to promote or constrain transitional conflict. In our scenarios, the conflict-promoting factors tend to win hands down. The constraining factors—the Kantian tripod and nuclear deterrence—exert little in the way of discernible constraint, with a few exceptions, except in the "liberal peace" scenario. Such an outcome may tell us something about the limitations of Kantian arguments and nuclear deterrence for systemic-transition cases. Ultimately, democracy, economic interdependence, and IGOs, along with nuclear deterrence, may interact to transform the world. Along the way to that transformed world, there are apt to be some problems and parts of the world that are less than amenable to these constraints. A twenty-first-century transitional war, for instance, may be one of those problems that are little affected by constraining processes that are highly uneven in application.

If our selected factors that are thought to promote conflict lead to a transitional war, does that mean that their theoretical importance is vindicated? The answer is no. It only means that their presence in the story may contribute to the scenario outcome. We need to compare and contrast these facilitating and constraining factors in the scenarios leading to the other possible outcomes in order to get a better sense of their importance, at least for this particular question.

The pattern that emerges allows us to simplify the things for which to watch:

1. Reconcentrated technological innovation and global reach capabilities, other things being equal, are likely to lead to a new or reinvigorated world order with less probability of transitional war; deconcentrated movement is likely to lead to a higher probability of transition and, other things being equal, transitional warfare.
2. Bipolarization and multiple, intensified rivalries, other things being equal, are likely to lead to a movement toward transitional warfare.

3. Chinese perceptions of dissatisfaction with the systemic status quo and/or US perceptions of threat from the challenger, other things being equal, are likely to lead to a higher probability of transitional conflict and perhaps warfare.

4. Continuing and increased economic interdependence, as well as revived IGOs for at least trade management purposes, other things being equal, are likely to encourage movement toward liberal peace with less probability of transitional warfare.

5. Continuing prevalence of the appearance of nuclear deterrence, other things being equal, is likely to lead to a diminished probability of transitional warfare.

6. Numbers 1–5 interact with one another and other things are rarely equal. What is least clear is the relative weight of the drivers, not so much in theoretical terms, but how future events play themselves out in the real world.

Not too long ago, Aaron Friedberg suggested that informed academic opinion on the implications of the rise of China could be segmented by international relations theoretical paradigm and optimism/pessimism.[5] Combining paradigmatic allegiance and attitudes about the future yields a number of different groups. Optimistic liberals, for instance, stress the constraining effect of interdependence. Pessimistic liberals point to the dangers of an authoritarian China. Optimistic realists argue that China's capabilities are less than they seem, while pessimistic realists note that China's capabilities are improving and, in any event, that there are always security dilemmas to sustain tension and otherwise cause trouble.

What is most striking is that the basis for being in one group or another is predicated on hunches about very general processes and/or very specific country characteristics. But whether future Chinese decision makers might feel insecure or future US decision makers might give in to crusading impulses seems rather illusory bases on which to form expectations. On other issues, we simply have no idea whether US or Chinese relative capabilities will be limited or foreign policy aims will be restricted twenty years from now. Similarly, we do not know whether a security dilemma might go awry or whether the long-term strategic culture of China will prevail in vastly different contexts than China has experienced in the past.

Ideally, we should be able to do better than relying on the vagaries of pretheoretical paradigms and our instinctual attitudes about the future. Analyzing future possibilities is guesswork but can at least be informed by a strong theoretical base. If our disciplinary studies have value, we should be able to develop theoretically based expectations about how the future might work. The ones that we rely on in this analysis are certainly not the only ones that could be developed. Perhaps even some of the ideas suggested in table 11.4 could be used to generate alternative expectations. But the point is that we should be developing theoretically informed expectations about what may well prove to be one, if not the, most significant international relations problem of the century.

Transitional warfare, or Pax Americanas/Sinicas, or liberal peace are neither predetermined, inevitable, or near to hand. We have the opportunity to observe the development of processes that might or might not lead to such outcomes. There are a number of "early indicators" for which to watch. In this respect a scenario is not just a fictional tale of what might come to pass. It is also a set of clues to interpret real world developments as they emerge and evolve. Even if the particular trajectories that we outline in our scenarios do not take place, we may be able to arrive at an assessment about where the scenarios went right or wrong. In the final analysis, it is not so much a question of whether the world system zigzags the way we think it might. The real question is whether we can decipher the zigzags theoretically and as they occur. That goal remains our principal mission in this ongoing project.

Notes

Chapter One

1. The source for great power status is Jack S. Levy, *War in the Modern Great Power System, 1495–1975* (Lexington: University Press of Kentucky, 1983), 48. Austria dropped out in 1918 while the Ottoman Empire left the great power ranks in 1699. Spain left in 1808.

2. The Netherlands left the great power system, according to Levy, *War in the Modern Great Power System*, in 1713, Sweden in 1721, Italy in 1943, and Japan in 1945.

3. We assume that states listed as great powers in 1495 entered the great power list at some point prior to 1495 and, therefore, are excluded from this examination of new entries.

4. See, e.g., R. J. B. Bosworth, *Italy the Least of the Great Powers: Italian Foreign Policy Before the First World War* (Cambridge: Cambridge University Press, 2005).

5. This process is similar to the tendency for ancient rulers to demonstrate their coercive prowess early in their rule as a demonstration effect thereby avoiding the need to rely on force constantly thereafter.

6. We assume here a distinction between regional and global politics. At the regional level, actors have tended to focus on local territorial expansion, with regional hegemony the ultimate prize. At the global level, a few actors have focused on long-distance and interregional commerce. Predominance in trade and, later, industrial production are the primary goals. This distinction has gradually emerged over the past millennium. One of the implications is that there are regional elite states and global elite states, some of which have both statuses (as in the contemporary US regional position in North America and the lead position at the global level), but others have been either one or the other (examples are Austria, the Ottoman Empire, Sweden, Italy, and, to date, China).

7. Note that another one of our assumptions is that east-west trade initially between parts of Asia and Western Europe has betrayed an increasing level of economic interdependence throughout the past five hundred years.

8. See, for instance, George Modelski, "Enduring Rivalry in the Democratic Lineage: The Venice-Portugal Case," in *Great Power Rivalries*, ed. William R. Thompson (Columbia: University of South Carolina Press, 1999).

9. The Dutch decision was a reaction to the belated Spanish decision to close Iberian ports to Dutch shipping long after the Dutch Revolt had begun. The Dutch choice was one between accepting being closed out of Asian and Mediterranean markets that had earlier been accessed through Spanish ports or going around the Spanish ports and developing Dutch routes beyond Europe.

10. On Dutch foreign policy problems of this era, see Jack S. Levy, "Economic Competition, Domestic Politics, and Systemic Change," in *Great Power Rivalries*, ed. William R. Thompson, 172–200; Jack S. Levy and Salvatore Ali, "From Commercial Conflict to Strategic Rivalry to War: The Evolution of the Anglo-Dutch Rivalry, 1609–52," in *The Dynamics of Enduring Rivalries*, ed. Paul F. Diehl (Urbana: University of Illinois Press, 1999), 29–63; Charles H. Wilson, *Profit and Power: A Study of England and Dutch Wars* (London: Longmans, 1957); and Jonathan I. Israel, *Dutch Primacy in World Trade, 1585–1740* (Oxford: Clarendon Press,1989).

11. Incumbent system leaders, other things being equal, tend to focus on more direct threats, as opposed to more abstract threats. See William R. Thompson, "The Evolution of Political-Commercial Challenges in the Active Zone," *Review of International Political Economy* 4 (1997): 285–317.

12. The Anglo-Russian/Soviet rivalry de-escalation proved temporary while the Anglo-French and Anglo-American ones were permanent.

13. Soviet pilots flying North Korean planes in the Korean War appears to have been the sole exception. A series of limited proxy wars in developing countries might also be considered as a kind of indirect, surrogate US-Soviet military competition.

14. This statement makes it sound as if Politburo members cast a ballot about whether to admit that they were losing the Cold War competition and unanimously agreed to attempt a different strategy. That is hardly what happened. There was disagreement among Soviet elites over preferred strategies and it is not inconceivable that different choices could have been made that would have led to the continuation of the Cold War. As it turned out, owing to the combination of internal fissures and external pressures, the Soviet adoption of a less confrontational approach was not something over which Soviet decision-makers had full control.

15. See, e.g., William R. Thompson, "The Evolution of Systemic Leadership, World Politics, and International Relations Theory: The Unipolarity Question," *International Studies Review* 8:1 (2006): 1–22.

16. John Mueller, *Retreat from Doomsday: The Obsolescence of Major War* (New York: Basic Books, 1989).

17. Aaron L. Freidberg, "The Future of U.S.-China Relations: Is Conflict Inevitable?" *International Security* 30 (Fall 2005): 8.

18. Avery Goldstein, "Parsing China's Rise: International Circumstances and National Attributes," in Robert S. Ross and Zhu Feng, eds., *China's Ascent: Power, Security and the Future of International Politics*, 55.

19. More recently, however, Freidberg has argued that China's rise will lead to a marginalization of the United States if it is unable to develop a more effective strategy of coping with China's improving status than it has demonstrated so far. See Aaron L. Friedberg, *A Contest for Supremacy: China, America, and the Struggle for Mastery in Asia* (New York: W. W. Norton, 2011).

20. There are, of course, many different positions on this issue. Views anticipating both transition and/or intensive conflict include Samuel P. Huntington, *The Clash of Civilizations and the Remaking of the World Order* (New York: Simon and Schuster, 1996); Richard Bernstein and Ross H. Munro, *The Long Conflict with China* (New York: Alfred A. Knopf, 1997); Steven W. Mosher, *Hegemon: China's Plan to Dominate Asia and the World* (San Francisco: Encounter Books, 2000); John Mearsheimer, *The Tragedy of Great Power Politics* (New York: Norton, 2001); Ronald L. Tammen, Jacek Kugler, Douglas Lemke, Allan C. Stam III, Carole Alsharabati, Mark A. Abhollahian, Brian Efird, and A. F. K. Organski, *Power Transitions: Strategies for the Twenty-First Century* (New York: Chatham House, 2000); and Martin Jacques, *When China Rules the World: The End of the Western World and the Birth of a New Global Order* (New York: Penguin, 2009). Dissenters are as many as their arguments are varied. But, basically, they see China as unlikely to catch up (no transition) or becoming reasonably well integrated into the systemic status quo (limited conflict). Examples include Andrew J. Nathan and Robert S. Ross, *The Great Wall and the Empty Fortress: China's Search for Security* (New York: W. W. Norton, 1997); Gerald Segal, "Does China Matter?," *Foreign Affairs* 78:5 (September/October 1999): 24–36; Robert S. Ross, "The Geography of the Peace: East Asia in the Twenty-first Century," *International Security* 23 (Spring 1999): 81–118 and "Bipolarity and Balancing in East Asia," in T. V. Paul, James J. Wirtz, and Michael Fortmann, eds., *Balance of Power: Theory and Practice in the 21st Century* (Stanford: Stanford University Press, 2004); Gordon G. Chang, *The Coming Collapse of China* (New York: Random House, 2001); Thomas J. Christensen, "Posing Problems Without Catching Up: China's Rise and Challenges for U.S. Security Policy," *International Security* 25 (Spring 2001): 5–40; Alastair I. Johnston, "Is China a Status Quo Power?" *International Security* 27 (2003): 5–56; Goldstein, *Rising to the Challenge*; David L. Shambaugh, "Return to the Middle Kingdom? China and Asia in the Early Twenty-first Century," in David L. Shambaugh, ed., *Power Shift: China and Asia's New Dynamics* (Berkeley: University of California Press, 2005); Richard N. Rosecrance, "Power and International Relations: The Rise of China and Its Effects," *International Studies Perspectives* 7:1 (2006): 31–35; Jonathan Kirschner, "The Consequences of China's Economic Rise for Sino-U.S. Relations," in Robert S. Ross and Zhu Feng, eds., *China's Ascent: Power, Security, and the Future of International Politics*; Robert J. Art, "The United States

and the Rise of China: Implications for the Long Haul," in Robert S. Ross and Zhu Feng, eds., *China's Ascent: Power, Security, and the Future of International Politics*; G. John Ikenberry, "The Rise of China: Power, Institutions and the Western Order," in Robert S. Ross and Zhu Feng, eds., *China's Ascent: Power, Security, and the Future of International Politics*; Steve Chan, *China, the U.S., and the Power Transition Theory* (London: Routledge, 2008); Steve Chan and Brock Tesseman, "Relative Decline: Why Does It Induce War or Sustain Peace," in William R. Thompson, ed., *Systemic Transitions: Past, Present, and Future* (New York: Palgrave Macmillan, 2009); Joseph S. Nye, "China's Century is Not Yet Upon Us," *Financial Times*, May 19, 2010; Charles Glaser, "Will China's Rise Lead to War? Why Realism Does Not Mean Pessimism," *Foreign Affairs* 90:2 (2011): 80–91; Randall L. Schweller and Xiaoyu Pu, "After Unipolarity: China's Visions of International Order in an Era of U.S. Decline," *International Security* 36:1 (Summer 2011): 41–72; and Steve Chan, *Looking for Balance: China, The United States, and Power Balancing in East Asia* (Stanford: Stanford University Press, 2012). Another important dissenting position focuses less on China's strengths and more on the relative strengths of the US position. A good example is Stephen G. Brooks and William Wohlforth, *World Out of Balance: International Relations and the Challenge of American Primacy* (Princeton: Princeton University Press, 2008). For Chinese perspective, see Zheng Bijan, "China's Peaceful Rise to Great Power Status," *Foreign Affairs* 84 (2005): 18–24; Tang Shipeng, "From Offensive to Defensive Realism: A Social Evolutionary Interpretation of China's Security Strategy," in Robert Ross and Zhu Feng, eds., *China's Ascent: Power, Security, and the Future of International Politics*. There are, of course, arguments that it all depends on how things work out. See, for instance, Bin Yu, "China and Its Asian Neighbors," in Y. Deng and F. Wang, eds., *In the Eyes of the Dragon: China Views the World* (Lanham: Rowman and Littlefield, 1999); Michael D. Swaine and Ashley J. Tellis, *Interpreting China's Grand Strategy: Past, Present, and Future* (Santa Monica: Rand Corporation, 2000); David Scott, *The "Chinese Century"?: The Challenge to Global Order* (London: Palgrave Macmillan, 2007); and Aaron L. Friedberg, "The Geopolitics of Strategic Asia, 2000–2020," in Ashley J. Tellis, Andrew Marble, and Travis Tanner, eds., *Strategic Asia 2010–11: Asia's Rising Power and America's Continued Purpose* (Seattle: National Bureau of Asian Research, 2010).

Chapter Two

1. Richards J. Heur, Jr., and Randolph H. Pherson, *Structured Analytic Techniques for Intelligence Analysis* (Washington, DC: Congressional Quarterly Press, 2011), 119. For useful methodological comparisons of estimates, forecasts, and scenarios, see Sam J. Tangredi, *Futures of War* (New York: Xlibris, 2008), chap. 3. *Estimates*, which tend to be shorter term, examine current information to try to iden-

tify future events; *forecasts* are longer term and tend to relay on analysis of existing trends; and, *scenarios* also tend to be longer term and more holistic.

2. Steven Bernstein, Richard Ned Lebow, Janice Gross Stein, and Steven Weber, "God Gave Physics the Easy Problems: Adapting Social Science to an Unpredictable World," *European Journal of International Relations* 6:1 (2000): 53.

3. Bernstein et al., "God Gave Physics the Easy Problems," 58.

4. Bernstein et al., "God Gave Physics the Easy Problems," 55.

5. Paul Humphreys, "Aleatory Explanations," *Synthese* 48:2 (August 1981): 225–32, and "Aleatory Explanations Expanded," *Proceedings of the Biennial Meeting of the Philosophy of Science Association* (1982): 208–23.

6. For a useful discussion of Russett's use of these terms, see Bruce Russett, "Violence and Disease: Trade as Suppressor to Conflict When Suppressors Matter," in Edward D. Mansfield and Brian M. Pollins, eds., *Economic Interdependence and International Conflict: New Perspectives on an Enduring Debate* (Ann Arbor: University of Michigan Press, 2003), 165–68; and Michael P. Colaresi, Karen Rasler, and William R. Thompson, *Strategic Rivalries in World Politics* (Cambridge: Cambridge University Press, 2007), chap.10.

7. Aaron Friedberg, "The Future of U.S.-China Relations: Is Conflict Inevitable?" *International Security* 30:2 (2005): 40.

8. Bernstein et al., "God Gave Physics the Easy Problems," 54.

9. Steven A. Rosell, *Renewing Governance: Governing by Learning in the Information Age* (New York: Oxford University Press, 1999), 122.

10. Bernstein et al.

11. James Kitfield, "Game Changers," *National Journal*, September 7, 2007.

12. This approach is consistent with Lempert: "Scenarios often come in groups that illuminate how the future might play out if key unanticipated events break one way or another." See Robert Lempert, "Can Scenarios Help Policymakers Be Both Bold and Careful?," in Francis Fukuyama, ed., *Blindside: How to Anticipate Forcing Events and Wild Cards in Global Politics* (Washington, DC: Brookings Institution Press, 2007), 110.

13. Richards J. Heur, Jr., and Randolph H. Pherson, *Structured Analytic Techniques for Intelligence Analysis* (Washington, DC: Congressional Quarterly Press, 2011), 126–27.

14. Heur and Pherson actually provide a list of ten steps that we have compressed to eight. We have also altered their instructions somewhat but again only to compress the messages, not to change their intent.

15. For a range of alternative approaches, see Liam Anderson and Gareth Stansfield, *The Future of Iraq: Dictatorship, Democracy, or Division?* (New York: Palgrave Macmillan, 2004); and Robert J. Shapiro, *Futurecast: How Superpowers, Populations, and Globalizations Will Change Your World By the Year 2020* (New York: St. Martin's, 2008), which provide scenario and forecasts that do not appear to be explicitly guided by theoretical considerations; see also George Friedman, *The*

Next 100 Years: A Forecast for the 21st Century (New York: Doubleday, 2009), for a forecast that does seem to be guided by theoretical considerations but not in a very explicit fashion. As we were preparing the final copy of this book, a similar, although much more abbreviated, approach to our own was discovered in Carl J. Dahlman, *The World Under Pressure: How China and India Are Influencing the Global Economy and Environment* (Stanford: Stanford University Press, 2012), 210.

Chapter Three

1. See I. F. Clarke, *Voices Prophesying War: Future War, 1763–3749* (New York: Oxford University Press, 1993), *The Tale of the Next Great War, 1871–1914: Fictions of Future Warfare and Battles Still-to-Come* (Syracuse: Syracuse University Press, 1996), and *Great War with Germany, 1890–1940: Fictions and Fantasies of the War-to-Come* (Liverpool: Liverpool University Press, 1997).

2. One US-China war scenario that we have omitted from scrutiny is found in Richard C. Bush and Michael E. O'Hanlon, *A War Like No Other: The Truth About China's Challenge to America* (Hoboken: John Wiley, 2007), 93–97. We omit it because it is advanced in a speculative manner and used to illustrate more general points about policy. David Shambaugh offers five scenarios on a Chinese attack on Taiwan, but the point is to illustrate different military modes of attack (as in amphibious assault versus a strategic strike). This sort of discussion is also not what we have in mind as fictional scenarios. See David Shambaugh, *Modernizing China's Military: Progress, Problems, and Prospects* (Berkeley: University of California Press, 2002), 319–27. William H. Overholt in *Asia, America, and the Transformation of Geopolitics* (Cambridge: Cambridge University Press, 2008), 265–94, offers some interesting scenarios that look like the ones we will develop later in this book. However, there are two important differences. Overholt's scenario drivers are countries or important actors, whereas ours are processes that have some theoretical sanction. He also does not seem to do anything with his scenarios other than to offer them as illustrations of alternative futures. Much the same thing occurs in National Intelligence Council, *Global Trends 2025: A Transformed World* (Washington, DC: U.S. Government Printing Office, 2008). Our scenarios are meant to interact with our theoretical concerns. Finally, Mohan Malik also offers five fairly brief scenarios for possible outcomes in Chinese and Indian interactions through 2040. In this case, the approach is focused more on the 2040 outcome and less on how it came about. See Mohan Malik, *China and India: Great Power Rivals* (Boulder: First Forum Press/Lynne Rienner, 2011), 397–404.

3. Compare the views on precipitants, for instance, aired in William R. Thompson, "A Streetcar Named Sarajevo: Catalysts, Multiple Causation Chains, and Rivalry Structures," *International Studies Quarterly* 47:3 (2003): 453–74; and Richard Ned Lebow, "A Data Set Named Desire: A Reply to William R. Thompson," *International Studies Quarterly* 47:3 (2003): 475–78.

4. Caspar Weinberger and Peter Schweizer, *The Next War* (Washington, DC: Regnery Publishing, 1996).

5. Chuck DeVore and Steven W. Mosher, *China Attacks*, 2nd ed. (Haverty: Infinity, 2001).

6. Humphrey Hawksley and Simon Holberton, *Dragon Strike: A Novel of the Coming War With China* (New York: St. Martin's Press, 1997).

7. Humphrey Hawksley, *Dragon Fire* (London: Macmillan, 2000).

8. Samuel P. Huntington, *The Clash of Civilizations and the Remaking of World Order* (New York: Simon and Schuster, 1996).

9. Eric L. Harry, *Invasion* (New York: Jove Books, 2000); Carl Berryman, *2013: World War III* (Bloomington: Author House, 2004).

10. It is not clear what had happened to American bases in Okinawa. Perhaps they had been abandoned along with the US departure from South Korea.

11. Andrew F. Krepinevich, *Seven Deadly Scenarios: A Military Futurist Explores War in the 21st Century* (New York: Bantam, 2009).

12. Rhoe Mallock, *The Eagle in Autumn: A Chronicle of the South China Sea War of 2022* (New York: iUniverse, 2005).

13. Berryman, *2013: World War III*.

14. Note that most of the scenarios that have been published thus far depict events in years that have already passed or are about to pass. The 2022 scenario that casts India as the main winner in a US-China confrontation could not possibly come about in the time frame (less than a decade in the future) indicated, at least in terms of its depiction of Indian economic and naval prowess.

15. The necessity of these ingredients may not seem equally apparent to all readers but the discussion in chapters three and four should contribute further to our case.

16. So far, fictional scenarios tend to fall back on a conspiracy approach to the unfolding of events. Simultaneous developments in, say, Korea and Kashmir, are united by Chinese subversion as opposed to happenstance.

Chapter Four

1. See, e.g., Robert Gilpin, *War and Change in World Politics* (Cambridge: Cambridge University Press, 1981); Charles F. Doran, *Systems in Crisis* (Cambridge: Cambridge University Press, 1991); Dale C. Copeland, *The Origins of Major War* (Ithaca: Cornell University Press, 2000); Robert J. Art, "The United States and the Rise of China: Implications for the Long Haul," in Robert S. Ross and Zhu Feng, eds., *China's Ascent: Power, Security and the Future of International Politics* (Ithaca: Cornell University Press, 2008); and R. Ned Lebow, *Why Nations Fight* (Cambridge: Cambridge University Press, 2010).

2. On offensive realism, see John J. Mearsheimer, *The Tragedy of Great Power Politics* (New York: Norton, 2001). The challenger/transition model is developed

in William R. Thompson, "The Evolution of Political-Economic Challenges in the Active Zone," *Review of International Political Economy* 4 (1997): 286–318, *The Emergence of the Global Political Economy* (London: Routledge, 2000), and "Structural Preludes to Systemic Transition Since 1494," in William R. Thompson, ed., *Systemic Transitions: Past, Present, and Future* (New York: Palgrave-Macmillan, 2009). For leadership long-cycle theory, see George Modelski, *Long Cycles in World Politics* (London: Macmillan, 1987); and George Modelski and William R. Thompson, *Sea Power in Global Politics, 1494–1993* (London: Macmillan, 1988), and *Leading Sectors and World Power: The Coevolution of Global Politics and World Economics* (Columbia: University of South Carolina Press, 1996).

3. See A. F. K. Organski, *World Politics* (New York: Alfred A. Knopf, 1958); A. F. K. Organski and Jacek Kugler, *The War Ledger* (Chicago: University of Chicago Press, 1980); and Ronald L. Tammen, Jacek Kugler, Douglas Lemke, Allan C. Stam III, Carole Alsharabati, Mark A. Abdollahian, Brian Efird, and A. F. K. Organski, *Power Transitions: Strategies for the 21st Century* (New York: Chatham House, 2000).

4. Tammen et al., *Power Transitions*, 31.

5. Tieh-shang Lee, "China's Rising Military Power and Its Impact," in Baogang Guo and Chung-chian Teng, eds., *China's Quiet Rise: Peace Through Integration* (Lanham: Lexington Books, 2011). Lee assumes a 6.5 percent economic growth rate for China between 2004 and 2025, and a 5.5 percent growth rate between 2025 and 2050.

6. A state first catches up to another in power-transition terminology when its gross domestic product equals 80 percent of the other's.

7. Of course, these alliance groupings complicate the calculations. If one adds India to the US-led group, the calculations would change considerably. Similarly, adding Russia to China's relative power size would also lead to different computations. Lee also calculates a schedule for China overtaking the United States, Taiwan, and Japan in terms of military spending, an unorthodox emphasis by power-transition conventions. The schedule for military spending has China overtaking Japan in 2010, the United States in 2056, the combination of the United States and Taiwan in 2063, and the trio of the United States, Taiwan, and Japan in 2072. This schedule is predicated on the assumptions that China will allocate 10 percent of GDP to military spending until 2025 and 7 percent thereafter; Japan will allocate 5 percent of its GDP to military spending; the United States will devote 3 percent of its GDP to the military. Although the estimated Taiwanese economic growth rate is not disclosed, the "dangerous war zone," based on catching up in military expenditures is reduced to a relatively brief 2063–79 window. Lee believes the schedule based on military spending is a better predictor of when to expect conflict. Focusing solely on GDP means ignoring war-making capability, which is more directly related to the probability of conflict in East Asia.

8. This statement is not entirely correct. One of the extensions of the power-

transition research project has involved applying the principles to regional systems. Examples of this type of analysis are found in Tammen et al., *Power Transitions*, chap. 3; Douglas Lemke, *Regions of War and Peace* (Cambridge: Cambridge University Press, 2002); and Jonathan M. DiCicco and Jack S. Levy, "Power Shifts and Program Shifts: The Evolution of the Power Transition Research Program," *Journal of Conflict Resolution* 43 (1999): 691–92. A specific critique of power-transition theory in the context of the ascent of China may be found in Jack S. Levy, "Power Transition Theory and the Rise of China," in Robert S. Ross and Zhu Feng, eds., *China's Ascent: Power, Security, and the Future of International Politics* (Ithaca: Cornell University Press, 2008). Nevertheless, power-transition analysts assume that conflict diffuses down from global to regional levels but not up from regional to global levels. The challenger/transition model sees the problem as an interaction of global and regional dynamics.

9. One problem with this line of argument is that power-transition analysts, usually parenthetically, suggest that Britain overtook France at some point in the late eighteenth century, which led to the French Revolution and Napoleonic Wars. Lacking data on GDP, they are reluctant to pursue this possibility. Yet, since Britain had a smaller population than France, its transition had to be based primarily on economic development. But, if this is the case, the power-transition historical script has one case of transition based on economic development (Britain-France) and two cases of transition based on population and economic development (the successful and relatively nonconflictual US-Britain case and the unsuccessful, conflictual Germany-Britain case). The very small number of cases provides a rather shaky foundation for generalizing about economic development, population size, and power transitions.

10. For an excellent review and extension of the "war initiation" models developed in association with power-transition theory, see Andrew Wedeman, "Prospects for a Sino-American Transition War," in Kwang Il Baek, ed., *Comprehensive Security and Multilateralism in Post-Cold War East Asia* (Seoul: Korean Association of International Studies, 2000).

11. Tammen et al., *Power Transitions*, 18.

12. Ibid., 19.

13. For the development of the argument that power equals population multiplied by GNP/population, which, in turn, equals GNP, see Organski and Kugler, *War Ledger*, 34. They also report that their GNP indicator is highly correlated ($r = 0.86$), with a Correlates of War index of capability concentration that aggregates six indicators of military, industrial, and demographic standings.

14. See Organski and Kugler, *War Ledger*, 49. For the most part, the 80 percent rule seems to have been maintained in subsequent power-transition analyses.

15. The estimates are based on purchasing power parity converters to avoid problems encountered in using exchange rates. Details on the procedures used are found in Angus Maddison, *Monitoring the World Economy, 1820–1992* (Paris:

Organization for Economic and Co-operation and Development Centre, 1995), 162–69.

16. The relative size of Germany's economy vis-à-vis Britain measured in GDP terms was 47.1 percent in 1820, 48.6 percent in 1850, 45.7 percent in 1870, 46.1 percent in 1880, 49.2 percent in 1890, 56.2 percent in 1900, 67.6 percent in 1913, 56.1 percent in 1920, 69.3 percent in 1930, 76.9 percent in 1940, 62.0 percent in 1950, and 104.5 percent in 1960.

17. Mearsheimer, *The Tragedy of Great Power Politics*.

18. Hans Morgenthau is often regarded as the exemplar of human nature realism while Kenneth Waltz has surely created the foundation for defensive realism. See Hans Morgenthau, *Politics Among Nations: The Struggle for Power and Peace* (New York: Alfred A. Knopf, 1948, and subsequent editions); and Kenneth Waltz, *Theory of International Politics* (Reading: Addison-Wesley, 1979).

19. These same examples also suggest that, once these states had achieved regional hegemony, they then tried to move into adjacent regions until they were stopped by successful resistance. There are no offshore balancers in this particular set of actors.

20. The US's army prowess in the post–World War II era is the exception to this generalization.

21. Richard N. Rosecrance, "War and Peace," *World Politics* 55:1 (2002):143.

22. In "War and Peace," Rosecrance does not really take the US and British examples in a theoretical direction other than to say that they do not seem to fit the assumptions of offensive realism. Elsewhere, however, Rosecrance addresses the tendency to assume all states behave alike with a binary alternative, focusing on military-political and commercial behavioral emphases that comes closer to the mark. See Richard N. Rosecrance, *The Rise of the Trading State: Commerce and Conquest in the Modern World* (New York: Basic Books, 1986). Even though the historical application of the perspective differs from Rosecrance's own interpretation, this binary approach is adopted in Karen Rasler and William R. Thompson, *Puzzles of the Democratic Peace* (New York: Palgrave-Macmillan, 2005).

23. Although some of their leaders would have said that they were simply pursuing defensive realism.

24. On this topic, the boundary between empirical and normative theory is most unclear. Should the emphasis be placed on what major powers actually do or what they should do?

25. In a strategic rivalry, two states view each other as competitive enemies. The strategic rivalry information is found in William R. Thompson and David R. Dreyer, *Handbook of International Rivalries, 1494–2010* (Washington, DC: Congressional Quarterly Press, 2011). Levy's major power dating scheme is employed here. See Jack S. Levy, *War in the Modern Great Power System, 1495–1975* (Lexington: University Press of Kentucky, 1983).

26. Most people are familiar with the 1588 Armada attempt at invasion but there were, in fact, four different attempts in the 1580s and 1590s.

27. Aspiring regional hegemons in Europe contributed mightily to their own multiple front problems by taking on other foes before they had decisively defeated an early foe. Examples are the Spanish turning to fight in France just as they were approaching victory over the Dutch in the early 1590s or the Germans turning on the Soviet Union before they had taken care of Britain.

28. There are qualifications advanced in offensive realism. Major powers with second-strike nuclear capabilities have less fear. Major powers that are very distant and separated by water are less threatening. Distributions of power in which all states have roughly the same capability share are less likely to inspire fear and threat. More powerful states also have less to fear from weaker states as long as they are acting rationally and avoiding miscalculation.

29. Every once in a while there are hints in Mearsheimer's *The Tragedy of Great Power Politics* that technology plays some role. Chinese high technology will make the Chinese army more complex and proficient. The Soviet Union stumbled badly because it could not keep up with the West in information technology. Iron and steel are good indicators of wealth prior to the development of GDP indicators. But they remain only glimmers.

30. The major caveat, of course, is that when they did occur, they tended to last for thirty years on average.

31. Thompson, "The Evolution of Political-Economic Challenges in the Active Zone," *The Emergence of the Global Political Economy,* and "Structural Preludes to Systemic Transition Since 1494," in William R. Thompson, ed., *Systemic Transitions: Past, Present, and Future* (New York: Palgrave Macmillan, 2009)

32. Somebody in China is paying attention. People's Liberation Army Senior Colonel Liu Mingfu, the author of *The China Dream* (about China supplanting the United States as the number one power in the world), has stated: "The duel in the 21st century between China and the United States is over which one will be the global champion. In the past 500 years, different countries have emerged as the global champion—Portugal in the 16th century, followed by Holland, then England in the 18th and 19th centuries, and the United States in the 20th century. It will be China's turn to be the global champion in the 21st century": see Chita Romano, "Does China Want to Be Top Superpower?," ABC News/International (March 2, 2010), http://abcnews.go.com/international/china-replace-us-top-superpower/story? Id = 9986355. Our point here is that the analytical framework to embrace Portugal as the sixteenth-century and Britain as the eighteenth-century system leaders is the leadership long cycle.

33. The leadership long-cycle argument is that each system leader has enjoyed at least two spurts of innovation-led economic growth. The first spurt in this "twin-peaks" model destabilizes the world political economy's pecking order and leads to global warfare. Emerging victorious from the global war at the head of a winning coalition improves immensely the chances of pioneering a second, postwar growth spurt. This topic is examined at greater length in Modelski and Thompson, *Leading Sectors and World Power.*

34. The subject of system leader relative decline is explored extensively in Karen Rasler and William R. Thompson, *The Great Powers and Global Struggle, 1490–1990* (Lexington: University Press of Kentucky, 1994).

35. See Peter J. Hugill, "Transitions in Hegemony: A Theory Based on State Type and Typology," in William R. Thompson, *Systemic Transitions: Past, Present, and Future.*

36. One way to look at these disagreements over the extent or existence of leadership is to imagine scholars of the American presidency insisting that all US presidents that "count" must have exhibited precisely the same powers wielded by the current US president. But the point is that US presidential capabilities and powers have evolved over time, too. It makes little sense, therefore, to require all earlier presidents to have exhibited the same political powers of the contemporary era.

37. Modelski, *Long Cycles in World Politics.*

38. William R. Thompson, "Dehio, Long Cycles and the Geohistorical Context of Structural Transitions," *World Politics* 45 (October 1992): 127–52; Karen Rasler and William R. Thompson, *The Great Powers and Global Struggle, 1490–1990*, and "Global War and the Political Economy of Structural Change," in Manus I. Midlarsky, ed., *Handbook of War Studies II* (Ann Arbor: University of Michigan Press, 2000).

39. Portugal was occupied by Spain in the late sixteenth century. France occupied the Netherlands in the late eighteenth century.

40. Modelski and Thompson, *Leading Sectors and World Power.*

41. This model is discussed in more detail and in the context of the global warfare of the past five hundred years in William R. Thompson, "The Evolution of Systemic Leadership, World Politics, and International Relations Theory: The Unipolarity Question," *International Studies Review* 8:1 (2006): 1–22. The model represents a synthesis of three earlier models advanced in Paul Kennedy, *The Rise of the Anglo-German Antagonism, 1860–1914* (London: George Allen and Unwin, 1980); Sen Gautam, *The Military Origins of Industrialized International Trade Rivalry* (London: Pinter, 1983); and Stephen G. Bunker and Paul S. Ciccantell, *Globalization and the Race for Resources* (Baltimore: Johns Hopkins University Press, 2005). Note that many of the problems are likely to be more acutely manifested in circumstances involving "doubled" twin peaks—i.e., when one state enjoys two sets of twin peaks. The gap between the lead economy and latecomers is likely to be all the greater.

42. William R. Thompson, "A Streetcar Named Sarajevo: Catalysts, Multiple Causation Chains, and Rivalry Structures," *International Studies Quarterly* 47:3 (2003): 453–74.

43. Thompson, "The Evolution of Political-Economic Challenges in the Active Zone."

44. The main caveat to the preceding point is that two states that are specialized in the same economic activities are more likely to have conflict than two states that are not. For a challenger to develop a major innovation in one of the leader's specialties—whether Asian spices, American sugar, or automobiles—the resulting

economic threat is apt to be seen as quite acute. A challenger that is threatening to undermine one or more legs of the lead economy's foundation is more dangerous than a challenger specializing in activities that are complementary to the leader's resource base. At the same time, the lead economy tends to monopolize those sectors in which it possesses technological edges. Challengers must literally break into markets that have not been characterized by much competition. As Japan's experiences in the 1980s and 1990s illustrate, it is difficult to do this without resorting to tactics that are viewed as unfair by the targets of the challenge. Indeed, leaders and challengers tend to converge in their choice of economic specializations rather than settle into a harmonious division of labor. It is not really that common for a challenger to innovate in some totally new activity in which more established actors are not already present. The leading sectors of industrialization have been fairly uniform, suggesting that lead economies will find it difficult to avoid direct competition with other industrial economies. More variable are the geographical locations and significance of markets in which leaders and challengers compete. For instance, Asian trade dominated in the late fifteenth through seventeenth centuries as the main locus of contention. But, it was German maneuvering in Middle Eastern markets in the late nineteenth and early twentieth centuries that contributed to the British sense of threat more so than did nineteenth-century American competition in Central America.

45. For a more extended discussion of these elements of order, see Robert Gilpin, *War and Change in World Politics* (Cambridge: Cambridge University Press, 1981). The contributors to Kupchan et al., especially the chapters by Kupchan and Khong, focus on these elements as key to understanding why some power transitions do not culminate in large-scale war. See Charles A. Kupchan, Emanuel Adler, Jean-Marc Coicaud, and Yuen Foong Khong, *Power in Transition: The Peaceful Change in International Order* (Tokyo: United Nations University Press, 2001).

46. Thompson finds that three variables (system leader naval-capability share, the difference between global and regional capability concentration, and alliance balancing behavior) account for nearly 50 percent of the variation in global transitions over the past five centuries (see Thompson, "Structural Preludes to Systemic Transition Since 1494"). If there was a reasonable way to introduce the first peak of technological change as a fourth variable and the frictions between technological pioneers and latecomers, we might anticipate an even stronger explanatory outcome. But part of the problem is that only some innovation peaks cause trouble. Other peaks, such as the second part of the twin-peaks phenomenon introduce statistical noise in this particular respect. Frictions, moreover, are notoriously difficult to pin down quantitatively.

47. Here the question is whether the ending of the longtime centrality of Western Europe implies the absence of a central region in the future or the substitution of other regions. One possibility is that East Asia might supplant Western Europe, creating a reversed mirror effect for the Dehioan geopolitical tendencies of eastern and western balancers for interior hegemons. Or, it could be that the

new central region will be Eurasia writ large. One can interpret the Cold War re-action to the Soviet threat of expansion as a continuation of a Eurocentric script or a new pan-Eurasian development. Since the Cold War was contested through-out Eurasia, rather than simply in Europe, the evidence leans toward a more pan-Eurasian possibility. If so, this development would conform with the long-term British-Russian rivalry that also was waged on a pan-Eurasian scale. However, should China become the twenty-first century's principal challenger, much of the pan-Eurasian contest will have a strong East Asian focus.

48. Earlier concentrations of power in East Asia are discussed in Gari Led-yard "Yin and Yang in the China-Manchuria-Korea Triangle," in Morris Rossabi, ed., *China Among Equals: The Middle Kingdom and Its Neighbors, 10th–14th Cen-turies* (Berkeley: University of California Press, 1983); David C. Kang, *East Asia Before the West: Five Centuries of Trade and Tribute* (New York: Columbia Univer-sity Press, 2010); Yuan-kang Wang, *Harmony and War: Confucian Culture and Chi-nese Power Politics* (New York: Columbia University Press, 2010); and William R. Thompson, "Patterns of Conflict and Stability in the Asian Region from a Long-Term Perspective," in Ali Ahmed, Jaganmath P. Panda, and Prashant K. Singh, eds., *Asian Security* (New Delhi: Shipra, 2012).

49. See the arguments developed by Rosecrance, *The Rise of the Trading State*; and Karen Rasler and William R. Thompson, *Puzzles of the Democratic Peace*.

50. Zheng Bijian, "China's 'Peaceful Rise' to Great Power Status," *Foreign Affairs* 84 (2005): 22.

51. Angus Maddison, *Chinese Economic Performance in the Long Run* (Paris: Organization for Economic Co-operation and Development, 1998).

52. Despite some alarms to the contrary, Chinese naval development has had more success in the conventional arena than in terms of nuclear submarines or aircraft carriers, still the hallmarks of maritime global reach. The applicability of such a generalization need not persist long into the future. Nor do we assume that diesel submarines cannot complicate carrier incursions in or near Chinese waters.

53. Hence, the question is not how big the challenger becomes but who arrives at the next technological frontier first, how concentrated global and regional sys-tems become, and what sort of alliances are constructed to contain threatening challengers or to evade containment.

54. This "recent past" extends back continuously to Song China or over a mil-lennium, according to Modelski and Thompson, *Leading Sectors and World Power*.

Chapter Five

1. Robert Gilpin, *War and Change in World Politics* (Cambridge: Cambridge University Press, 1981), 188–89.

2. Nanotechnology or miniaturization is particularly critical to these innova-tions. A nanometer is one billionth of a meter.

3. Richard Silberglitt et al., *The Global Technology Revolution 2020, In-Depth Analyses: Bio/Nano/Materials/Information Trends, Drivers, Barriers, and Social Implications* (Santa Monica: Rand Corporation, 2006), 19–31.

4. Angus Maddison's GDP time series are found at www.ggdc.net/maddison.

5. On this point and in a specific Chinese context, see Keith Crane, Roger Cliff, Evan Medeiros, James Mulvenon, and William Overholt, *Modernizing China's Military: Opportunities and Constraints* (Santa Monica: Rand Corporation, 2005), 9–17 and 44–48.

6. This particular series stops in 2003, but the Chinese share of world GDP had tripled by 2003 in contrast to its 1980 share.

7. Dominic Wilson and Roopa Purushothman, "Dreaming With BRICs: The Path to 2050." Global Economics Paper, no. 99, http://www.goldmansachs.com /our-thinking/topics/brics/brics-reports-pdfs/brics-dream.

8. The G6 includes France, Germany, Italy, Japan, the United Kingdom and the United States. The BRICs are Brazil, Russia, India, and China.

9. US long-term growth is pegged at about 1.3 percent. Chinese growth is assumed to drop from 8.1 percent in 2003 to 5.6 percent in 2020 and to 3.5 percent in the mid-2040s.

10. For a pioneering effort to reconceptualize national power that seeks to incorporate and operationalize the technological capacity of countries, including the ability to innovate, see Ashley Tellis, Janice Bially, Christopher Lane, and Melissa McPherson, *Measuring National Power in the Postindustrial Age* (Santa Monica: Rand Corporation, 2000). From this standpoint, "[t]he ability to dominate the cycles of innovation in the international economy is the critical mainspring beneath the production of power" (Tellis et al., 36).

11. Interestingly, the Rand study published in 2006 calculates the likelihood of states adapting the 2020 technologies to military/defense purposes along lines very similar to the array display in figure 5.1. For useful surveys of China's innovative potential with respect to military technologies, see Raymond E. Franck and Gregory G. Hildebrandt, "Competitive Aspects of the Contemporary Military-Technological Revolution: Political Military Rivals to the US," *Defense Analysis* 12 (1996): 239–58; Kathryn L. Gauthier, *China as Peer Competitor: Trends in Nuclear Weapons, Space, and Information Warfare* (Maxwell Air Force Base: Air War College, 1999), Maxwell Paper No. 18; and Mark A. Stokes, *China's Strategic Modernization: Implications for the United States* (Carlisle: US Army War College, Strategic Studies Institute, September 1999). Consensual points across these diverse, pre-Afghan war studies include the following: China is closing the gap with the United States in some critical technologies, but overall, still has a long way to go; integration of various technologies and weapons into complex systems remains a weak point (see also Eric A. McVadon, "Systems Integration in China's People's Liberation Army," in James Mulvenon, C. and Richard H. Yang, eds., *The People's Liberation Army in the Information Age* [Santa Monica: Rand Corporation, 1999], on this issue); and China does not have to catch up with the United States in over-

all strength of military technology in order to seriously complicate US military operations in the Asian theater.

12. Wendy Frieman, "The Understated Revolution in Chinese Science and Technology: Implications for the PLA in the Twenty-First Century," in James P. Lilley and David Shambaugh, eds., *China's Military Faces the Future*, Armonk: M. E. Sharpe,1999), 250.

13. Ibid. 263.

14. Roger Cliff, *The Military Potential of China's Commercial Technology* (Santa Monica: Rand Corporation, 2001).

15. Ibid., 30.

16. Ibid., 58.

17. Ibid., 62.

18. Paul H. B. Godwin, "The PLA Faces the Twenty-First Century: Reflections on Technology, Doctrine, Strategy, and Operations," in James P. Lilley and David Shambaugh, eds., *China's Military Faces the Future* (Armonk: M. E. Sharpe, 1999), 59. See also Roger Cliff, Mark Burles, Michael S. Chase, Derek Eaton, and Kevin L. Pollpeter, *Entering the Dragon's Lair: Chinese Antiaccess Strategies and Their Implications for the United States* (Santa Monica: Rand Corporation, 2007), 18–23.

19. Eliot A. Cohen, "A Revolution in Warfare," *Foreign Affairs* 75 (1996): 51.

20. Burles and Shulsky cite Chinese strategists as identifying five types of "local war": small-scale border conflicts, contests for territorial seas and islands, surprise air attacks, partial hostile intrusions, and punitive counterattacks. See Mark Burles and Abram N. Shulsky, *Patterns in China's Use of Force: Evidence from History and Doctrinal Writings* (Santa Monica: Rand Corporation, 1999), 31.

21. Burles and Shulsky, *Patterns in China's Use of Force*, 45.

22. Godwin, "The PLA Faces the Twenty-First Century," 60.

23. Cited in Mark Burles and Abram N. Shulsky, *Patterns in China's Use of Force: Evidence from History and Doctrinal Writings* (Santa Monica: Rand, 2000), 48. Cohen, "A Revolution in Warfare," provides a persuasive general argument that, owing to the ongoing revolution in military affairs, "the balance between quality and quantity has shifted in favor of quality" (48). For the contention that the Chinese military needs to "trade quantity for quality," see Zalmay M. Khalilzad, Abram N. Shultsky, Daniel L. Bynam, Roger Cliff, David T. Orletsky, David Shlapak, and Ashley J. Tellis, *The United States and a Rising China: Strategic and Military Implications* (Santa Monica: Rand Corporation, 1999), 61.

24. Shambaugh, "China's Military in Transition," in David Shambaugh and Richard H. Yang, eds., *China's Military in Transition* (New York: Oxford University Press, 1997), 25. That does not imply that the Chinese navy is not improving. See Ronald O'Rourke, *China Naval Modernization: Implications for US Navy Capabilities — Background and Issues for Congress*, CRS Report for Congress (Washington, DC: Congressional Research Service, 7–5700, June 8, 2011).

25. Shambaugh, "China's Military in Transition," 29.

26. See Gary Li, "China's Military in 2020," in Kerry Brown, ed., *China 2020: The Next Decade for the People's Republic of China* (Oxford: Chandos Publishing, 2011), 87. Li also notes that the Chinese PLAAF is no longer inferior to Taiwan's.

27. John Wilson Lewis and Xue Litai, "China's Search for a Modern Air Force," *International Security* 24 (1999): 64–94.

28. See Jeremy Page, "A Chinese Stealth Challenge?" *Wall Street Journal* (January 5, 2011), http://online.wsj.com/article/SB10001424052748703808704576061674166905408.html; and Ken Dilanian, "China's Development of Stealth Fighter Takes US by Surprise." *Los Angeles Times* (January 7, 2011), http://articleslatimes.com/2011/jan/07/world/la-fg-china-military-20110107.

29. "Chinese General Says His Military is No Match for US," *Military.Com* (May 19, 2011), http://www.military.com/news/article/Chinese-general-says-his-military-is no-match-for-US.html. See also Roy Kamphausen and Andrew Scobell, eds., *Right Sizing the People's Liberation Army: Exploring the Contours of China's Military* (Carlisle: Strategic Studies Institute, 2007), http://www.strategic studiesinstitute.army.mil/pdfiles/PUB 784pdf; and Michael D. Swaine, "China's Military Muscle," Carnegie Endowment for International Peace (1/19/2011), http://www.carnegieendowment.org/2011/01/19/china-s-military-muscle/19. Even Colonel Liu Mingfu in his book *The China Dream: The Great Power Thinking and Strategic Positioning of China in the Post-American Age* (Beijing: Zhongguo youyi chuban gongsi, 2010) estimates that it will take sixty years to match US military strength. See Chita Romano, "Does China Want to be Top Superpower?," ABC News/International (March 2, 2010), http://abcnews.go.com/international/china -replace-us-top-superpower/story? Id=9986355.

The general also noted that the PLAN was twenty years behind the US Navy. But compare this assertion with retired General Xu Guangyu's warning in the same year: "We only want one thing: Don't harm our interests. The U.S. must accept the changing situation. As China becomes more powerful, we'll start voicing our opinions about maritime demands and any conflicts regarding surrounding territories" (see Louis Lim, "China's Growing Military Muscle: A Looming Threat," *National Public Radio* (July 26, 2011), http://www.npr.org/2011/06/20 /136901727/chinas-growing-military-muscle-a-looming-threat. Alternatively, consider PLAAF Lieutenant General Liu Yazhou who told a reporter in 2005 that "When a nation grows strong enough, it practices hegemony. The sole purpose of power is to pursue even greater power ... The frontiers of our national interests are expanding. Our military strategy should embody characteristics of the time" (cited in Richard D. Fisher, Jr., *China's Military Modernization: Building for Regional and Global Reach* [Westport: Praeger, 2008, 171]). Genuine disagreement within China about the most appropriate path to pursue and the timeline on which to pursue it should not be surprising. Shambaugh reminds us that there are a number of different schools of thought (he counts seven) on what China should do in foreign policy and when it should do it. See David Shambaugh, "Coping with a Conflicted China," *Washington Quarterly* 34:1 (2011): 7–27.

30. This argument that dissimilar strategic orientations are more likely to result in global war is directly at odds with Robert Ross's interpretation that complementarity of different strategic orientations is conducive to peace: "The U.S.-China bipolar conflict is a rivalry between a land power and a maritime power," which by definition will reduce the potential for conflict; see Robert S. Ross, "The Geography of the Peace: East Asia in the Twenty-First Century," *International Security* 23 (1999): 81–118. Ross is also confident that, contrary to our argument in this section, "Beijing's continental interests and U.S. maritime capabilities should deter China from making naval power a priority" (Ross, "The Geography of the Peace," 193). As noted earlier, however, though complementarity of strategic orientations makes for a more dangerous situation than similarity, Ross's argument does hold when applied to position within a global division of labor. When economic interaction is interindustry, as in the classic Ricardian sense of comparative advantage, complementarity can more easily lead to a harmony of interests. Conversely, when great powers are converging on the same set of industrial specializations, or leading sectors, commercial relations among them are more likely to be conflictual.

31. Dennis J. Blasko, "A New PLA Force Structure," in Mulvenon and Yang, *People's Liberation Army in the Information Age*, 267.

32. Michael D. Swaine, and Ashley J. Tellis, *Interpreting China's Grand Strategy: Past, Present, and Future* (Santa Monica: Rand Corporation, 2000), 124.

33. Paul H. B. Godwin, "The PLA Faces the Twenty-First Century," 49.

34. David M. Finkelstein, "China's Military Strategy," in Mulvenon and Yang, *People's Liberation Army in the Information Age*, 117.

35. Michael Pillsbury, *China Debates the Future Security Environment* (Washington, DC: National Defense University Press, 2000), 267, 302.

36. Paul H. B. Godwin, "From Continent to Periphery: PLA Doctrine, Strategy and Capabilities Towards 2000," in Shambaugh and Yang, eds., *China's Military in Transition*, 220.

37. David Shambaugh, "China's Military Views the World: Ambivalent Security," *International Security* 24 (1999/2000): 60. Note that two hundred to three hundred miles was the maximum offshore range of the PLA's land-based aircraft at that time.

38. John Frankenstein and Bates Gill, "Current and Future Challenges Facing Chinese Defence Industries," in Shambaugh and Yang, *China's Military in Transition*, 133, fn. 7.

39. Swaine and Tellis, *Interpreting China's Grand Strategy*, 160–61.

40. Updates on the mixed progress made in developing projection capability at sea can be found in Bernard D. Cole, *The Great Wall at Sea: China's Navy in the Twenty-First Century*, 2nd ed. (Annapolis: Naval Institute Press, 2010); Andrew S. Erickson, Lyle J. Goldstein, and Nan Li, eds., *China, the United States, and 21st Cen-*

tury Sea Power: Defining a Maritime Security Partnership (Annapolis: Naval Institute Press, 2010); and Toshi Yoshinhara and James R. Holmes, *Red Star Over the Pacific: China's Rise and the Challenge to US Maritime Strategy* (Annapolis: Naval Institute Press, 2010).

41. Michael D. Swaine, *America's Challenge: Engaging a Rising China in the Twenty-First Century* (Washington, DC: Carnegie Endowment for International Peace, 2011), 159.

42. In some cases, though, Chinese decision makers may be content with more limited capabilities. Jeffrey Lewis argues that the intentionally small Chinese strategic force has not moved toward emulating the size of the strategic forces of Russia or the United States. As a consequence, according to Lewis, "China's nuclear forces today look remarkably like they have for decades." Jeffery Lewis, *The Minimum Means of Reprisal: China's Search for Security in the Nuclear Age* (Cambridge: MIT Press, 2007), 206.

43. For explication of this concept, see Shen Kaigun, "Dialectics of Defeating the Superior with the Inferior," in Michael Pillsbury, ed., *Chinese Views of Future Warfare* (Washington, DC: National Defense University Press, 1997).

44. Godwin, "The PLA Faces the Twenty-First Century," 42.

45. For a provocative scenario in which China uses deception and surprise to wage a successful military campaign to take control of Taiwan, see Richard L. Russell, "What if ... 'China Attacks Taiwan!'," *Parameters* 31 (2001): 76–91. For the cognate concept of "unrestricted warfare," see Qiao Liang and Wang Xiangsui, *Unrestricted Warfare* (Beijing: Literature and Arts Publishing House, 1999), http://www.terrorism.com/documents/unrestricted.pdf.

46. Michael Pillsbury, "Chinese Views of Future Warfare," in James P. Lilley and David Shambaugh, eds., *China's Military Faces the Future* (Armonk: M. E. Sharpe, 1999), 69–71.

47. On the politicized interaction between military and civilian technology in the Chinese domestic context, see Evan A. Feigenbaum, *China's Techno-warriors: National Security and Strategic Competition from the Nuclear Age to the Information Age* (Stanford: Stanford University Press, 2003).

48. Tim Ross, Holly Watt, and Christopher Hope, "Wiki Leaks: US and China in Military Standoff Over Space Missiles," *The Telegraph*, July 26, 2011. More general material on the Chinese space program can be found in Ann E. Robertson, *Militarization of Space* (New York: Facts on File, 2011), 87–94.

49. See, for instance, Bryan Krekel, *Capability of the People's Republic of China to Conduct Cyber Warfare and Computer Network Exploitation* (McLean: Information Systems Sector, Northrop Grumman Corporation, 2009), http://www.uscc.gov/researchpapers/2009/Northrop Grumman_PRC_Cyber_Paper_FINAL; and Andrew Erickson and Gabe Collins, "A Smoking Cursor? New Window Opens on China's Potential Cyberware Development: CCTV 7 Program Raises New Questions about Beijing's Support for Hacking," *China Sign Post*, no. 46

(August 24, 2011), http://www.chinasignpost.com/2011/08/1-smoking-cursor-new
-window-opens-on-china%E2%80%99s-potential-cyberwarfare.

50. Note that these roles correspond with the contrast between continental and maritime strategic orientations discussed below.

51. Lemke stresses this facet from a power transition perspective. See Douglas Lemke, *Regions of War and Peace* (Cambridge: Cambridge University Press, 2002).

52. Kenneth Boulding, *Conflict and Defense: A General Theory* (New York: Harper and Row, 1962).

53. Thomas S. Szayna, Daniel L. Bynam, Steven C. Bankes, Derek Eaton, Seth G. Jones, Robert E. Mullins, Ian O. Lesser, and William Rosenau, *The Emergence of Peer Competitors: A Framework for Analysis* (Santa Monica: Rand Corporation, 2001), 67.

54. Burles and Shulsky, *Patterns in China's Use of Force*, 63.

55. Thomas Christenson, "Posing Problems Without Catching Up: China's Rise and Challenges for US Security Policy," *International Security* 25:4 (2001): 7. On this point see also James Lilley and Carl Ford, "China's Military: A Second Opinion," *The National Interest* 57 (1999): 71–77.

56. Christenson, "Posing Problems Without Catching Up," 13.

57. Paul H. B. Godwin, "From Continent to Periphery: PLA Doctrine, Strategy and Capabilities Towards 2000," in Shambaugh and Yang, *China's Military in Transition*, 220.

58. Thus a Dutch lead was replaced by a British lead which, in turn, was replaced by a US lead.

59. Ronald L. Tammen, Jacek Kugler, Douglas Lemke, Allan C. Stam III, Carole Alsharabati, Mark A. Abdollahian, Brian Efird, and A. F. K. Organski, *Power Transitions: Strategies for the 21st Century* (New York: Chatham House, 2000), 9–15.

60. Tammen et al., *Power Transitions*, 9.

61. See Szayna et al., *Emergence of Peer Competitors*, 51–52.

62. Richard K. Betts and Thomas J. Christensen, "China: Getting the Questions Right," *The National Interest* 62 (Winter 2000): 7. But the resentment is not on hold for all. Kerry Brown has translated Wang Xiaodung, Song Shaojun, Huang Jilao, Song Qiang, and Liu Yi, eds., *Zhongguo bu gaoxing* [China is Not Happy] (Jiangsu: Phoenix Publishing and Jiangsu People's Press, 2009) and finds that the authors (Wang Xiaodung is described as a popular blogger and an earlier author of the 1998 book, *The China That Can Say No*) conclude that China basically has three choices: continue being a sweatshop for the world economy, embrace Western economic models, or prepare for full-fledged conflict. Their recommendation is to build more aircraft carriers. See Brown, "China 2020: International Relations," in Kerry Brown, ed., *China 2020: The Next Decade for the People's Republic of China* (Oxford: Chandos Publishing, 2011), 22.

63. Richard Bernstein and Ross H. Munro, *The Coming Conflict with China*

(New York: Vintage, 1998). We have already listed some of the entries in this expanding literature in fn. 20 in chapter 1.

64. Current and recent US Defense Department documents understandably remain focused on Iraqi drawdown processes and Afghani deployments, but there is usually some reference to the need to prepare for "potential major adversaries" and also some nonexplicitly related mention of the rise of Chinese geopolitical significance. See, for instance, the *Quadrennial Defense Review Report*, February 2010 (Washington, DC: Government Printing Office, 2010). Immediately prior to the advent of the wars in Iraq and Afghanistan, Defense Department references to the potential Chinese threat were less oblique and may be expected to return to greater specificity in future years.

65. At the same time, the European powers have yet to create an independent European Union pole of their own. The economic wealth is certainly there but the will to create a political-military actor that could absorb British, French, and German (as well as other) capabilities is not yet manifested fully. However, some increased military cooperation between France and Germany (a joint army brigade) and France and the United Kingdom (an arrangement to "share" a future aircraft carrier) is observable. The real question is just how multipolar the world will become in the next two decades. Bipolarization could, of course, proceed without any further tendencies toward multipolarity than already have been demonstrated.

66. See Aaron L. Friedberg, "The Geopolitics of Strategic Asia, 2000–2020," in Ashley J. Tellis, Andrew Marble, and Travis Tanner, eds., *Strategic Asia 2010–11: Asia's Rising Power and America's Continued Purpose* (Seattle: National Bureau of Asian Research Press, 2010), 42–43.

67. It is not inconceivable that Vietnam might ultimately join the maritime group.

68. These are referred to as "central power transitions" in the fifth of six transitional submodels.

69. Part of this issue is which state has more people in the 18–65 optimal producing age bracket. China's numbers will be declining while India's most productive group is increasing in size. This demographic quirk due to China's one child policy does not necessarily translate into the Indian economy surpassing the Chinese economy's considerable head start. See Paranjoy Guha Thakurta, "Can India's Economy Overtake China?," *BBC News* (October 3, 2009), http://news.bbc.co.uk/2/hi/south_asia/8273464.stm and Tushar Poddar and Eva Yi, "India's Rising Growth Potential," in Goldman Sachs Global Economics Group, ed., *BRICSs and Beyond* (2007), http://www2.golmansachs.com/ideas/brics/book/Bric-Full.pdf.

70. This compilation of potential Chinese challenges is drawn largely from Khalilzad et al., *The United States and a Rising China* (chapter 2); Swaine and Tellis, *Interpreting China's Grand Strategy* (chapter 1); and Fisher, *China's Military Modernization*, 5–6. There are, of course, other issues on which US and Chi-

nese interests are at odds. One frequent source of tension is China's human rights practices; another is its exports of nuclear and missile technologies, especially to the Middle East and Pakistan. Though human rights is an important element in US foreign policy, it is not an issue area that engages US "vital interests" and thus is not likely to lead to militarized conflict; the same cannot be said concerning proliferation of weapons of mass destruction.

71. Romano, "Does China Want to Be Top Superpower?"

Chapter Six

1. See, for instance, Bruce Russett, "Violence and Disease: Trade as Suppressor to Conflict When Suppressors Matter," in Edward D. Mansfield and Brian M. Pollins, eds., *Economic Interdependence and International Conflict: New Perspectives on an Enduring Debate* (Ann Arbor: University of Michigan Press, 2003).

2. For a variety of opinions, see Edward Freidman and Barrett L. McCormick, eds., *What if China Doesn't Democratize? Implications for War and Peace* (Armonk: M. E. Sharpe, 2000); Zhang Yongnian, *Will China Become Democratic? Elite, Class and Regime Transition* (Singapore: Eastern Universities Press, 2004); Minxin Pei, *China's Trapped Transition* (Cambridge: Harvard University Press, 2006); Bruce J. Dickson, "The Future of the Chinese Communist Party: Strategies of Survival and Prospects for Change," in Jae Ho Chung, ed., *Charting China's Future: Political, Social, and International Dimensions* (Lanham: Rowman and Littlefield, 2006); Yawei Liu, "The Rule of Law and Electoral Processes: Present and Future Forecasts," in Chung, *Charting China's Future*; and Robert Grafstein, "Democracy in China? Go Figure," in Robert Grafstein and Fan Wei, eds., *A Bridge Too Far? Commonalities and Differences Between China and the United States* (Lanham: Lexington Books, 2009).

3. Elsewhere, we have examined the democratic peace; see Karen Rasler and William R. Thompson, *Puzzles of the Democratic Peace: Theory, Geopolitics and the Transformation of World Politics* (New York: Palgrave-Macmillan, 2005). Economic interdependence was evaluated in David Rapkin and William R. Thompson, "Economic Interdependence and the Emergence of China and India in the 21st Century," in Ashley J. Tellis and Michael Wills, eds., *Strategic Asia 2006–07: Trade, Interdependence and Security* (Seattle: National Bureau of Asian Research, 2006). International organizations receive close scrutiny in David Rapkin and William R. Thompson, "Kantian Dynamics and Systemic Transitions: Can International Organizations Influence U.S.-China Conflict?," in William R. Thompson, ed., *Systemic Transitions: Past, Present, and Future* (New York: Palgrave-Macmillan, 2008).

4. Bruce Russett and John R. Oneal, *Triangulating Peace: Democracy, Interdependence and International Organizations* (New York: Norton, 2001).

5. See Sebastian Rosato, "The Flawed Logic of Democratic Peace Theory,"

American Political Science Review 97:4 (2003): 585–602. We have paraphrased his summary.

6. See Henry S. Farber and Joanne Gowa, "Common Interests or Common Politics? Reinterpreting the Democratic Peace," *Journal of Politics* 59 (1995): 393–417; and Lars-Erik Cederman, "Back to Kant: Reinterpreting the Democratic Peace as a Macrohistorical Learning Process," *American Political Science Review* 95:1 (2001): 15–31.

7. Michael Mousseau, Havard Hegre, and John R. Oneal, "How the Wealth of Nations Conditions the Liberal Peace," *European Journal of International Relations* 9 (2003): 277–314.

8. On the causal arrow direction problem, see Christopher Layne, "Kant or Cant: The Myth of the Democratic Peace," *International Security* 19 (1994): 5–49; Manus I. Midlarsky, "Environmental Influences on Democracy; Aridity, Warfare and a Reversal of the Causal Arrow," *Journal of Conflict Resolution* 39 (1995): 224–62; William R. Thompson, "Democracy and Peace: Putting the Cart Before the Horse?," *International Organization* 50 (1996): 141–74; Scott Gates, Torbjorn L. Knutsen, and Jonathan W. Moses, "Democracy and Peace: A More Skeptical View," *Journal of Peace Research* 33 (1996): 1–10; Steve Chan, "In Search of Democratic Peace: Problems and Promise," *Mershon International Studies Review* 41 (1997): 59–91; Michael J. Crescenzi and Andrew J. Enterline, "Ripples for the Waves? A Systemic, Time-Series Analysis of Democracy, Democratization, and Interstate War," *Journal of Peace Research* 36 (1999): 75–94; Michael Mousseau and Yuhang Shi, "A Test for Reverse Causality in the Democratic Peace Relationship," *Journal of Peace Research* 36 (1999): 639–63; Patrick James, Eric Solberg, and Murray Wolfson, "An Identified Systemic Model of the Democracy-Peace Nexus," *Defense and Peace Economics* 10 (1999): 1–37; John R. Oneal and Bruce Russett, "Why 'An Identified Systemic Analysis of the Democracy-Peace Nexus' Does not Persuade," *Defense and Peace Economics* 11 (2000): 197–214; Patrick James, Eric Solberg, and Murray Wolfson, "Democracy and Peace: A Reply to Oneal and Russett," *Defense and Peace Economics* 11(2000): 215–29; Dan Reiter, "Does Peace Nurture Democracy?," *Journal of Politics* 63 (2001): 935–48; Karen Rasler and William R. Thompson, "The Democratic Peace and a Sequential, Reciprocal Causal Arrow Hypothesis," *Comparative Political Studies* 37 (2004): 879–602; Douglas M. Gibler and Jaroslav Tir, "Settled Borders and Regime Type: Democratic Transitions as Consequences of Peaceful Territorial Transfers," *American Journal of Political Science* 54:4 (2010): 951–68.

9. See Michael Mousseau, "Market Prosperity, Democratic Consolidation, and Democratic Peace," *Journal of Conflict Resolution* 44 (2000): 472–507, and "The Social Market Roots of Democratic Peace," *International Security* 33 (2009): 52–86; Havard Hegre, "Development and the Liberal Peace: What Does It Take to Be a Trading State?," *Journal of Peace Research* 37 (2000): 5–30; Erich Weede, "Globalization: Creative Destruction and the Prospect of a Capitalist Peace," in Ger-

ald Schneider, Katherine Barbieri, and Nils Petter Gleditsch, eds., *Globalization and Armed Conflict* (Lanham: Rowman and Littlefield, 2003); Erik Gartzke, "The Capitalist Peace." *American Journal of Political Science* 51 (2007): 161–91; and Patrick J. McDonald, *The Invisible Hand of Peace, Capitalism, the War Machine, and International Relations Theory* (Cambridge: Cambridge University Press, 2009).

10. Jack S. Levy and William R. Thompson, *The Arc of War: Origins, Escalation, and Transformation* (Chicago: University of Chicago Press, 2011).

11. Douglas M. Gibler, "Bordering on Peace: Democracy, Territorial Issues and Conflict," *International Studies Quarterly* 51 (2007): 509–32, and "The Implications of a Territorial Peace," in John A. Vasquez, ed., *What Do We Know About War*, vol. 2 (Lanham: Rowman and Littlefield, 2012); and Gibler and Tir "Settled Borders and Regime Type"; Karen Rasler and William R. Thompson, "Boundary Disputes, Rivalry, Democracy, and Interstate Conflict in the European Region, 1816–1994," *Conflict Management and Peace Science* 28:3 (2011): 280–305; and Andrew P. Owsiak, "The Pen Is Mightier Than the Sword: International Boundary Agreements, Democracy, and Militarized Interstate Conflict," *International Studies Quarterly* 56:1 (2012): 51–66.

12. See John A. Vasquez "Why Do Neighbors Fight? Proximity, Interaction, or Territoriality," *Journal of Peace Research* 32:3 (1995): 277–93.

13. See Nils Petter Gledtisch and Havard Hegre, "Peace and Democracy: Three Levels of Analysis," *Journal of Conflict Resolution* 41 (1997): 283–310; and Rasler and Thompson, *Puzzles of the Democratic Peace.*

14. See, e.g., Rasler, and Thompson, *Puzzles of the Democratic Peace.*

15. Thomas G. Moore and Dixia Yang, "Empowered and Restrained: Chinese Foreign Policy in the Age of Economic Interdependence," in David M. Lampton, ed., *The Making of Chinese Foreign and Security Policy in the Era of Reform* (Stanford: Stanford University Press, 2001), 193–98.

16. Space constraints do not permit more detailed consideration of the different effects likely to result from different forms of economic interaction, e.g., trade and direct foreign investment. For a thorough explication of this distinction, see Stephen G. Brooks, *Producing Security: Multinational Corporations, Globalization, and the Changing Calculus of Conflict* (Princeton: Princeton University Press, 2005).

17. Dale Copeland, "Economic Interdependence and War: A Theory of Trade Expectations," *International Security* 20:4 (1996): 5–41, and "Economic Interdependence and the Future of U.S.-Chinese Relations," in G. John Ikenberry and Michael Mastanduno, eds., *International Relations Theory and the Asia-Pacific* (New York: Columbia University Press, 2003). The former examines the cases of Germany prior to World Wars I and II; the latter looks at Japan prior to World War I and contemporary China. See also, Rex Li, "Security Challenge of an Ascendant China: Great Power Emergence and International Stability," in Suisheng Zhao, ed., *Chinese Foreign Policy: Pragmatism and Strategic Behavior* (New York:

M. E. Sharpe, 2004), for another application of Copeland's framework that finds that, "[f]or the moment, China's expectations of future trade with both its Asian neighbors and Western nations are by and large positive" (39).

18. This finding is based on a review of thirty-four empirical analyses reported in Karen Rasler and William R. Thompson, "Assessing Inducements and Suppressors of Interstate Conflict Escalation," paper delivered at the Annual Meeting of the International Studies Association, San Diego, California, March 2006. Two strongly contrasting views on the role of economic interdependence are Russett and Oneal, *Triangulating Peace: Democracy, Interdependence and International Organizations*; and Katherine Barbieri, *The Liberal Illusion: Does Trade Promote Peace?* (Ann Arbor: University of Michigan Press, 2002). For collections of various views on this question, see Gerald Schneider, Katherine Barbieri, and Nils Petter Gleditsch, eds., *Globalization and Armed Conflict* (Lanham: Rowman and Littlefield, 2003); and Edward D. Mansfield and Brian M. Pollins, eds., *Economic Interdependence and International Conflict: New Perspectives on an Enduring Debate* (Ann Arbor: University of Michigan Press, 2003).

19. These findings are reported in Rasler and Thompson, "Assessing Inducements and Suppressors of Interstate Conflict Escalation." They are based on a quantitative analysis of militarized interstate disputes for the post–World War II period using databases that allow analysts to avoid the extensive missing data problems that characterized empirical analyses involving gross domestic product information prior to the last three to four years. Some readers may be surprised by the finding of the comparative weakness of the "democratic peace" effect. Two things need to be said here, albeit briefly. One is that the regime-type conflict relationship proved to be statistically significant. Thus, no argument is made here that democratic regimes have nothing to do with conflict propensities. But the finding that regime type exerted the weakest constraint on conflict escalation suggests that the "democratic peace" interpretation has been exaggerated. For an effort to explain the emergence of pacific relations in some dyads in terms of a combination of escalated costs of warfare and altered policy priorities, see Rasler and Thompson, *Puzzles of the Democratic Peace*.

20. Perhaps the strongest support for economic interdependence restraining conflict is the unusually pacific history of the European region after World War II. Though major power warfare was quite common in Western Europe prior to 1945, there has since been no warfare in a region that has become increasingly integrated economically. The connection between greater economic interdependence and less conflict seems apparent. Yet this case requires careful interpretation. European integration contributed over time to the ending of the Franco-German strategic rivalry, but it is also the case that the Franco-German rivalry, which was not entirely extinguished in 1945, contributed to European integration. In fact, European integration emerged as a plan for suppressing the reemergence of German centrality in Europe only after the French were frustrated by US and

British opposition to their initial postwar attempts to keep Germany permanently weak. French decision makers gravitated reluctantly to alternative schemes that involved shared control of resource extraction and production. This approach was embraced by German decision makers, who were apprehensive of undertaking economic reconstruction on their own and thus sought a multilateral approach. In the process, French fears of renewed German expansion were ameliorated. A second important consideration is that western European economic integration, which had been attempted coercively by Napoleon and by Charlemagne before Hitler, depended in large part on the exhaustion of the leading European great powers in World War II. Their militaries had been destroyed, and their industrial bases were in dire need of rebuilding. Aspirations to dominate the western European region thus had to be interred. Hence, it is questionable whether any western European state retained genuine great power status after 1945. It is also clear that political-military aggrandizement policies have not reemerged and may never do so. Though Europe was able to regain an impressive measure of economic competitiveness, the question of whether European actors could still be competitive as great powers presumably was resolved by the 1945 outcome. In that sense, the relative lack of conflict between western European states after 1945 seems more a special case than an exemplar of the pacifying powers of economic interdependence.

21. On the overlap in basing choices over the last half-millennium, see Robert Harkavy, "Long Cycle Theory and the Hegemonic Powers' Basing Networks," *Political Geography* 18 (1999): 941–72.

22. The dissatisfaction of latecomers is a point that is featured prominently in power transition arguments. See A. F. K. Organski, *World Politics* (New York: Random House, 1958); and A. F. K. Organski and Jacek Kugler, *The War Ledger* (Chicago: University of Chicago Press, 1980).

23. The Dutch had attempted to seize Brazil from the Portuguese; once that project had failed, they were important agents in shifting sugar production to Caribbean islands controlled by England.

24. The Portuguese, in essence, were extending by assumption and practice the centuries long, Christian-Muslim struggle in the Mediterranean to the Indian Ocean.

25. The Gerschenkron effect refers to the argument that late developers must overcome more obstacles to growth than early developers and thus are more likely to rely on authoritarian governments, central planning, and banking-business partnerships in attempts to catch up with the growth leaders. See Alexander Gerschenkron, *Economic Backwardness in Historical Perspective* (Cambridge: Belknap Press, 1962).

26. See Paul Kennedy, *The Rise of the Anglo-German Antagonism, 1860–1914* (London: George Allen and Unwin, 1980), 291–305.

27. Note that "the rules" tend to be set by the early developers and are not nec-

essarily accepted by later developers. Free trade, for instance, is most appealing to an economy that can out produce all other economies.

28. In general, see John A. C. Conybeare, *Trade Wars: The Theory and Practice of International Commercial Policy* (New York: Columbia University Press, 1987). For more specific examples relating to late-nineteenth-century business competition, see Kennedy, *Rise of Anglo-German Antagonism*, 41–58, 291–305.

29. These elements are emphasized in Gautam Sen, *The Military Origins of Industrialized International Trade Rivalry* (London: Pinter, 1983).

30. For an argument that increasingly globalized production by multinational corporations substantially reduces major power conflict, see Brooks, *Producing Security*. Interestingly, though, Brooks explicitly excludes developing countries from this generalization.

31. Resources are emphasized in Stephen G. Bunker and Paul S. Ciccantell, *Globalization and the Race for Resources* (Baltimore: Johns Hopkins University Press, 2005).

32. The length of a wooden sailing ship, and thus its carrying capacity to some extent, was determined by the length of the trees used to make the keel. Taller trees meant longer keels, as well as taller masts.

33. On the US effort to acquire secure access to oil prior to World War II, see Ed Shaffer, *The United States and the Control of World Oil* (New York: St. Martin's Press, 1983); and William R. Thompson, "Global War and the Foundations of U.S. Systemic Leadership," in James Fuller and Lawrence Sondhaus, eds., *War and Power: Defining the American State* (London: Routledge, 2007).

34. See, for instance, Jonathan Marshall, *To Have and Have Not: Southeast Asian Raw Materials and the Origins of the Pacific War* (Berkeley: University of California Press, 1995); and David P. Rapkin, "The Emergence and Intensification of the US-Japan Rivalry in the Early Twentieth Century," in William R. Thompson, ed., *Great Power Rivalries* (Columbia: University of South Carolina Press, 1999).

35. Support for this observation is found in, among other places, Richard Overy, *Why the Allies Won* (New York: Norton, 1995), 228–34.

36. Consider some illustrative examples of recent growth in China's resource consumption: between 1990 and 2003, China's iron ore imports increased from 14 to 148 million tons; aluminum from 1 to 5.6 million tons; refined copper from 20,000 to 1.2 million tons; platinum from 20,000 to 1.6 million ounces; and nickel from zero to 61,500 tons. Reported in David Hale, "China's Growing Appetites," *National Interest* 76 (Summer 2004): 1.

37. Hale, "China's Growing Appetites," 4.

38. Cited in David E. Sanger, "China's Oil Needs Are High on U.S. Agenda," *New York Times*, April 18, 2006.

39. From a report, "Energy Futures in Asia," by Booz Allen Hamilton (a US defense contractor), cited in Sudha Ramachandran, "China's Pearl in Pakistan's Waters," *Asia Times*, March 4, 2005.

40. For the conventional economic view that the bilateral imbalance is a conse-quence of low US and high Chinese savings rates and thus is not amenable to solu-tion by changes in exchange rates, see Ronald I. McKinnon, "Currency Manipula-tor?," *Wall Street Journal*, April 20, 2006.

41. Lawrence B. Lindsey, "Yuan Compromise?," *Wall Street Journal*, April 6, 2006.

42. T. N. Srinivasan, "Economic Reforms and Global Integration," in Fran-cine R. Frankel and Harry Harding, eds., *The India-China Relationship: What the United States Needs to Know* (New York: Columbia University Press, 2004), 240.

43. Vineet Toshniwai, an executive with the Indian software firm, Infosys, cited in Pallavi Aiyar, "China-India IT Cooperation: One 'Pagoda' Short," *Asia Times*, March 23, 2006.

44. See Anand Giridharadas, "In India, Next Great Industrial Story," *Interna-tional Herald Tribune*, April 17, 2006.

45. Barry Posen, "Command of the Commons: The Military Foundation of U.S. Hegemony," *International Security* 28:1 (Summer 2003): 5–46.

46. Antoaneta Bezlova, "Beijing: We Have Lift Off," *Asia Times*, October 14, 2005.

47. Ashley Tellis, "India as a New Global Power: An Action Agenda for the United States," Carnegie Endowment for International Peace," Washington, DC, 2005, 34, http://carnegieendowment.org/2005/07/14/india-as-global-power-action -agenda. See Tellis's ambitious agenda for enhanced US-India cooperation on space (34–38).

48. Cited in Siddarth Srivistava, "India Races into Space," *Asia Times*, May 20, 2005.

49. For a cautionary view of the likely effects of US weaponization of space, see Michael Krepon, "Lost in Space: the Misguided Drive Toward Antisatellite Weap-ons," *Foreign Affairs* 80:3 (May/June 2001): 2–8.

50. Kenneth S. Deffeyes, *Beyond Oil: the View from Hubbert's Peak* (Princeton: Princeton University Press, 2005).

51. The optimist position is based on the premises that new oil fields will be discovered and that new extraction technology will be developed to make it more affordable to pump oil now difficult to extract cheaply. The argument is not so much about the world's oil supply as it is about what can be extracted at what price.

52. For more detailed data on China's and India's energy consumption pat-terns, as well as those of other Asian countries, see Mikkal E. Herberg, "Asia's Energy Insecurity: Cooperation or Conflict," in Ashley J. Tellis and Michael Wills, eds., *Strategic Asia 2004–05: Confronting Terrorism in the Pursuit of Power* (Seattle: National Bureau of Asian Research, 2004), 339–78.

53. Thus, in addition to trying to diversify the kinds of energy resources it uses (more natural gas and coal so as to lessen oil dependence) and its sources (Africa,

Latin America, and Central Asia, as well as the Persian Gulf), China is also moving to diversify the modes of transportation by which its energy supplies are delivered: overland pipelines from Central Asia and Russia are partly intended to reduce its vulnerability to potential supply disruption by the US Navy.

54. James Clad, "Convergent Chinese and Indian Perspectives on the Global Order," in Francine R. Frankel and Harry Harding, eds., *The India-China Relationship: What the United States Needs to Know* (New York: Columbia University Press, 2004), 271–76. We are inclined to think that Clad overestimates the extent to which China and India have shifted to market-oriented approaches toward their energy problems.

55. Cited in Sarutha Rai, "China and India: Bidding Partners, at least on Paper," *International Herald Tribune*, January 20, 2006.

56. Keith Bradsher, "2 Big Appetites Take Seats at the Oil Table," *New York Times*, February 18, 2005.

57. Herberg, "Asia's Energy Insecurity: Cooperation or Conflict," 340.

58. We tentatively suggest that dissymmetric interdependence may make it more difficult to resolve economic disputes because negotiations are over dissimilar "goods" (apples and oranges) that are hard to directly compare. In contrast, in negotiations over similar goods—market openings, tariff reductions, increased exports or imports, national treatment, customs, or sanitary standards—it is easier to quantify the value of concessions and to "split the difference" to reach agreement.

59. Cited in Frederick Kempe, "U.S., China Stage an Economic Balancing Act," *Wall Street Journal*, March 28, 2006.

60. Cited in in Anand Giridharadas, "India Portrays Itself as a New Type of Superpower," *International Herald Tribune*, July 21, 2005.

61. A recent example of an independent Indian position, at least rhetorically, that the U.S. is unlikely to find congenial involves Prime Minister Singh questioning the patterns of trade and capital flows described in the preceding section: "Given the potential for investment demand in the region, we must find ways of making better use of our savings. How can we make sure that the savings and surpluses generated in our region can find investment avenues within our region?" Cited in Anand Giridharadas, "Singh Urges Less Money for Financing U.S. Debt," *International Herald Tribune*, May 5, 2006. It is difficult to interpret this statement as other than a call for regional coordination and self-reliance and a shift away from Asian financing of American consumption.

62. Ashley Tellis, "China and India in Asia," in Francine R. Frankel and Harry Harding, eds., *The India-China Relationship: What the United States Needs to Know* (New York: Columbia University Press, 2004), 172.

63. For a useful survey of these and other strategies for coping with rising powers, see Randall L. Schweller, "Managing the Rise of Great Powers: History and Theory," in Alastair Iain Johnston and Robert S. Ross, eds., *"Engaging China:*

The Management of an Emerging Power" (New York: Routledge, 1999), 7–18. As Schweller points out, these strategies are not necessarily mutually exclusive, i.e., states can undertake mixed strategies. It is also necessary to distinguish between bilateral engagement strategies and those pursued via IGOs, though in practice they are likely to be jointly pursued. For economic engagement strategies, see also Michael Mastanduno "The Strategy of Economic Engagement: Theory and Practice," in Edward D. Mansfield and Brian M. Pollins, eds., *Economic Interdependence and International Conflict: New Perspectives on an Enduring Debate* (Ann Arbor: University of Michigan Press, 2003), 175–86.

64. Samuel S. Kim, "China's International Organizational Behavior," in Thomas W. Robinson and David Shambaugh, eds., *Chinese Foreign Policy: Theory and Practice* (Oxford: Oxford University Press, 1994), 405.

65. Cited in J. David Singer and Michael Wallace, "Intergovernmental Organization and the Preservation of Peace, 1816–1964," *International Organization* 24:3 (Summer 1970): 521.

66. Schweller, "Managing the Rise of Great Powers: History and Theory"; and Charles A. Kupchan, Emanuel Adler, Jean-Marc Coicaud, and Yuen Foong Khong, *Power in Transition: The Peaceful Change in International Order* (Tokyo: United Nations University Press, 2001).

67. See Ann Kent, *Beyond Compliance: China, International Organizations, and Global Security* (Stanford: Stanford University Press, 2007), for a useful general overview of the compliance literature, for the distinction between compliance and the broader concept of cooperation, and for an assessment for China's record of compliance with IGOs rules and norms across an array of security, economic, environmental, and human rights IGOs.

68. Russett and Oneal, *Triangulating Peace*, 158.

69. See Russett and Oneal, *Triangulating Peace,* 163–66. Pevehouse and Russett suggest three mechanisms which link IGOs comprised mainly of democratic states to peaceful outcomes. See Jon Pevehouse and Bruce Russett, "Democratic International Governmental Organizations Promote Peace," *International Organization* 60:4 (Fall 2006): 969–1000. Renewed emphasis is given to mediation/dispute settlement and socialization (numbers 2 and 5) and another mechanism is added: IGOs make more credible the commitments of members.

70. Russett and Oneal, *Triangulating Peace*, 162.

71. Ian Hurd, "Too Legit to Quit," *Foreign Affairs* 82:4 (July/August 2003): 205.

72. Alastair I. Johnston and Paul Evans, "China's Engagement with Multilateral Security Institutions," in Johnston and Ross, *Engaging China: The Management of an Emerging Power*, 237.

73. Some IGOs may aim at both promotion of cooperation and suppression of conflicts; others at one or the other. Other potentially relevant distinctions among IGOs—that we cannot pursue further here—turn on the degree to which they are institutionalized (see Charles Boehmer, Erik Gartzke, and Timothy Nordstrom,

"Do International Organizations Promote Peace?," *World Politics* 57:1 [October 2004]: 1–38); whether they address security issues or economic issues (Charles Lipson, "International Cooperation in Economic and Security Affairs," *World Politics* 37:1 [October 1984]: 1–23), both, or other kinds of issues; whether their membership is universal or regional; and whether members' domestic regimes are densely democratic (Pevehouse and Russett, "Democratic International Governmental Organizations Promote Peace").

74. Margaret M. Pearson, "The Major Multilateral Economic Institutions Engage China," in Johnston and Ross, *Engaging China: The Management of an Emerging Power*, 211.

75. Pearson, "Major Multilateral Economic Institutions Engage China," 212–13.

76. Systematically collapsing this plethora of causal mechanisms, processes, and functions into a smaller number of semantic clusters is a task for another occasion, but we do offer the following rough-and-ready categorization: (1) use of force and coercion; (2) arbitration, mediation, provision of "good offices," and arena for negotiation; (3) convey information and reduce transaction costs; (4) learning, internalization of norms, socialization, and preference change; (5) reputation, image, and status; and (6) entanglement and constraints on action.

77. Steve Chan "Discerning the Causal Relationships Between Great Powers' Membership in Intergovernmental Organizations and Their Initiation of Militarized Disputes," *Conflict Management and Peace Science* 22:3 (Fall 2005): 239–56.

78. Chan, "Discerning the Causal Relationships Between Great Powers' Membership in Intergovernmental Organizations and Their Initiation of Militarized Disputes," 240.

79. For recent reviews of the empirical literature, see Boehmer, Gartzke, and Nordstrom, "Do International Organizations Promote Peace?"; Chan, "Discerning the Causal Relationships Between Great Powers' Membership in Intergovernmental Organizations and Their Initiation of Militarized Disputes"; and Pevehouse and Russett, "Democratic International Governmental Organizations Promote Peace."

80. For discussions of the issues that arise in conceptualizing and measuring IGOs, see Michael Wallace and J. David Singer, "Inter-Governmental Organization and the Preservation of Peace, 1816–1965: Some Bivariate Relationships," *International Organization* 24:2 (1970): 520–47; Singer and Wallace, "Intergovernmental Organization and the Preservation of Peace, 1816–1964"; Jon Pevehouse, Timothy Nordstrom, and Kevin Warnke, "The Correlates of War 2 International Governmental Organizations Data Version 2.0," *Conflict Management and Peace Science* 21:2 (Summer 2004): 101–19; and Thomas Volgy, Keith A. Grant, Elisabeth Fausett, and Stuart Rodgers, "Search for Changing Organizational Architecture During Global Transition: Where Is the Post-Cold War Order?," in William R. Thompson, ed., *Systemic Transitions: Past, Present, and Future* (New York: Palgrave-Macmillan, 2009).

81. Bruce Russett, John Oneal, and David R. Davis (1998) "The Third Leg of the Kantian Tripod for Peace: International Organizations and Militarized Disputes, 195–85." *International Organization* 52:3 (Summer 1988): 441–67; Russett and Oneal, *Triangulating Peace*; John R. Oneal, Bruce Russett, and Michael Berbaum, "Causes of Peace: Democracy, Interdependence, and International Organizations, 1885–1992," *International Studies Quarterly* 47:3 (September 2003): 371–93.

82. Singer and Wallace, "Intergovernmental Organization and the Preservation of Peace, 1816–1964"; Harold K. Jacobsen, William M. Reisinger, and Todd Mathers, "National Entanglements in International Governmental Organizations," *American Political Science Review* 80:1 (March 1986): 141–59; William Domke, *War and the Changing Global System* (New Haven: Yale University Press); D. Scott Bennett and Alan C. Stam, "Research Design and Estimator Choices in the Analysis of Interstate Dyads: When Decisions Matter," *Journal of Conflict Resolution* 44:5 (October 2000): 653–85; Boehmer, Gartzke, and Nordstrom, "Do International Organizations Promote Peace?"; and Chan, "Discerning the Causal Relationships Between Great Powers' Membership in Intergovernmental Organizations and Their Initiation of Militarized Disputes."

83. Boehmer, Gartzke, and Nordstrom, "Do International Organizations Promote Peace?"

84. Pevehouse and Russett, "Democratic International Governmental Organizations Promote Peace."

85. Russett and Oneal, *Triangulating Peace*, 160.

86. Richard Cupitt, Rodney Whitlock, and Lynn Richards Whitlock, "The (Im)mortality of International Governmental Organizations," *International Interactions* 21:4 (1996): 399.

87. Wallace and Singer, "Inter-Governmental Organization and the Preservation of Peace, 1816–1965: Some Bivariate Relationships," 520–47.

88. See Cheryl Shanks, Harold K. Jacobson, and Jeffrey H. Kaplan, "Inertia and Change in the Constellation of International Governmental Organizations, 1981–1992," *International Organization* 50 (1996): 593–627. At the same time, the primary source of growth in IGOs since World War I has been a matter of organizations creating more specific auxiliary organizations as opposed to states creating new organizations in the traditional fashion.

89. James Kurth, "The Political Consequences of the Product Cycle: Industrial History and Political Outcomes," *International Organization* 79 (1979): 1–34.

90. Bruce D. Porter, *War and the Rise of the State: The Military Foundations of Modern Politics* (New York: Free Press, 1994).

91. These factors come together most clearly in the cases of NATO and EU encouragement of democratic forces in order to satisfy minimal prerequisites for organizational membership.

92. Mearsheimer, "The False Promise of International Institutions," *International Security* 19:3 (Winter 1994/1995): 5–49.

93. Michael J. Glennon, "Why the Security Council Failed," *Foreign Affairs* 82:3 (May/June 2003): 33.

94. Contrary to widespread popular and scholarly perceptions, Drezner argues that "the Bush administration has tried to reshape international organizations to make them more accommodating to rising powers." See Daniel W. Drezner, "The New New World Order," *Foreign Affairs* 86:2 (March/April 2007): 42. To the extent that Drezner is correct about the engagement efforts of the Bush administration in IGOs, as well as to the extent that subsequent administrations follow a similar course in the decades to come, the case for realist skepticism expressed in this section would lose force. On the other hand, there is likely to be something of a gap between attempts to reform/reshape IGOs and actually attaining the desired outcome. Whatever the case about Bush administration efforts on behalf of rising powers, it seems clear that US attempts to make the UN more accommodating to US interests have not been especially successful. Nor should one find that surprising given the changes that have taken place since the UN's founding.

95. Shanks, Jacobson, and Kaplan, "Inertia and Change in the Constellation of International Governmental Organizations, 1981–1992," 593–627.

96. See, for instance, Thomas Volgy, Thomas J., Keith A. Grant, Elisabeth Fausett, and Stuart Rodgers, "Search for Changing Organizational Architecture During Global Transition: Where is the Post-Cold War Order?," in Thompson, *Systemic Transitions: Past, Present, and Future*.

97. Michel Oksenberg and Elizabeth Economy, "Introduction: China Joins the World," in Elizabeth Economy and Michel Oksenberg, eds., *China Joins the World: Progress and Prospects* (New York: Council on Foreign Relations, 1999), 25.

98. Robert Z. Lawrence, "China and the Multilateral Trading System," Harvard University, Faculty Research Working Paper Series RWP06–045 (October 2006), http://ksgnotes1.harvard.edu/Research/wpaper.nsf/rwo/RWP06–045, 2.

99. David M. Lampton, *Same Bed, Different Dreams: Managing U.S.-China Relations, 1989–2000* (Berkeley: University of California Press, 2001), 4.

100. Kent, *Beyond Compliance: China, International Organizations, and Global Security*, 4. On economic IGOs, see also Margaret M. Pearson, "The Major Multilateral Economic Institutions Engage China," in Johnston and Ross, *Engaging China: The Management of an Emerging Power*, 207–34, and "China's Integration into the International Trade and Investment Regime," in Economy and Oksenberg, *China Joins the World: Progress and Prospects*; Johnston and Evans, "China's Engagement with Multilateral Security Institutions"; and Michael D. Swaine, Andrew N. D. Yang, and Evan S. Medeiros, with Oriana Skylar Mastro, eds., *Assessing the Threat: The Chinese Military and Taiwan's Security* (Washington, DC: Carnegie Endowment for International Peace, 2007).

101. The obvious comparison is with Germany's fairly enthusiastic participation in international institutions after World War II as an acceptable approach to developing an active foreign policy in a world that was anything but eager to see German foreign policy revived.

102. See Bernard Brodie, ed., *The Absolute Weapon: Atomic Power and World Order* (New York: Harcourt, Brace and Company, 1946); Robert Jervis, "Rational Deterrence: Theory and Evidence," *World Politics* 41 (1989): 183–207, and *The Meaning of the Nuclear Revolution: Statecraft and the Prospect of Armageddon* (Ithaca: Cornell University Press, 1989; and Waltz, Kenneth N., *The Spread of Nuclear Weapons: More May Be Better*, Adelphi Paper, no. 171(London: International Institute for Strategic Studies, 1981), and "The Emerging Structure of International Politics," *International Security* 18 (1903): 44–79.

103. This section relies heavily on literature surveys on this question. See, in particular, Daniel S. Geller, "Nuclear Weapons and War," in John A. Vasquez, ed., *What Do We Know About War?*, vol. 2 (Lanhan: Rowman and Littlefield, 2012).

104. See Bruce Bueno de Mesquita and William H. Riker, "An Assessment of the Merits of Selective Nuclear Proliferation," *Journal of Conflict Resolution* 26 (1982): 283–306; Jacek Kugler, "Terror Without Deterrence: Reassessing the Role of Nuclear Weapons," *Journal of Conflict Resolution* 28 (1984): 470–506; Susan G. Sample, "Military Buildups, War, and Realpolitik: A Multivariate Model," *Journal of Conflict Resolution* 42 (1998): 156–75; Victor Asal and Kyle Beardsley, "Proliferation and International Crisis Behavior," *Journal of Peace Research* 44 (2007): 139–55; and Kyle Beardsley and Victor Asal, "Nuclear Weapons as Shields," *Conflict Management and Peace Science* 26 (2009): 235–55.

105. For evidence that nuclear weapons do not influence the probability of crisis escalation, see Barry M. Blechman and Stephen S. Kaplan, *Force Without War: U.S. Armed Forces as a Political Instrument* (Washington, DC: The Brookings Institution, 1978); Organski and Kugler, *The War Ledger*; Kugler "Terror Without Deterrence: Reassessing the Role of Nuclear Weapons"; Paul Huth, D. Scott Bennett, and Christopher Gelpi, "System Uncertainty, Risk Propensity, and International Conflict Among the Great Powers," *Journal of Conflict Resolution* 36 (1992): 478–517; and Erik Gartzke and Dong-Joon Jo, "Bargaining, Nuclear Proliferation, and Interstate Disputes," *Journal of Conflict Resolution* 53 (2009): 209–233. On the increased likelihood of escalation, see Daniel S. Geller, "Nuclear Weapons, Deterrence, and Crisis Escalation," *Journal of Conflict Resolution* 34 (1990): 291–310; Paul Huth, Christopher Gelpi, and D. Scott Bennett, "The Escalation of Great Power Militarized Disputes: Testing Rational Deterrence Theory and Structural Realism," *American Political Science Review* 87 (1993): 609–23; Asal and Beardsley, "Proliferation and International Crisis Behavior"; Beardsley and Asal, "Nuclear Weapons as Shields"; and Robert Rauchhaus, "Evaluating the Nuclear Peace Hypothesis: A Quantitative Approach," *Journal of Conflict Resolution* 54 (2009): 258–77.

106. Henry A. Kissinger, *Nuclear Weapons and Foreign Policy* (New York: Harper and Row, 1957); Thomas C. Schelling, *The Strategy of Conflict* (Oxford: Oxford University Press, 1960), and *Arms and Influence* (New Haven; Yale University Press, 1966); Herman Kahn, *Thinking About the Unthinkable* (New York:

Avon Books, 1962), and *On Escalation: Metaphors and Scenarios* (New York: Prae-ger, 1965); Glenn H. Snyder, "The Balance of Power and the Balance of Terror," in Paul Seabury, ed., *Balance of Power* (San Francisco: Chandler, 1965); Robert E. Osgood and Robert W. Tucker, *Force, Order, and Justice* (Baltimore: Johns Hop-kins University Press, 1967); Glenn H. Snyder and Paul Diesing, *Conflict Among Nations: Bargaining, Decision Making, and System Structure in International Crises* (Princeton: Princeton University Press, 1977); and Colin S. Gray, Nuclear Strategy: The Case for a Theory of Victory," *International Security* 4 (1979): 54–58.

107. T. V. Paul, "Causes of the India-Pakistan Enduring Rivalry," in T. V. Paul, ed., *The India-Pakistan Conflict: An Enduring Rivalry* (Cambridge: Cambridge University Press, 2005).

108. Geller, "Nuclear Weapons, Deterrence, and Crisis Escalation"; T. V. Paul, *Asymmetric Conflicts: War Initiation by Weaker Powers* (Cambridge: Cambridge University Press, 1994), and "Nuclear Taboo and War Initiation in Regional Con-flicts," *Journal of Conflict Resolution* 39 (1995): 696–717; Beardsley and Asal, "Nuclear Weapons as Shields"; and Rauchhaus, "Evaluating the Nuclear Peace Hypothesis: A Quantitative Approach."

109. For arguments and evidence that nuclear weapons make some differ-ence in achieving success in deterrence cases, see Erich Weede, "Preventing War by Nuclear Deterrence or by Détente," *Conflict Management and Peace Science* 6 (1981): 1–8, and "Extended Deterrence by Superpower Alliance," *Journal of Con-flict Resolution* 27 (1983): 231–54; and Lisa J. Carlson, "Crisis Escalation: An Em-pirical Test in the Context of Extended Deterrence," *International Interactions* 24 (1998): 225–53. On the other hand, Paul Huth and Bruce Russett have published a number of studies arguing, among other things, that conventional weapons are more critical than nuclear ones—see Bruce Russett, "The Calculus of Deterrence," *Journal of Conflict Resolution* 7 (1963): 97–109; Paul Huth, *Extended Deterrence and the Prevention of War* (New Haven: Yale University Press, 1988), "Extended Deterrence and the Outbreak of War," *American Political Science Review* 82 (1988): 423–43, and "The Extended Deterrent Value of Nuclear Weapons," *Journal of Conflict Resolution* 34 (1990): 270–90; and Paul Huth and Bruce Russett, "What Makes Deterrence Work? Cases from 1900 to 1980," *World Politics* 36 (1984): 496–526, and "Deterrence Failure and Crisis Escalation," *International Studies Quar-terly* 32 (1988): 29–45.

110. For an argument questioning whether deterrence was responsible for the Cold War remaining cold, see George Modelski and Patrick Morgan, "Under-standing Global War." *Journal of Conflict Resolution* 29 (1985): 391–417.

111. For an argument that asserts that nuclear weapons are irrelevant because wars have become increasingly unthinkable, see John Mueller, "The Essential Irrelevance of Nuclear Weapons," *International Security* 13:2 (Autumn 1988): 55–79. A weaker but more general assertion that wars are becoming increasingly unaffordable for industrialized states to contemplate fighting other industrialized

states is found in Jack S. Levy and William R. Thompson, *Arc of War: Origin, Escalation, Transformation* (Chicago: University of Chicago Press, 2011).

112. Liz Alderman, "In U.S. Impasse, Global Concern Over Possible Collateral Damage," *New York Times*, July 30, 2011, B1.

113. See, for instance, Handel Jones, *ChinAmerica: The Uneasy Partnership that Will Change the World* (New York: McGraw Hill, 2010).

114. See, among others, Keith Bradsher, "China Conveys 'Regret' Over Trade Complaints." *New York Times*, April 11, 2007, http://www.nytimes.com/2007/04 /11/business/worldbusiness/11yuan.html?pagewanted =1&acbxbbkx=13118762; Reuters, "Factbox- U.S. Trade Complaints About China" (May 19, 2010), http:// www.Reuters.com/article/2010/05/19/usa-china-trade-idUSN19106492010 0519; and Elizabeth Williamson and Ian Talley, "Steelworkers Blast China on Subsidies," *Wall Street Journal*, September 10, 2010, http://online.wsj.com/article/SB100014240 527487046444045754817437471706 92.html.

115. See Ding Qingfen, "More Trade Complaints Urged," *China Daily*, March 12, 2010, http://www.chinadaily.com.cn/china/2010npc/201003/12/content_9576963 .htm.

116. Azar Gat, "The Return of Authoritarian Great Powers," *Foreign Affairs* 86:4 (July/August 2007): 59–69.

117. Russett and Oneal, *Triangulating Peace*, 287.

Chapter Seven

1. We make no claim that contrasting situations involving mixtures of strong and weak conflict inducements or facilitators and constraints constitute a complex theory. It is a very simple pairing of influences that should have opposite effects, as well as lead to different types of outcomes as the combinatorial pairings are altered. It is a theory of sorts, but a rather weak one.

2. Some readers may question this statement in view of the recession that began in 2008. It is possible that the pace of relative decline has accelerated with this latest shock. However, it will be easier to assess the accuracy of a statement along these lines only after the recession ends.

Chapter Eleven

1. See Kurt M. Campbell, Jay Gulledge, John R. McNeill, John Podesta, Peter Ogden, Leon Furth, R. James Woolsey, Alexander T. J. Lennon, Julianne Smith, Richard Weitz, and Derek Mix, *The Age of Consequences: The Foreign Policy and National Security Implications of Global Climate Change* (Washington, DC: Center for Strategic and International Studies, November 2007), http://csis.org/files/media/ csis/pubs/071105_ageofconsequences.pdf.

2. See Damian Carrington, "IPCC Officials Admit Mistake Over Melting Himalayan Glaciers," *The Guardian*, January 20, 2010, http://www.guardian.co.uk /environment/2010/jan 20/IPPC-himalayan-glaciers-mistake. The initial claim that Himalayan glaciers might melt by 2035 proved to be unfounded. The glaciers are melting but not that quickly.

3. Alternatively, in the "More of the Same" scenario described in chapter 6, we have borrowed from Andrew Erickson and Gabe Collins, "China's S-shaped Threat," *The Diplomat*, September 6, 2011, http://the-diplomat.com/2011/09/06 /china-s-shaped-threat/; Nicholas Eberstadt, "Asian Pacific Demographics in 2010–2040: Implications for Strategic Balance," in Ashley J. Tellis, Andrew Marble, and Travis Tanner, eds., *Asia's Rising Power and America's Continued Purpose* (Seattle: National Bureau of Asian Research, 2010); and Barry Eichengreen, Dongh yun Park, and Kwanho Shin, "When Fast Growing Economics Slow Down: International Evidence and Implications for China," National Bureau of Economic Research (NBER) Working Paper, no. 16919 (Cambridge: NBER, March 2011). The notion of the Chinese using their large US public debt holdings as a weapon in a crisis with the United States to force is raised in Arvind Subramanian, "The Inevitable Superpower," *Foreign Affairs* 90:5 (2011): 66–78, but in this case we use a more subtle variation in the scenarios that feature a Diaoyu crisis (see chapters 6 and 8), because we find it dubious that a threat concerning public debt holdings could persuade the United States to withdraw militarily from the western Pacific. It does not seem dubious, however, that China might use its debt-holding leverage as a reminder of US dependence on access to Chinese capital. Cyberwarfare, which some Chinese strategists see as the information age's equivalent of nuclear war in the industrial era, seems far more likely. It appears in the rise of Pax Sinica described in chapter 8. Some of the sources useful for appreciating possibilities associated with cyberwarfare include Charles Billo and Welton Chang, *Cyber Warfare: An Analysis of the Means and Motivations of Selected Nation States* (revised December 2004) (Hanover: Institute for Security Technology Studies, Dartmouth College), http://www.ists.dartmouth.edu/docs/cyberwarfare.pdf; Bryan Krekel, *Capability of the People's Republic of China to Conduct Cyber Warfare and Computer Network Exploitation* (McLean: Northrop Grumman Corporation, October 2009), http://www.uscc.gov/researchpapers/2009/NorthropGrum man_PRC_Cyber_Paper_FINAL_Approved%Report_16oct2009.pd; and Christopher Bronk, "Blown to Bits: China's War in Cyberspace, August-September 2020m," *Strategic Studies Quarterly* 5:1 (2011): 1–20, http://www.au.af.mil/au/ssq /2011/spring/bronk.pdf.

4. Martin Jacques, *When China Rules the World: The End of the Western World and the Birth of a New Global Order* (New York: Penguin, 2009), 367.

5. Aaron L. Freidberg, "The Future of U.S.-China Relations: Is Conflict Inevitable?," *International Security* 30 (Fall 2005): 39.

Index